LIMITS

Medical Ethics Series
David H. Smith and Robert M. Veatch, series editors

Norman L. Cantor. *Advance Directives and the Pursuit of Death with Dignity*

Norman L. Cantor. *Legal Frontiers of Death and Dying*

Arthur L. Caplan. *If I Were a Rich Man Could I Buy a Pancreas?*
And Other Essays on the Ethics of Health Care

Cynthia B. Cohen, ed. *Casebook on the Termination of Life-Sustaining Treatment and*
the Care of the Dying

Cynthia B. Cohen, ed. Commissioned by the National Advisory Board on Ethics in
Reproduction. *New Ways of Making Babies: The Case of Egg Donation*

Larry Gostin, ed. *Surrogate Motherhood: Politics and Privacy*

Christine Grady. *The Search for an AIDS Vaccine: Ethical Issues*
in the Development and Testing of a Preventive HIV Vaccine

A Report by the Hastings Center. *Guidelines on the Termination*
of Life-Sustaining Treatment and the Care of the Dying

Paul Lauritzen. *Pursuing Parenthood: Ethical Issues in Assisted Reproduction*

Joanne Lynn, M.D., ed. *By No Extraordinary Means: The Choice to*
Forgo Life-Sustaining Food and Water, Expanded Edition

William F. May. *The Patient's Ordeal*

Richard W. Momeyer. *Confronting Death*

S. Kay Toombs, David Barnard, and Ronald Carson, eds. *Chronic Illness:*
From Experience to Policy

Robert M. Veatch. *The Patient as Partner: A Theory of Human-Experimentation Ethics*

Robert M. Veatch. *The Patient-Physician Relation: The Patient as Partner, Part 2*

LIMITS

*The Role of the Law in
Bioethical Decision Making*

Roger B. Dworkin

INDIANA UNIVERSITY PRESS

Bloomington and Indianapolis

© 1996 by Roger B. Dworkin

The paper used in this publication meets the minimum requirements of American National Standard for Information Sciences—Permanence of Paper for Printed Library Materials, ANSI Z39.48-1984.

Manufactured in the United States of America

Library of Congress Cataloging-in-Publication Data

Dworkin, Roger B.
Limits : the role of the law in bioethical decision making / Roger B. Dworkin.
p.   cm. — (Medical ethics series)
Includes index
ISBN 0-253-33075-0 (cl : alk. paper)
1. Medical laws and legislation—United States.   2. Genetic engineering—Law and legislation—United States.   3. Bioethics—United States.   I. Title.   II. Series.
KF3821.D87   1996
344.73′041—dc20
[347.30441]   95-50697

2   3   4   5   01   00   99   98   97

THIS BOOK IS DEDICATED
TO MY MOTHER, IRENE S. FIGILIS,
WITH LOVE, GRATITUDE,
AND RESPECT.

CONTENTS

Contents

PREFACE

Writing a book is among the more social of solitary activities. This book could not have been completed without the contributions of a great many other persons.

I am grateful to the Indiana University School of Law-Bloomington and to its Dean, Alfred C. Aman, Jr., for creating a happy and supportive environment in which to work. The law school also provided me with summer research support, which made it possible for me to devote extended amounts of time to this project.

My other academic home, Indiana University's Poynter Center for the Study of Ethics and American Institutions and its inspired Director, David H. Smith, have been equally supportive, both spiritually and financially, and have provided me with an interdisciplinary sounding board for my ideas.

Colleagues of many years have contributed to my understanding of law and of the role of the law in bioethics. Among these, three stand out. Walter Wadlington of the University of Virginia Law School has been a generous friend and adviser for many years. I am grateful for his support and for his kindness in reading the manuscript of this book and offering very helpful suggestions. David H. Smith has also made major contributions to my understanding of the issues discussed in this book and has also read and made very valuable suggestions about the manuscript. The late Herbert L. Packer, my teacher at Stanford Law School, first introduced me to systematic thought about the legal process. For many years I said he taught me everything I know. It is probably no longer fair to tar him with that brush, but his influence on my thinking and my career continues to be profound.

Many of my students have wrestled with the ideas in this book, and, like any teacher, I have learned much from them. Several students have provided research assistance. Most notable for the very high quality of their contributions are Suzanne Buchko, Scott Idleman, and Elissa Preheim.

Shirley Walker cheerfully provided excellent secretarial services throughout the preparation of the manuscript. Robert Sloan of the Indiana University Press has been a model of patience.

My most important debts, of course, are to my family, without whose love and support nothing would be possible. To my wife, Terry Morehead Dworkin, my sons, Craig and Andrew, and my mother, Irene Figilis, to whom this book is dedicated, all my thanks and love.

LIMITS

ONE

Introduction

Biomedical Advance and the American Legal System

Everyone who reads, listens to a radio, or watches television now realizes that an unprecedented explosion in biological research and medical applications offers humanity relief from some of its bleakest suffering while posing ethical dilemmas of mind-numbing complexity. Respirators, heart-lung machines, and multiple techniques for artificial feeding and hydration allow us to maintain life, often for years, in persons who as recently as two decades ago would have died in short order. Yet the prolongation of life comes only at great expense, and it often deprives the dying person of dignity and any vestige of autonomy while prolonging the suffering of those who love the patient.

Similarly, life, and even health, can be prolonged through organ transplantation, but again only at great cost and amid troubling questions of selection of donors and recipients, coping with scarcity, and avoiding abuse.

Scarcely four decades after Watson and Crick described the double helix structure of DNA,[1] the nation has embarked upon a massive effort to map the entire human genome; recombinant DNA technology offers genetically engineered insulin, human growth hormone, and other products; genetic counseling and prenatal diagnosis permit sophisticated family planning and the avoidance of genetic disease; mass screening programs offer those benefits to entire populations; presymptomatic testing for late onset diseases is becoming a reality; and genetic therapy is just around the corner. These developments, though, pose troubling questions of abortion, sterilization, privacy, genetic discrimination, loss of respect for individual choices and variety, human experimentation, and the limits of human wisdom.

New reproductive techniques—surrogate motherhood and in vitro fertilization, as well as their older cousin, artificial insemination—contribute to the conquest of genetic disease and the pain of infertility. But these techniques also challenge conventional notions of family, raise serious issues of personal relationships, force consideration of gay and lesbian parenthood, and, in the eyes of some, threaten the status, rights, and aspirations of women.

These developments and others force us to pay careful attention to ethics, the branch of philosophy directed at developing moral principles and modes of moral reasoning. Courses in medical ethics are now common in medical and other health professional schools, and even at the undergraduate level. The literature about bioethics is enormous, and the number of centers devoted to its study grows steadily. This is hardly surprising. Careful and rigorous thought rooted in the wisdom of the ages seems a sensible approach for coming to grips with the tormenting issues posed by biomedical advance.

But careful thinking is hard and often does not point clearly in one direction. People are impatient; they want to know the right thing to do right now. If they are doctors, patients, or family members, their desire for quick, clear answers is easy to appreciate. A doctor who needs to decide today whether to accede to the wishes of a twenty-five-year-old quadriplegic to cease artificial feeding will want some firmer, faster basis for decision than a seminar on Aristotle, Plato, Mill, Kant, and Rawls.

Partly because of the desire for speedy, certain answers; partly because of a popular lack of understanding of the relationship between law and ethics; partly because of ignorance about law and the legal system; and partly because of the belief that law is magic, concern for medical ethics has often become a plea for medical law. Thus law exists about death and dying, organ transplants, genetic counseling and screening, reproductive technologies, etc., and more law is made about these subjects every day. The law is asked and often tries to resolve questions of medical ethics.

This is not improper. Real questions about real people and about public policy are posed by biomedical developments. Real disagreements exist. The law is a primary vehicle for resolving disagreements about public policy and the treatment of real persons. To suggest that the law has no role to play in the area of biomedical advance would be both stupid and unrealistic. Yet blind faith in the law's ability to resolve bioethical problems or unthinking acquiescence in the dominant role of law would be equally unsound. Much of the law that exists today is ill advised. Law is a collection of tools of limited utility. Sound public policy requires evaluation of each legal tool to ascertain which one(s) can deal best with which problems of biomedical advance and to understand the limits of the ability of each legal tool and the entire legal system to regulate biomedical developments. The purpose of this book is to make such an evaluation. The book is designed to point would-be lawmakers in the right direction when they decide to make law and, more importantly, to encourage them to refrain from lawmaking when the legal system has no positive contribution to make. The law is a limit on biology and medicine. It is not, however, the only limit; and law itself has limits that suggest deference and humility in considering whether and how to use it.

LAW AND THE AMERICAN LEGAL SYSTEM

Law is hard to define, and one cannot hope to find agreement about its definition. Importantly, though, one can readily describe several important things law is not.

Most importantly, and contrary to popular belief, law is not a collection of rules to govern human behavior. Certainly the law contains rules. However, if "rule" means a directive that one can learn and must follow, many legal rules are not rules at all, because they are created only after someone has acted, thus making advance learning and compliance impossible. Even preexisting rules are seldom clear. Someone must interpret and apply them. The interpretation and application, not the rule, are what matters.

To borrow a standard example,[2] even so clear a rule as "No vehicles are permitted in the park," requires someone to decide through some method whether to penalize drivers of motorcycles and bicycles as well as cars and trucks; a pilot who crashed in the park; persons who carried their canoe through the park to the lake; a child with a battery-powered car or a matchbox car; and the civic leaders who installed a tank on a pedestal in the park in order to honor veterans. Even the clearest case, an automobile, requires someone to decide whether to refrain from applying the rule if the driver was cutting through the park to get an accident victim to the hospital as fast as possible, to avoid armed thugs, etc.

In newly emerging areas like those that are the subject of this book, few obviously relevant rules exist. Of course, one may ask such questions as whether a rule about doctor-patient confidentiality applies in the genetic disease setting, but again, the process of deciding the answer to that question, not the existence of the rule, is what is important.

Secondly, law is not science. The role of science is to discover (or approach) the truth about the way the universe and the things inside it are and work. The methods of science are observation and experimentation. Law, by contrast, cares little for how things are or would be apart from human intervention. Law examines things believed to be within human control, decides how they ought to be, and attempts to make them that way through the use of threats, promises, and rewards. The methods of law are observation, value judgment, prediction, and intervention. No experiment or set of experiments will reveal the truth about what the law is.

This does not mean that one cannot study law through the methods of social science. It does mean that law can never be expressed with the certainty of the Pythagorean theorem or the proposition that eyes are required for sight.

The obvious observation that law is not science is quite important. It goes a long way toward explaining the difficulty that scientists and lawmakers have in communicating with each other; it complicates the efforts of lawmakers to make law that is scientifically sensible; and it frustrates scientists who see the law take positions that seem absurd.

The point of law is to make the social condition as good as possible. From a social point of view that may require the law to excuse a person from criminal liability on the ground of "insanity" even if no psychiatrist would find that person insane or even if insanity is not a scientifically meaningful concept. The scientist wants to describe the state of a person's mind. The lawmaker wants to know whether society will be better off to imprison, hospitalize, or release the perpetrator of a forbidden act. Knowing the state of the perpetrator's mind may help to answer that question, but it may not be determinative. Expense, impact on others, the moral sense of the community, and ease of administration are all part of the question for the law. The scientist has no special claim to expertise about any of those considerations except the state of the perpetrator's mind.

Recognizing that law is a question of how things ought to be rather than how they are can lead easily to yet another erroneous belief about law, the idea that law is ethics or the conscious embodiment of some ethical view. The relationship between law and ethics has been a subject of inquiry for millennia, and we can hardly expect to revisit it meaningfully here. For now it should suffice to say that law and ethics are not the same. Ethics is a branch of philosophy that considers how persons and institutions ought to behave. It claims for itself no temporal sanctions to ensure compliance or punish deviation. Law, conversely, is entirely temporal and very much involved with sanctions. Justice Holmes brilliantly captured the difference between reliance on temporal and eternal sanctions when, in discussing the mundane question of whether a person will be liable for injuring another if he acted as well as he personally could, Holmes wrote

> The law . . . does not attempt to see men as God sees them, for more than one sufficient reason. . . . If, for instance, a man is born hasty and awkward, is always having accidents and hurting himself or his neighbors, no doubt his congenital defects will be allowed for in the courts of Heaven, but his slips are no less troublesome to his neighbors than if they sprang from guilty neglect. His neighbors accordingly require him, at his proper peril, to come up to their standard, and the courts which they establish decline to take his personal equation into account.[3]

Additionally, at least some ethicists argue that ethics involves primarily or exclusively questions about what ought to be done rather than about how to decide what ought to be done and even to suggest that one could not adopt procedures without knowing in advance what outcomes one wanted the procedures to reach. In contrast, procedure is the heart of the legal enterprise, and any suggestion that the system's procedures were designed to reach preconceived substantive conclusions would be anathema to the legal mind.

One can agree that law is not ethics but argue that law is the embodiment of ethics or of some view or system of ethics. In a meaningless sense that is true. Each legal position will serve some ethical norm, and the totality of "law" will also serve some norm or norms, even if it is only the norm of pluralistic decision making. So what? Unless the law *consciously* embodies ethics, observing that it serves some ethic is simply to note a coincidence or a fact of group psychology. Persons routinely argue for the adoption of legal positions on the basis of ethical norms. Whether they succeed, however, depends on how much weight the system accords those norms when it weighs them with administrability, economic efficiency, and countless other factors. How much it ought to weight them is the question of the relationship of law and ethics, which, as noted, has been much mooted.

If then, law is not rules, science, or ethics, is law simply politics? Some currently active legal scholars suggest that the answer is yes.[4] They argue that law is simply the imposition of the will of the powerful (rich, white men) on the powerless (women, racial minorities, and the poor). They argue that the empowered make and utilize the law to maintain their position of hegemony and that by capturing the forms of legal discourse (insisting on dispassionate, linear, analytical thinking rather than empathic storytelling) they strive permanently to exclude the unempowered from achieving justice. If this is so, then nihilism seems the most sensible attitude to adopt toward law, and revolution or disingenuous subversion seem the most efficient routes to power.

But surely this view is wrong. While it may be true that some or even most law protects the status quo, that does not make law pure power politics without two crucial showings: (1) that the *purpose* of the law is to preserve the status quo and (2) that the status quo is worse than some realistic alternative for the members of the entire society. One learns nothing more about law by noting that protective wage and hour legislation curtailed the opportunities of women than one does by noting that prohibiting abortion coincides with the views of the Catholic Church. If the purpose of protective legislation really was to protect, then the problem with the wage and hour laws was that they were based on incorrect factual premises about the strength and abilities of women and about the role of mothers in raising the next generation, and an arguably incorrect assessment of social policy that saw safety, health, and upbringing as more important to the society than economic independence and free choice. The fact that law has trouble getting facts and makes mistakes is a reason not to make much law, not a reason to impugn motives and reduce law to politics.

Moreover, protective legislation no longer exists. That mistake has been corrected. The fact that the nation is not yet perfect is hardly an occasion for cynicism or revolution. The politics theory assumes that the existence of many wrong, or bad, legal positions means that the law itself is "bad." Is that necessarily true? Would the society as a whole or even the dispossessed be better off if power politics fundamentally transformed the legal system? One cannot give a definitive answer without knowing what is to replace the system we have now. If it were to be replaced by a system in which incentive to achieve were capped, opportunity to argue against the system were curtailed, procedural restraints on police were abandoned, wealth was redistributed, and janitors taught at the Harvard Law School,[5] one may well doubt whether the society would be improved. Politics can keep our failings before our eyes and help us to correct them. But the acts of correction or noncorrection are not and cannot be synonymous with politics. Law has a life of its own.

What is the essence of that life? What is this law that deals in rules but is not rules, considers science but is not scientific, fosters ethics but is not ethics, and utilizes politics but is not politics? What is separate, special, or unique about the law?

As suggested, the law can be thought of as the acts, that is the activities, of correcting or refusing to correct perceived social ills. It is the official creation, interpretation, and application of social rules through distinctive methodologies of observation, value judgment, prediction, and intervention that consider ethics along with economics, sociology, psychology, administrative convenience, etc., all for the purpose of deciding whether to intervene and, if so, who should intervene and in what way in relationships between persons or between persons and the government. That is, law is procedure. More precisely, it is a collection of procedures or processes for making the kinds of decisions described. What is unique about law is not its rules, not its power, not its claim to moral sanction. What is unique about law is its methods, its procedures, the ways it works.[6]

As the Supreme Court notes, quoting from an article in *Social Casework*, "Procedure is to law what scientific method is to science."[7] And as Justice Frankfurter explained, "The history of American freedom is, in no small measure, the history of procedure."[8]

For the law, procedure is everything. It is what allows a society to reach conclusions on terribly difficult problems without knowing in advance what the solutions to the problems should be and without resort to brute force. One reason that nonlawyers have so much trouble understanding the law and use it so ineffectively is that nonlawyers seldom recognize what every lawyer knows: In law, what one does is almost never as important as how one does it. In this book we shall have ample opportunities to observe the truth of that proposition as we see good intentions and apparent victories come to naught because reformers paid too little attention to means, i.e., processes, and too much attention to their desired goals.

If law is simply procedures for resolving social questions, what general attitude ought one to adopt in studying the processes to ascertain which ones are best suited for what? I suggest the proper starting point is the recognition that the processes are to answer *questions*, resolve *problems*, solve *controversies*. That is, they are to operate in areas in which something is to be said on more than one side of an issue. Not surprisingly, Paul Freund put it best: "The law is dialectic in a deeper sense than its adversary process. It mediates most significantly between right and right."[9]

Nobody needs a lawyer to tell them the difference between right and wrong. The only questions that matter for the law are those in which there is something "right," or good, on both or all sides of the controversy. All the social dilemmas posed by biomedical advance share this characteristic. That is what makes them dilemmas.

Confronted with a conflict between right and right, the law's job is much more difficult than it would be if it had the luxury of confronting right and wrong. One can *choose* between right and wrong, but choice between right and right will be a serious mistake. When right exists on both sides of an issue, the job of the law is to mediate between the "rights," to accommodate, to adjust, to attempt to sacrifice as little as possible of what is "right" on both sides. Thus, even if one knows nothing about law except that legal problems are difficult because they involve competing values, one can begin one's analysis in the proper frame of mind. The goal of any choice of legal processes ought to be to minimize the sacrifice of goods, i.e., matters of value. How well adapted are our legal mechanisms for achieving that goal?

Basically, the American legal system consists of four major processes or modes of operation—common law adjudication, legislation, administrative lawmaking, and constitutional adjudication. Often two or more processes combine to deal with a social issue.

COMMON LAW ADJUDICATION

Common law adjudication[10] is the most important American legal process. It is a method of lawmaking derived from our English forebears and adapted to the exigencies of a diverse and rapidly expanding young nation. Until well into the twentieth century most law in the United States was common law. As legislation has become more dominant, the common law may no longer account for the most law, but its overriding importance remains. Its modes of analysis dominate legal education and, therefore, legal thinking. Its methods are often applied in what are technically statutory interpretation, administrative law, or even constitutional cases. All federal and state legislation is drafted on a background of common law. And common law adjudication is the fall back or default process within our legal system. That is, unless a conscious decision is made to pass a statute, adopt administrative controls, or utilize the Constitution, the common law is the legal process that will deal with a social issue.

Common law is a legal system in which (1) judges (2) who get their information from lawyers, make law (3) mostly on a state-by-state basis through (4) the resolution of real, existing disputes, (5) one case at a time, (6) basing their decisions largely on analogy and precedent, and (7) having at their disposal a limited number of remedies, the most important of which is to order one person to pay money to another.

Common law is made by judges, mostly sitting in state supreme and appellate courts. Judges are often appointed and are almost never elected in any meaningful sense of the term. Typically they serve very long terms; in the federal system appointment is for life. Thus, the fact that common law is made by judges means that it is undemocratic. The reason judges are appointed and serve long terms is to insulate them from the pressures of the majority and popular will.

Judges (at least at the appellate level) are chosen from the ranks of lawyers. To the extent that they have expertise, it is expertise in law. No reason exists to believe that judges have any expertise, or even any literacy, in any area of medicine or the biological sciences. Certainly law school gives them no such exposure; and they are unlikely to have gained it before law school. After all, persons who choose to attend law school typically are equally terrified of numbers and the sight of blood. They majored in business, history, political science, English, philosophy, or whatever, and typically satisfied their science distribution requirements by taking Introductory Psychology or "Rocks for Jocks." Thus, common law decision making is inexpert as well as undemocratic.

The inexpert, undemocratic lawmakers get the information on which to base their decisions from lawyers, advocates for litigants, and bright new law graduates who serve as judges' clerks. Unlike legislatures, courts have no large staffs or facilities for holding investigational hearings and no power to compel otherwise uninvolved persons with expertise to share it. Most of the time they probably don't even know who the experts in a particular field are. Appellate judges get their information from trial transcripts and lawyers' briefs. They know what lawyers tell them. Thus, in a sense, the blind are leading the blind, as inexpert instructors provide information to inexpert decision makers.

In fact, the lack of expertise is exacerbated by the fact that lawyers who represent litigants are required to be zealous advocates of their client's point of view. Zealous advocacy does not include intentional falsification, but it does involve "characterizing" facts to make them appear as supportive as possible of the client's position. This means that judges (quite properly) receive purposely biased information selected to support a litigant's claim or defense. If some legitimate scientific information does not support any party's position, it won't be presented at all. Therefore, the inexpert decision makers receive selected and biased inexpert information. Their law clerks lack the advocates' biases, but have no independent expertise or power to correct scientific information. The inexpert judges have no ability to see through the biases and make sophisticated selections of information on which to rely. The lack of scientific expertise among judges and the fact that lawyers are the judges' virtually exclusive source of information make the common law ill suited for providing sophisticated solutions to problems that have a significant scientific dimension.

Most common law is made by state courts. This means that for most purposes common law development is unlikely to provide uniform, national resolutions of issues. If one believes that social problems posed by biology and medicine have one right solution, the common law—which can provide different solutions for each state—is unlikely to provide it. Conversely, common law is unlikely to impose a wrong solution on everybody either. Thus, the state-based nature of the common law reduces the costs of its mistakes by reducing their geographical scope.

Additionally, not everyone agrees that one best answer exists for every problem. If some persons wonder why an American who lives in Mississippi should be denied a benefit available to her cousin in Wisconsin, others would ask why a citizen of Utah should be forced to behave as if she lived in New York. One can argue that the cultural diversity of the United States is one of its greatest strengths; to the extent that different communities celebrate different values, that is a strength, not a weakness. Moreover, one can adopt the respected view that the states are laboratories, conducting experiments that will lead over time to the best position on social issues.[11] That too supports the desirability of state-by-state decision making, which usually characterizes the common law.

Common law is made through the resolution of real, existing disputes. Common law judges have no power to issue advisory opinions or proffer generalized codes of conduct. They have no power to rule for the future even about problems that seem certain to arise. This means that for the common law to deal with a technology the technology must exist and have operated in a way that angered someone enough for that person to have claimed injury and sought legal redress. Thus, to the extent that a rapid response or a response in advance to a biosocial development is important, the common law cannot provide it. Common law is reactive, not proactive. If speed and advance regulation by nonexpert, ill-informed, undemocratic decision makers seems likely to lead to unsound results, then, of course, being reactive is a virtue rather than a vice.

In a common law system disputes are resolved one case at a time. Naturally, they are decided largely in the order in which they arise. This means that the common law will develop in an uneven, unsystematic, often illogical way.

Theoretically, one can imagine a system in which the decision maker tried to envision all the social issues posed by a technology. The decider could then think about those issues until it decided what basic question(s) had to be answered first in order to begin resolving the issues. After that, one could construct a decision tree. If the answer to question 1 is A, then question 2 arises; if it is B, question 3 arises instead. Question 2, in turn, may have multiple possible answers, each of which may lead to different new questions until finally all questions have been answered and a logical system of responses to the technology exists. The common law does not work that way.

Because disputes arise in the order in which people are angered rather than in a logical order, the first dispute to arise may raise question 24. The immediacy of the dispute, the exigencies of time, and the common law tradition of deciding only what is necessary to resolve the dispute at hand make a resort to first principles nearly inconceivable. Thus, the common law is ill suited to comprehensive, systematic lawmaking. It develops unevenly in fits and starts, and at any one time it is likely to contain more holes than fabric.

The real, existing disputes that the common law tackles one case at a time are decided largely through resort to analogy and precedent. Justice demands that like cases be decided alike. Moreover, if persons are to guide their conduct by the law, they must be able to predict on the basis of past cases what the results of new cases will be; and if the society is to enjoy stability, the law cannot be constantly changing.

Therefore, judges are taught to look to previously decided cases to see whether those cases have already decided the question before them. If the same question has been decided by the court where a dispute is pending or by a higher court in its jurisdiction, then ordinarily the court is bound to follow the earlier decision. If a court in a different jurisdiction has decided the question, the court should at least consider the desirability of following its lead.

If the question before the court has not been decided previously, then the court is to look for resolutions of analogous disputes and be guided by the way they were resolved. Deciding which cases are analogous is a very difficult business, but for our purposes what matters is that courts make the effort.

Looking for analogy and precedent means that the courts are seeking solutions to today's problems in yesterday's wisdom. As noted, there are good reasons for doing that. However, the backward-looking nature of the common law is still another reason to doubt the common law's ability to deal with new problems posed by rapid changes in science and technology.

Finally, common law courts have very little authority to craft remedies. If one is willing to play fast and loose with history and to treat equitable remedies applied by modern courts as "common law" remedies, then the courts may be said to have some power to order behavior (e.g., issue injunctions, require specific performance of contracts). As a practical matter, however, the primary remedy available to a common law court is to award money (damages) from one party to another. Common law courts have neither the ability, staff, nor authority to regulate behavior in detail or to supervise ongoing activities. Thus, if such regulation or supervision is important for dealing with a problem, common law adjudication is not likely to be the legal response of choice. Many problems posed by biomedical advance seem to call for relatively detailed regulation and supervision.

At first blush the common law seems unlikely to deal well with biomedical social issues. Therefore, it is not surprising that persons often look elsewhere for solutions or relief.

LEGISLATION

Legislation is, in many ways, the opposite of common law adjudication. To some it may seem to offer correctives for the common law's deficiencies.

Legislation is law (1) made by elected representatives, who may be (2) informed by a large number and wide variety of sources. It can deal with problems (3) prospectively and (4) comprehensively, and it offers both (5) greater speed and (6) more certainty than the common law.

Legislation is obviously more democratic than common law adjudication. Therefore, in a liberal, democratic society it enjoys greater prima facie attractiveness and legitimacy than the common law. This advantage, however, is easily overstated. After all, courts do not occur in nature like trees. State and federal constitutions created the courts and empowered them to decide cases. To the extent that deciding cases necessarily involves making law, constitutions have empowered the courts to make law. As constitutions are popularly enacted, courts are democratic institutions, at least in the sense that they have democratic sanction for what they do.

Moreover, democracy has its downside. The ugly underbelly of democracy is politics. In this context I take politics to mean the consideration of matters that are irrelevant to the merits of the question at hand. Thus, if Legislator A will vote for Legislator B's bill about surrogate motherhood only if B will vote to fund a branch campus of the state university in A's district, A's decision about surrogate motherhood is political. Obviously political decisions make no contribution to wise social policy formulation. One would have to assume both incredible public knowledge and sophistication and a far larger pool of candidates for any one office than is realistic in order to believe that such decisions contribute to any of the other values that make us extol democracy either.

Unlike courts, legislatures have access to a large amount of information gleaned from many sources. Legislatures have staffs and hold hearings and therefore, theoretically, are better able to inform themselves than courts.

In reality, little reason exists to expect well-informed or sophisticated decision making from legislatures. In the first place, legislators are too busy to become expert about very much. When the state needs a budget, when public attention is focused on a very few things (abortion, the war on drugs, garbage), when constituents have to be served, speeches given, etc., the opportunity to become well informed is not very real.

Second, experts become and remain experts by working in laboratories or clinics, not by testifying at legislative hearings. Legislative information comes primarily from lobbyists and other persons with axes to grind, not from objective, detached experts. To the extent that purveyors of points of view may come to the legislature draped in the mantle of expertise, they are more dangerous than advocates in litigation. At least everybody knows what trial lawyers are trying to do.

Third, even if experts truly offer their best and least biased insights, issues of science, including social science, are seldom clear-cut. Experts will often present information on both or all sides of an issue. Legislators are no more likely as a group to be able to make intelligent choices between conflicting expert claims than are judges. One very seldom finds Ph.D. biochemists in the legislature. Therefore, like common law adjudication, legislation is the product of inexpert decision makers utilizing biased, partial, and ill-understood information to form the bases for their actions. Add politics and overwork to all of this and the legislature loses some of its lustre as a potential source of sound decision making.

At least, however, the legislature can act prospectively. Unlike a court the legislature need not await a real case to make law. It can act in advance.

Two things reduce this apparent advantage of legislation over the common law: It is less true than one might think, and to the extent that it is true, it may not be desirable. Certainly, legislation can be forward looking. However, legislators are not oracles. They have no more ability to predict scientific and technological developments than anybody else, and therefore, their ability to act for the future is constrained by their human limitations.

Those limitations also raise questions about the desirability of prospective lawmaking. While preventing harm is more attractive than cleaning up after harm has occurred, the inability to foretell the future or to envision every possible scenario suggests that advance solutions may turn out to be unwise or even counterproductive.

Similarly, comprehensive lawmaking, another feature of legislation, may not be as attractive as it seems because of the legislators' human failings. If a problem with the common law is its inability to paint in broad strokes, a problem with legislation is its inability to use a fine brush. Human experience is too rich and too varied to be captured forever in any form of words, and a broad solution that seems sound in light of today's realities may well be very foolish when applied to an unanticipated set of facts.

Changing values, advances in science, and unanticipated situations combine to create the possibility that prospective, comprehensive lawmaking will be fundamentally flawed. Moreover, even generally sound legislation cannot truly provide the universal answer people often seek. For example, the Uniform Anatomical Gift Act facilitates organ donation after death;[12] it is widely viewed as a "good statute." One of its features is to list in order persons who may donate a dead person's organs if the dead person has not made provisions to the contrary. At the top of the list is a spouse. Several years ago a surgeon called me with a question: Was it all right for a man to donate his dead wife's kidneys after he had murdered her? The statutory drafters had not considered that point!

Because legislation need not await a case and because it can be prospective and comprehensive, it may be a faster way to deal with problems than case-by-case common law adjudication. The concerns just noted raise questions about whether speed is a virtue. Even if it is a virtue, the legislature is not all that fast. A problem must be recognized before the legislature can act. The political process slows bills on their way to passage, often for multiple legislative sessions. And once the legislature has acted, the press of business and the enormity of effort required to pass a statute make revisiting an issue in the near future highly unlikely. Thus, rather than being able to respond quickly to new developments, law often becomes frozen at one historical moment in scientific development. Depending on the nature of the statute adopted, the legislation may freeze science and technology as well.

Finally, legislation is said to be more certain than common law. To an extent this is true. The legislature can provide rules in advance that tell people what they are supposed to do and what the consequences of noncompliance will be. That is why criminal law is statutory. Legislation is much more likely to achieve conduct control than is common law adjudication.

As with other asserted legislative virtues, certainty may be a mixed blessing, and the degree of certainty attainable may be overstated. Certainty is only a virtue if the certain answer is the right answer, or if the situation is one in which stability and predictability are all that matter so that nobody *cares* what the answer is as long as everybody *knows* what the answer is. If the legislature makes a mistake, certainty is a vice, not a virtue, and the fact that legislation is hard to change and affects the entire jurisdiction means that the costs of the mistakes of certainty will be large. They will be borne for a long time, by many persons, in a large area. The fact-specific nature of common law, on the other hand, makes mistakes fairly easy to confine. Courts often distinguish cases in order not to follow them, and the phenomenon of exceptions becoming so numerous that they swallow a rule is well known.

Additionally, certainty is related to the virtue of comprehensiveness. Part of what makes legislation certain is that it applies to a wide range of facts. Once again, if a legislative pronouncement makes no sense in a specific application, certainty has been purchased at the expense of sound results. To put it another way, "rigidity" is the negative way to say "certainty"; "flexibility" is the positive term for "uncertainty."

In any event, legislation is not really very certain. Language is the only tool legislators have at their disposal, and the uncertainties of language are well known. Moreover, statutes are not self-executing. Their enforcement requires courts. Courts, of course, have the power to interpret statutes, and the certainty of language disappears rapidly in the mists of judicial interpretation. Indeed, willful courts can often interpret statutes to mean precisely the opposite of what their drafters obviously had in mind. Thus, the California Supreme Court read a statute that required motels with swimming pools to have a lifeguard or a sign stating that there was no lifeguard to impose a primary obligation to have a lifeguard. The court simply read the sign requirement out of the statute.[13] The Supreme Court of Washington rejected professional standards as the measure of negligence in malpractice cases.[14] The legislature passed a statute reinstating professional standards.[15] The court then read the statute as supporting its view.[16]

In some cases very well drafted legislation can restrict the room for judicial construction, but the vagaries of language and the fallibility of drafters prevent that from happening very often. And, of course, if all else fails, a court may declare a statute unconstitutional. Despite the myth of legislative dominance courts almost always have the last word.

Before leaving the subject of legislation we should note that not all legislation is the same. The legislature has many choices open to it. It can enact criminal statutes, civilly enforceable statutes, or administratively enforceable statutes. It can require, prohibit, tax, license, or fund behavior. It can create and empower administrative agencies or remit matters to courts. Each of these options has independent characteristics, and we shall see several of them at work throughout this book. In general, however, the specific characteristics of legislation either reflect and build upon or are conscious efforts to try to avoid the general characteristics discussed so far.

ADMINISTRATIVE LAWMAKING

One thing a legislature can do is create an administrative agency to deal with a particular range of problems. The invention of administrative agencies during the New Deal period was the last major legal innovation in the United States.

Administrative agencies, which exist at both the state and federal levels, are designed to overcome some of the deficiencies of both common law adjudication and legislation. Administrative law is made by (1) appointed officials who are not directly accountable to the public. These persons are to be (2) experts in the area being regulated; they are to proceed (3) informally; and they can engage in both (4) rule making and (5) adjudication. Thus, administrative law is supposed to be fast, responsive, expert decision making that can be implemented in a variety of ways. Unfortunately, the performance of administrative agencies has not matched their promise.

In a sense, administrative agencies are caught on both horns of the accountability-nonaccountability dilemma. Most agency lawmakers are civil servants, career government workers who are shielded from public view and public accountability. They are the much reviled "faceless bureaucrats." High-level agency lawmakers, on the other hand, are political appointees, committed to the agenda of whoever appoints them, usually those in control of the executive branch. These officials are likely to reflect political considerations in their lawmaking while not being subject to direct democratic control.

If administrative agencies really dealt only with matters that were susceptible to expert decision making, the fact that they are populated by bureaucrats and political appointees might not be very important. But, of course, no legal question is simply a matter of one kind of expertise. Law deals with social questions as to which values and many kinds of expertise are relevant. The Department of Health and Human Services under President Reagan adopted regulations to require treatment for handicapped newborns,[17] not because biology dictated that result, but because the administration's values dictated it. Unaccountable, political decisions in areas not susceptible to expert decision making are difficult to justify.

Even within areas as to which expertise is relevant, the likelihood of an agency making truly unbiased expert decisions is very small. Persons become experts by working in a field. For example, doctors are the experts on medicine. Therefore, if an agency really is populated by experts, it will consist of members of the very group the agency is supposed to regulate. The regulated group captures the regulating agency; the fox guards the chicken coop. Obviously, expertise in lawmaking is not an unmixed blessing.

The hope that administrative agencies could work quickly and informally has turned out to be evanescent. Federal statutes[18] and the requirements of due process dictate the procedures agencies must follow. Whatever the theory, administrative lawmaking is, in fact, highly formalized, remarkably technical, and extremely complex. A large part of the practice of major law firms, especially in Washington, D.C., involves guiding clients through the administrative maze.

Administrative agencies can engage in both rule making and adjudication. That is, they can act like legislatures and like courts. This is a major advantage, because it permits agencies to paint with both broad and fine brushes and to tailor their responses to the particular kind of problem they are confronting. Similarly, agencies have a broad range of remedies available to them and can engage in the kind of ongoing supervision that courts or legislatures cannot undertake. Of course, all this flexibility cannot overcome the defects inherent in either rulemaking or adjudication—lack of foresight, limitations of language, inadequate presentation of facts, etc. To some extent a shift from legislature to agency is simply a shift of the place where intractable problems of lawmaking will occur.

Even the shift of locus is not complete. Administrative agencies are created, empowered, financed, and to some extent overseen by legislatures. Thus, to say that a new problem should be dealt with administratively is to say the legislature should remit it to an agency. In other words, many of the problems of legislation will affect the law's response to the problem. Even getting the problem into agency hands requires exposing it to the legislature, which may choose to do something else with it. Finally, if someone is dissatisfied with something an agency has done, the dissatisfied person may seek judicial review of the agency's action. While notions of deference to expertise constrain such review,[19] they cannot overcome the time, cost, formality, and other limits of the judicial approach. Sometimes administrative lawmaking simply adds an extra layer of lawmaking to efforts to deal with a social issue, thereby adding costs and complexity in the name of simplification and informality.

CONSTITUTIONAL ADJUDICATION

The ultimate weapon in the American legal arsenal is constitutional adjudication. If Americans want something decided once and for all at the highest levels of principle and authority, they look to the Constitution. Like a statute the Constitution is not self-executing. Therefore, judicial decisions interpreting and applying the Constitution are the ultimate repository of American constitutional law.

Constitutional adjudication looks, to the casual observer, like common law adjudication. It involves trials, appeals to judges who decide real cases and issue opinions that are used as precedent, etc. In fact, in many ways constitutional adjudication is an even clearer polar opposite of common law adjudication than legislation is. Common law is thinking small; constitutional law is thinking big. If common law is the legal system's beebee gun, constitutional adjudication is its nuclear bomb—much more likely than the common law to destroy its target, but also much more likely to produce fallout, which may prove noxious even to those who dropped the bomb.

Constitutional adjudication is law (1) made by judges (2) who get their information from lawyers. It involves (3) the national imposition of solutions, is (4) sweeping in its analogical as well as its geographical impact, and it is (5) difficult to change. It is made through (6) case by case adjudication, and (7) real, existing disputes serve as vehicles for lawmaking.

Like common law adjudication, constitutional adjudication is performed by judges who are informed by lawyers. As a practical matter, constitutional law is made by nine judges, the Justices of the United States Supreme Court. State and lower federal courts may pass on questions of constitutional law, but only the decisions of the Supreme Court are definitive. Thus, constitutional law, like common law, is law made by nonexperts. It is law made by persons with life tenure, who are insulated from political pressures, but who may well have been appointed to foster political agendas. Even if those agendas lose popular support, they may retain vitality because of the life tenure of Supreme Court Justices.

These nondemocratic, inexpert decision makers have enormous power. Their decisions are binding throughout the United States, much like federal legislation. That means that if the Court makes mistakes, the costs of those mistakes will be visited on all of us. Moreover, their decisions have impact far beyond the facts of the cases they decide.

The basic building block of common law adjudication is the case. By the time a case reaches the lawmaking (appellate) stage, its facts are either known or assumed. The job of the appellate court is to decide the dispute to which those facts gave rise. Over a period of years the resolutions of disputes that arose out of discrete factual situations will permit generalization and the formulation or tentative formulation of rules. Those rules, which emerge *up* out of disputes, are what lawyers and citizens rely on to make predictions about the way future disputes will be resolved. Often the predictions are weak because the facts of a new dispute are always different than the facts of an old one, and in evaluating a previously decided case the only thing one can be sure of is that in A year B facts led to C outcome. A lawyer is always free to argue that social conditions are so different in X year, or Y facts are so different from B facts, that Z outcome should follow instead of C outcome. In some ways the essence of common law decision making is the comparison of the *facts* of cases to decide which facts are similar enough to lead to similar results.

In constitutional adjudication, on the other hand, the basic building block is the Constitution. One may argue about how to read the Constitution—strictly, in light of the intent of the framers, incorporating modern values, or whatever—but the Constitution, however construed, is what the lawmaking process is about. The Constitution sets forth the basic principles that create our governmental structure and govern the relationship between the citizen and the government. The principles and their meanings are not self-evident. The Court must interpret and explicate them. Once it has done so, however, it applies the principles *down* to the facts of a particular case in order to resolve it. The principles are what matter; the case is merely an occasion for explaining them.

Since constitutional adjudication is, or purports to be, principled, its decisions have broad analogical reach. In theory they apply to every situation covered by the same principle they have announced. That is why many persons thought the right of privacy recognized in *Roe v. Wade*,[20] the famous 1973 abortion case, included a right to commit sodomy.[21] The principle of bodily privacy rooted in personal autonomy suggests that. On the other hand, the facts of committing sodomy are so different from the facts of having an abortion that a fact-based rather than a principle-based jurisprudence would not have suggested the analogy.

Thus, constitutional decisions influence an enormous range of issues over the full geographical sweep of the United States. Moreover, constitutional decisions are very difficult to change. The only ways to change constitutional decisions are to amend the Constitution or convince the Supreme Court to reverse itself. The process of amendment is difficult, burdensome, costly, and impractical, as any proponent of the Equal Rights Amendment will attest. Since the adoption of the Bill of Rights the Constitution has been amended only seventeen times in the history of the republic. Overruling is only slightly easier. The Supreme Court is properly reluctant to overrule its decisions. After all, one reason for rendering a constitutional decision is to resolve a matter definitively. Overruling defeats that purpose and upsets governmental and private actions taken throughout the United States in reliance on the decision. Overruling a constitutional decision is very disruptive. In addition, deciding that the United States Constitution says one thing today and the opposite tomorrow makes the Court look foolish and leads to disrespect for law by increasing the appearance that constitutional law is simply the personal opinions of any five members of the Supreme Court.[22] Thus, even decisions that are plainly unattractive to the majority of the Court, like the 1961 decision preventing the use in state trials of evidence obtained illegally,[23] remain on the books long after they have lost judicial support.

The difficulty of changing constitutional decisions means two things. First, it adds to the overwhelming impact of those decisions, thereby making mistakes even more costly than geographical and analogical breadth alone make them. Second, it means that when the Court decides that an earlier decision was wrong, or ought not to be followed, it is likely to distinguish cases and create exceptions in *common law* fashion, thus destroying the principled basis of constitutional decisions, muddying the law, precluding sound predictions, and increasing litigation. Both the history of the exclusionary rule mentioned above and of *Roe v. Wade* illustrate this phenomenon.

This introduces one of the great paradoxes of constitutional law. National, principled, difficult to change law is made through case by case adjudication. Thus, one can always argue that the facts of the case before the Court, rather than some principle located in the Constitution, controlled the outcome. Therefore, one can never really count on constitutional adjudication to resolve matters definitively or to illuminate the principles by which our society is to be governed. We have, if you will, the worst of all possible worlds, combining the failings of federal legislation and common law adjudication without providing the benefits of either. One really would not want to turn often to a system of lawmaking that combined those characteristics.

Finally, as may be apparent from what has been said, in constitutional adjudication, real, existing disputes serve as vehicles for lawmaking. In a common law system resolution of disputes makes the law. In the constitutional realm, however, the disputes are simply vehicles, opportunities, excuses to make law. Therefore, once again, one can argue either that the law transcends the disputes or that it is determined by them. The opportunities for expansiveness and contraction are enormous.

CONCLUSION

As this brief survey of legal institutions suggests, our tools for dealing with social problems posed by rapid change in biology and medicine are limited at best. Two lessons should emerge. First, different institutional responses should be chosen for different problems depending on such factors as the need for expertise in decision making, the importance of conduct control, the importance of national solutions, etc. Second, attention to the costs of mistakes counsels caution in resorting to law at all and suggests a preference for relatively low-level responses (common law, some administrative responses, some noncriminal state legislation) unless and until one is persuaded that a real and pressing need, which can only be met by extreme measures, exists, and that the costs of resorting to the extreme measures will not outweigh the gains.

Now we turn to examine areas in which the law has confronted social issues posed by biomedical advance. The law's responses to these issues will demonstrate the practical importance of paying attention to process concerns; the desirability of using the lowest level legal responses capable of dealing with the social issues a technology presents; and the damage that is done when lawmakers and law reformers fail to pay attention to the characteristics, strengths, and weaknesses of each of our legal institutions.

TWO

Abortion
The Perils of Thinking Big

The abortion controversy, which has divided America, illustrates the misuse of the legal system's most powerful tools to achieve ends for which they are ill designed. From 1821 until 1973, criminal legislation prohibited abortion. Since 1973 the Constitution has purported to allow it. Criminal law and constitutional law are the system's two big guns. The law, women seeking abortions, and the country at large would all be better off if moderation, small thinking, and attention to process had won the day.

Criminal law is the state's most powerful weapon against the individual. The worst thing our system can do to a person is to declare him a criminal and punish him accordingly. Beginning in Connecticut in 1821[1] that is the way our country dealt with abortion. Eventually every state made abortion a felony. Typically the law prohibited both women from seeking abortions and persons from performing them.

Apparently the early law was designed to protect women from the dangers of surgery in the days before aseptic and antiseptic techniques.[2] Consistently with that protective view the statutes contained an exception that allowed an abortion to be performed if it was necessary to save the mother's life.[3] Alabama and the District of Columbia permitted abortions to preserve either the mother's life or health.[4]

One need not take any position about women's rights or the morality of abortion to conclude that the statutes were probably unwise when they were enacted and were surely unwise by the middle of the twentieth century. By mid-twentieth century antisepsis and asepsis were routine; early abortions, performed by physicians in clean settings had become safer for women than carrying pregnancies to term.[5] Therefore, the original rationale could no longer justify criminalizing abortion.

However, the modern abortion debate no longer focuses on maternal safety. By the 1950s, and certainly today, criminal anti-abortion legislation is supported by so-called "right-to-life" groups, whose concern, as their name implies, is with protecting fetal life. Now the moral lines are plainly drawn—one must either be for life or (presumably) against it; one must either be for women's rights, independence, and autonomy or against them. In that climate, criminalizing abortion makes no sense.

As Professor Herbert Packer taught us a quarter century ago, criminalizing behavior requires substantial justification.[6] This is both because criminalization is extreme and because the use of the criminal sanction—the intentional infliction of suffering by the state—is morally problematic. Accordingly, Packer offered a series of prudential considerations to the rational legislator who was trying to decide whether to criminalize or remove criminal sanctions from behavior. Those considerations suggest that abortion in most circumstances ought not to be a crime.

The existence of deep and wide division about abortion is one fundamental reason not to criminalize it. Extreme, morally questionable law should be reserved for areas in which moral consensus exists in the society. Otherwise, we intentionally inflict pain on behavior many persons find appropriate, thereby using the state's power in an immoral way that can be justified only by asserting that might makes right.

The fact that many women feel driven to seek abortions because they find no other tolerable options suggests a range of reasons to refrain from using the criminal sanction. First, criminalization will be inefficacious. It will not (and did not) prevent abortions; it simply prevented safe abortions, driving women into the hands of dangerous back-alley butchers. Second, it is not even maximally effective in deterring safe abortions, as the demand for the service makes women who are able to pay a premium an attractive market for some physicians. This high demand results in what Packer called a "crime tariff."[7] Criminal anti-abortion laws did not prevent abortions. They simply raised the price of abortions to cover the abortionist's legal risks and funneled the inflated price into the hands of persons who, by definition, were willing to break the law. The impossibility of anything close to full enforcement meant that enforcement was sporadic, uneven, and, inevitably, discriminatory. Discriminatory enforcement obviously adds another evil to those of punishing conduct because one does not agree with someone else's point of view and endangering the health and lives of women.

If the legislatures made a mistake by enacting (or at least by failing to repeal) their criminal anti-abortion statutes, the most obvious place to look for reform would seem to be the legislatures. The most important reform would simply be to repeal the criminal prohibitions. Repeal would get the states out of the abortion area, free women and doctors from fear of prosecution, increase the availability of safe abortions, reduce costs, funnel moneys to legitimate practitioners, and remove from the law a source of discrimination and blackmail. In fact, a significant legislative reform movement flourished from the mid-1950s until 1973.

LEGISLATIVE REFORM

The middle of the twentieth century was a period of rationalization and reform of American criminal law. Sparked by the work of the American Law Institute in preparing a Model Penal Code,[8] and encouraged by scholars like Packer and others who argued for reducing society's reliance on the criminal law, twenty-one states revised their penal codes between 1956 and 1973.[9] Specific provisions of the Model Penal Code were influential even in states that did not do full-scale revisions.

Thus, by 1973, fourteen states had revised their criminal anti-abortion statutes along the lines recommended by the Model Penal Code.[10] These modern, "therapeutic" abortion statutes continued to prohibit abortion but expanded the number of exceptional situations in which abortions were permitted. Therapeutic abortion statutes permitted abortions not only to preserve the mother's life but also to preserve her physical or mental health, when there was reason to believe the child would be born with a serious physical or mental defect, and when the pregnancy was the result of rape or incest. Four states went farther and permitted abortion without regard to the reason for it until about the time of fetal viability.[11] Thus, by 1973 eighteen states had significantly reformed their law. Four permitted abortion on demand until viability, and fourteen others probably came close to capturing the views of most persons about when abortion was an appropriate response to a pregnancy. These eighteen statutes adopted over a period of seventeen years render wholly unconvincing the argument that the legislatures were unresponsive to the claims of women and pro-choice advocates and that seeking legislative reform was pointless.

Moreover, a 1971 United States Supreme Court decision[12] rendered moderate anti-abortion laws unenforceable. This made abortion readily available in eighteen states and (depending on who was asleep at what switches) may have provided pro-choice reformers in states that had not reformed their laws with an effective law reform strategy.

The District of Columbia statute prohibited abortions unless they were necessary to preserve the mother's life or health. In *United States v. Vuitch* a physician challenged the statute as unconstitutionally vague. The Due Process clauses of the Fifth and Fourteenth Amendments require that criminal statutes be sufficiently clear so that potential offenders do not have to guess what behavior is prohibited and what is permitted and so that potential law enforcers not be given excessive discretion that would allow them to use the statutes as a tool of discrimination or oppression.[13] In *Vuitch* the physician argued that "necessary to preserve . . . health" was such a vague phrase that it violated the requirements of due process. The Supreme Court disagreed and upheld the statute. However, it did that only by adopting two essential statutory constructions. It held (1) that "health" must be construed to include mental health as well as physical health and (2) that the prosecution has the burden of proving beyond a reasonable doubt that the abortion was not necessary for preservation of the mother's life or health. Thus, after *Vuitch* a prosecutor could only obtain a conviction under a District of Columbia type statute by proving beyond a reasonable doubt that an abortion was not necessary to save a mother's life or physical or mental health. Given the needs of women who seek abortions, that showing would be almost impossible to make. Thus, *Vuitch* should have reduced even further the fears of women in the District of Columbia, Alabama, and the fourteen states with therapeutic abortion statutes because it made their statutes nearly unenforceable.

After *Vuitch* a clever pro-choice strategy in a state without reform legislation might have been to introduce an abortion-on-demand-until-viability statute; mollify many opponents by compromising and accepting a therapeutic abortion statute; and then compromising again to pick up all but the most intransigent votes by settling for a statute that permitted abortions only to preserve maternal life or health. Getting that kind of statute would have accomplished many of the reformers' goals by making the state's anti-abortion statute virtually unenforceable.

We will never know whether that strategy would have worked, because rather than try it or simply continue the orderly process of legislative reform, pro-choice advocates sought to establish the existence of a constitutional right to abortion. Their reasons for pursuing that path are easy enough to understand. Legislative reforms gave them only half a loaf, and further legislative reform would be slow and uneven, and might not succeed. The reformers wanted a total victory, everywhere, right away. They wanted a principled recognition that abortion is a "right," not a "wrong" to be tolerated in certain exceptional circumstances. They wanted that principle to be recognized throughout the United States. And they wanted everything the principle of a "right" to abortion implied—not just freedom from criminal punishment, but an entitlement to an abortion, performed by and paid for by the state, free of the supervision of the fathers of their fetuses, their own parents or guardians, or any organs of the state.

CONSTITUTIONAL REFORM

The Road to Roe

The period of legislative reform of criminal anti-abortion laws was also a time of considerable ferment in constitutional law. It was the heyday of the Warren Court—of school desegregation, one man-one vote, and expanded protection for those accused of crime. It was also a period of judicial innovation and newfound interest in the relationship of the state to matters of sex and reproduction.

The story really begins even earlier, around the turn of the century. Both the Fifth Amendment, which applies to the federal government, and the Fourteenth Amendment, which applies to the states, protect persons against being deprived of life, liberty, or property without due process of law. Due process of law has always been understood to have a procedural thrust. Fair procedures are the essence of due process. Thus, one is entitled to a trial, to an unbiased judge, to confront the witness against him, etc. For most of the nation's history "procedure" has been taken as synonymous with "process."

However, due process may have another meaning as well. In a substantive sense one might say that a law that prevented a person from doing something deprived that person of liberty without due process of law unless there was a good reason for the law. How could the process we are due lead to laws unsupported by good reasons? A good reason would be that the statute actually served some legitimate goal of the state. Thus, under this substantive due process approach one could disallow a state's intrusion upon freedom of action on the ground either that the end the state sought to pursue was inappropriate or that the means adopted did not actually further the end.

Substantive due process has always been controversial.[14] It is obviously a tool of judicial activism and, since it is unconstrained by any specific, written grant or prohibition in the text of the Constitution, it opens the Court to charges that decisions based on it are unprincipled and nothing more than the personal preferences of the Justices. It expands the counter-majoritarian power of the Supreme Court and weakens respect for law. It reduces predictability because one cannot know what ends the Court will find important or how rigorously it will evaluate the means chosen to attain them. Moreover, the means-end analysis forces the Court to engage in complex factual analyses of areas in which it lacks expertise.

Nonetheless, from the end of the nineteenth century until the middle of the New Deal era, the Supreme Court frequently struck down statutes on substantive due process grounds.[15] The invalidated statutes typically were reform statutes that were opposed by business and conservative interests. Thus, a technique of judicial activism was used in the service of political and economic conservatism.

The conservative caste of the Supreme Court frustrated President Franklin Roosevelt and led to his famous Court-packing plan, which was averted in part by the rejection of substantive due process. Beginning in 1937, the Supreme Court largely stopped overseeing both state and federal interventions into areas not mentioned in constitutional text.[16] The Court rejected the main substantive due process cases in 1949,[17] and in 1963 it plainly held that substantive due process was dead.[18] This caused the Court some trouble in 1965, when it confronted the question of the relationship between contraceptives and the Constitution.

A Connecticut statute prohibited the use of contraceptives.[19] Not surprisingly, the statute had been under attack for many years. Until 1965, however, the Supreme Court had managed to avoid deciding whether the statute was constitutional by resorting to doctrines designed to guarantee that only real, sharply contested controversies will be resolved at the highest level of principle. After all, why decide a hard question and risk making a mistake that, along with its analogues, will be visited upon all the states if you don't have to?

Thus, in *Tileston v. Ullman*[20] in 1943, a doctor challenged the Connecticut statute as violating the rights of his patients. The Court dismissed the case because the doctor was not asserting his own rights; only a personally aggrieved person has "standing" to raise a constitutional challenge.

In 1961 a physician, a married couple, and a married woman challenged the statute. In *Poe v. Ullman*[21] the Supreme Court again refused to decide the case. Prosecuting attorneys in Connecticut had shown no interest in prosecuting the petitioners or anybody else for violating the statute despite the fact that contraceptives were widely available in Connecticut. Thus, said the Court, there is no controversy to be adjudicated; the controversy is not justiciable because it is not ripe.

Reformers then decided to ripen the controversy. The Court decided *Poe* on June, 19, 1961. On November 1, 1961, Planned Parenthood opened a birth control center in New Haven amid considerable fanfare. It succeeded in getting the prosecutor to move against it. In *Griswold v. Connecticut*[22] the state charged the executive director of the Planned Parenthood League and the League's medical director at the New Haven clinic with aiding and abetting violation of the anti-contraceptive use statute. The defendants were convicted and fined $100.00 each.

Although the Supreme Court could have used arguments similar to those in *Tileston* and *Poe* to avoid confronting the merits of the case, it chose not to do so. It now took the position that the criminal convictions made the question of statutory validity ripe for decision and that the defendants had standing to raise the rights of those who wanted to use contraceptives.

One can lament the Court's unwillingness to rely further on technical doctrines to avoid deciding hard questions. It does seem silly to allow reformers to force the Court to decide an issue it does not want to decide and is ill equipped to decide. Moreover, one could argue that the pre-*Griswold* situation in Connecticut was the best of all possible worlds—contraceptives were readily available; users incurred no practical risk of prosecution; and those who liked the law had the satisfaction of its continued existence on the books. However, the Court did not adopt that kind of realpolitik attitude. It confronted the question of statutory validity head on.

Once it decided to do that, it faced a serious problem. The statute was asinine; the Court could not let it stand. However, no written provision of the Constitution seemed to invalidate it, and the Court had rejected substantive due process as recently as two years before. What was the Court to do?

The Court, in an opinion by Justice Douglas, invalidated the Connecticut statute. It noted that specific provisions of the Bill of Rights cast long shadows. Specifically, despite the failure of the Constitution to mention privacy, the

Court found that a constitutional right of privacy existed in "penumbras, formed by emanations from" specific Bill of Rights guarantees.[23] First Amendment freedoms of speech and press; the Third Amendment's prohibition of quartering soldiers in persons' homes during peacetime; Fourth Amendment protection against unreasonable search and seizure; and the Fifth Amendment protection from compulsory self-incrimination all protect aspects of privacy. The Ninth Amendment's provision that the enumeration of some rights shall not be construed to deny other rights retained by the people prevents the argument that protection of some aspects of privacy shows that others are not to be protected.[24] Therefore, a constitutional right of privacy exists.

The marital relationship lies within the zone of protected privacy:

> Would we allow the police to search the sacred precincts of marital bedrooms for telltale signs of the use of contraceptives? The very idea is repulsive to the notions of privacy surrounding the marriage relation.
> ... Marriage is a coming together for better or for worse, hopefully enduring, and intimate to the degree of being sacred. . . . [I]t is an association for as noble a purpose as any involved in our prior decisions.[25]

The Connecticut statute, which impinged upon this right of marital privacy, was invalid because it was broader than necessary. By forbidding the use of contraceptives rather than simply regulating their manufacture or sale, it sought to achieve its goals by means having a maximally destructive impact on the protected privacy right.[26]

The *Griswold* opinion is easy to criticize. Most obviously, the fact that some aspects of privacy are constitutionally protected is no evidence that others are, even if the Ninth Amendment prevents it from being evidence that they are not. But criticizing *Griswold* is not what is important. What is important is to see that however hard Justice Douglas tried to tie his opinion to specific Bill of Rights guarantees, he had really decided that the Connecticut statute violated substantive due process. It had invaded an area of personal liberty without a good enough reason to do so; even if the state had valid goals in mind, its means were too extreme—they were unnecessarily broad.

In separate opinions Justices White[27] and Harlan[28] advocated basing the decision explicitly on substantive due process grounds. Justice Goldberg, who placed heavy emphasis on the Ninth Amendment,[29] did essentially the same thing. Justice Black[30] and Justice Stewart[31] dissented. Justice Stewart thought the Connecticut statute was "an uncommonly silly law,"[32] but he found nothing in the Constitution to invalidate it. Years later in *Roe v. Wade* Justice Stewart noted that the Court in *Griswold* had essentially adopted substantive due process, and he finally decided he agreed with the result.[33] Justice Douglas, however, steadfastly denied that he had applied substantive due process in his opinion for the Court in *Griswold*.[34]

If *Griswold* did represent the rebirth of substantive due process and its application to personal, noneconomic settings, then its implications were enormous. It would open all sorts of restrictions on personal liberty to constitutional attack. In fact, though, between 1965 and 1973 the Court seemed loath to go where the implications of *Griswold* seemed to lead.

As noted before, in 1971 the Court responded to an attack on the District of Columbia abortion statute not by invalidating it on substantive due process or privacy grounds, but by construing the statute and upholding it against the charge of unconstitutional vagueness.[35]

In 1972, only a year before *Roe v. Wade*, the Court seemed to continue its retreat from *Griswold* and from substantive due process. *Eisenstadt v. Baird*[36] involved a Massachusetts statute that prohibited the distribution of contraceptives to unmarried persons for the purpose of preventing conception. Both married and unmarried persons could obtain contraceptives to prevent disease. Married persons could also obtain them to prevent conception, but only from licensed doctors or pharmacists. Mr. Baird, who was neither a doctor nor a pharmacist, was convicted of giving contraceptive foam to an unmarried woman. The Supreme Court reversed his conviction on the ground that the statute deprived unmarried persons of the equal protection of the laws.

The Fourteenth Amendment prohibits states from denying persons the equal protection of the laws. If state action creates different classes of persons who are to be treated differently, the Court evaluates the state's classification scheme. If a classification is "suspect" (racial classifications are the clearest example) or if the state's scheme intrudes upon a fundamental right, the Court will subject the classification to "strict scrutiny" and invalidate the classification scheme unless the scheme is necessary to achieve a compelling state interest. If, however, the classification is not suspect and the statute does not intrude upon a fundamental right, then the Court will uphold the classification as long as it bears a rational relationship to a legitimate state end.[37] Many state interests are legitimate, few are compelling. Many means are rational, few are necessary. Therefore, as a practical matter, the decision that a classification is suspect or impinges on a fundamental right comes close to being a decision to invalidate it. The decision to apply mere rational basis analysis is close to a decision to uphold the classification.

The Massachusetts statute treated married and unmarried persons differently. Despite the fulsome language in *Griswold* about the sanctity of marriage and the importance of marital privacy, the Court in *Eisenstadt* said, "If the right of privacy means anything, it is the right of the *individual*, married or single, to be free from unwarranted governmental intrusion into matters so fundamentally affecting a person as the decision whether to bear or beget a child."[38] Having decided that unmarried as well as married persons enjoy a right of privacy, the Court then evaluated the state's reasons for treating them differently. It spoke the language of rational basis review; but in what has come to be called mid-level scrutiny,[39] it evaluated the reasons much more rigorously than the rational basis label seemed to suggest. The Court found that none of the state's proffered reasons to distinguish single persons from married ones was persuasive. It therefore held that contraceptive availability had to be the same for married and unmarried persons and that the Massachusetts statute deprived unmarried persons of the equal protection of the laws.

In one sense *Eisenstadt* was an expansion of *Griswold*. While *Eisenstadt* did not consider the substance of the right of privacy, it did extend the right from married persons to include the unmarried as well.

In another sense, though, it was a retreat. A substantive due process approach to the Massachusetts statute would have decided something about what the right of privacy includes in regard to contraception. Instead, the Court simply decided that whatever the right includes, it must give the same protection to married and unmarried persons. Theoretically, the state could prohibit furnishing contraceptives to anybody. The equal protection approach is narrower than substantive due process. It focuses only on the propriety of the means (classification) the state has adopted. Substantive due process focuses on ends as well. Moreover, equal protection analysis is well established, not controversial like substantive due process. Thus, as late as 1972 the Supreme Court seemed to have put the *Griswold* analysis on the shelf and to have turned away from substantive due process. Then came *Roe v. Wade*.

Roe v. Wade

In two cases decided on January 22, 1973, the Supreme Court revolutionized abortion law. It appeared to give pro-choice reformers the total, principled victory they had sought. How far short it had stopped of providing that victory has become increasingly clear over the last twenty years.

Roe v. Wade[40] presented a challenge to Texas's old-fashioned anti-abortion law, which prohibited all abortions except those "for the purpose of saving the life of the mother." *Roe*'s companion case, *Doe v. Bolton*,[41] challenged Georgia's more modern, therapeutic abortion statute. The Supreme Court struck down both statutes.

As in *Griswold* the Court decided that the statutes impinged upon the right of privacy. In *Roe*, however, the Court found that right not in penumbras formed by emanations from specific Bill of Rights guarantees but in the Fourteenth Amendment's concept of liberty.[42] No state may deprive any person of liberty without due process of law. The liberty that is protected includes a right of privacy, and the right of privacy is "broad enough to encompass a woman's decision whether or not to terminate her pregnancy."[43]

Only rights that are fundamental or implicit in the concept of ordered liberty are included in the right of privacy.[44] Thus, the right to decide whether to terminate a pregnancy is fundamental or implicit in the concept of ordered liberty. Because the right is fundamental, a state may not infringe the right unless doing so is necessary to a compelling state interest. In the abortion context two state interests deserve to be weighed against the woman's right, the interest in maternal health and the interest in the potential life of the fetus. The interest in maternal health becomes compelling at the end of the first trimester because until that point having an abortion is safer than carrying the pregnancy to term.[45] The interest in the potential life of the fetus becomes compelling at the time of fetal viability because then the fetus may be able to survive outside the mother's womb.[46] Accordingly, except for being allowed to insist that only physicians perform abortions,[47] the state may not impose any restrictions on abortion during the first trimester. Beginning at the end of the first trimester it may restrict abortions to the extent necessary to preserve maternal health.[48] After the fetus becomes viable, the state may also protect the fetus's potential life by restricting or prohibiting abortions except those that are necessary to preserve the mother's life or health.[49]

Applying the *Roe v. Wade* rules in *Doe v. Bolton* the Supreme Court invalidated provisions of Georgia's law that required abortions to be performed in accredited hospitals; that required them to be performed in licensed hospitals; that two physicians concur with the judgment of the physician who was to perform the abortion; that a hospital staff committee also agree; and that the woman obtaining the abortion be a Georgia resident.

Persons interested in abortion reform, at least those who were not legal scholars, were exultant. After *Roe* and *Doe* there seemed to be a fundamental right to abortion; the state had a well-nigh impossible burden to carry in justifying an infringement on that right until the time of fetal viability; and *Doe* seemed to suggest that the Court meant to enforce that burden vigorously against the state.

Legal scholars were less enthusiastic. While the public focused on the result of *Roe v. Wade*, i.e., the invalidation of virtually all the anti-abortion laws in the country, and rapidly took sides along the a-fetus-is-a-human-being-and-abortion-is-murder or a-woman-is-entitled-to-do-whatever-she-wants-with-her-own-body axis, scholars began dissecting the reasoning of *Roe v. Wade*. While analytical criticism of Supreme Court opinions is unlikely ever to capture the public's fancy, it is nonetheless very important. If it reveals that an opinion is devoid of reason, it alerts lawyers and judges to the opinion's vulnerability and presages the opinion's ultimate demise. Scholarly attacks on *Roe v. Wade* demonstrated that it could not stand.

While opponents of abortion hated the result of *Roe v. Wade*, scholarly critics often approved it. The most effective critic, Professor John Hart Ely,[50] prefaced his devastating attack on *Roe* with a lengthy explanation of his own prochoice preference. But regardless of one's views on abortion, *Roe* was a disaster for people who care about law. Scholars fell into two camps, those who criticized the opinion the Court wrote in *Roe* and those who made suggestions about the opinion the Court should have written.[51]

The basic problem with *Roe v. Wade* is that it is devoid of analysis. The opinion is very long and is filled with discussion of views on abortion from antiquity to the present, but it contains not one shred of analysis for any of its key propositions. Thus, no analysis supports either the assertion that Fourteenth Amendment liberty includes a right of privacy or the conclusion that the right of privacy is broad enough to encompass a woman's decision whether to terminate her pregnancy. Nothing except the Court's say-so supports the assertion that the right to make the abortion decision is fundamental or implicit in the concept of ordered liberty. The closest the Court comes to supporting its assertions is to note that carrying an unwanted pregnancy to term may have adverse effects on a woman's life. So may lots of other things, but that does not turn the satisfaction of desires to avoid a stressful life into a constitutional right.

The Court's analysis of the other side of the abortion equation is equally unpersuasive. The roots of the state's interests in maternal health and potential fetal life are nowhere described. The assertion that the interest in maternal health only becomes compelling at the end of the first trimester is ludicrous. (My women students are seldom attracted to the idea that the state has a compelling interest in their health only during the six-month periods when they are in the last two trimesters of pregnancy.) Presumably, the Court meant to say that the interest in maternal health is always compelling, but that no restriction on abortions other than insisting that physicians perform them is necessary to serve that end. Otherwise, it is hard to understand why the first trimester restriction to physicians is permissible.

Similarly, the assertion that the state's interest in potential life becomes compelling at viability because then the fetus may be able to survive outside the mother's womb begs the question. As Professor Ely pointed out, potential ability to survive outside the mother's womb is a definition of viability, not a reason anything should depend upon it.[52] Indeed, if one really cares about potential life, why isn't the fetus's possibility of survival a reason to be more permissive after viability, when the fetus may survive abortion, than before, when it cannot?

The facts that viability is a scientific concept, that the time of viability changes with technology, and that whether a fetus is viable depends on whether one determines viability before or after the abortion were all reasons not to make matters of constitutional significance depend upon viability. The fact that maternal health also depends on technology was a similar reason not to make such matters turn on maternal health. The facts that maternal health and potential fetal life are inextricably related and may sometimes be at war with each other suggests the folly of making them independent variables in the abortion regulation process. Each of these problems came back to haunt the Court, as we shall see.

Not surprisingly, the Court's failure of analysis in *Roe v. Wade* proved devastating to the opinion. It deprived *Roe* of any chance of persuading abortion opponents and left the Court defenseless before the charge that *Roe v. Wade* was lawless law, simply the imposition of the personal preferences of a majority of the members of the Supreme Court. Moreover, the fact that the absence of analysis emerged from an enormous opinion meant that language that suggested implications and further applications as well as language that sowed the seeds of retreat was plentiful in *Roe v. Wade*.

Whatever else one says about *Roe*, it plainly resurrected substantive due process. The Texas statute was unconstitutional because it violated an aspect of the liberty protected by the due process clause of the Fourteenth Amendment without a good enough reason for doing so. This clear rebirth of substantive due process invited persons to make substantive due process attacks on a variety of statutes that restricted personal choices. The Court's approach to the right of privacy encouraged that. The Court made no effort to define or circumscribe the right of privacy. It simply asserted that it was "broad enough" to encompass the decision of whether to terminate a pregnancy. What else was it broad enough to encompass—a right to die, to commit sodomy, to use heroin? How was anyone to know? The only limitation seemed to be that the asserted behavior had to be fundamental or implicit in the concept of ordered liberty to be protected. Since every western democracy has at some time prohibited abortion, since all of them wrestle with the issue, and since abortion was prohibited throughout the United States when we fought wars to end slavery, make the world safe for democracy, and crush Nazi totalitarianism, one might find it odd to think of abortion as implicit in the concept of ordered liberty. If it is, then what isn't?

Other examples of troublesome language in *Roe* are legion. Was one to pay attention to the use of the word "decision" in the Court's observation that the right of privacy is broad enough to include a woman's decision whether to terminate her pregnancy?[53] What is one to make of the Court's discussion of fetuses? The Court denied that it would decide when life begins[54] but noted that *no case could be cited* holding that a fetus is a person within the meaning of the Fourteenth Amendment[55] and that the "unborn have never been recognized in the law as persons in the whole sense."[56] One wonders whether other groups, for example, the comatose, the terminally ill, the handicapped, or the mentally retarded, might also exist who have some of the attributes of humanness but who are not "persons in the whole sense." A chilling prospect!

One could go on and on, but the point should be clear—whatever one thinks about abortion, the Supreme Court's opinion in *Roe v. Wade* was terrible. What remains to be shown is that the opinion worked significant mischief *from the point of view of those who had sought the ruling*, that it sowed the seeds of its own demise, and that all of this was predictable in 1972. Pro-choice reformers would have been better off to have continued the legislative reform strategy of the 1960s than to have pushed for constitutional reform.

The Aftermath of Roe v. Wade

The constitutional victory of the pro-choice reformers seemed secure for the first few years after *Roe v. Wade*. Indeed, the early post-*Roe* cases seemed to consolidate the victory and to recognize the logical implications of the abortion right recognized in *Roe*. If a constitutional right exists, two questions that must be answered quickly are (1) to whom does the right belong and (2) what is the nature of the right. In *Planned Parenthood Association v. Danforth*,[57] in 1976, the Court addressed the first of those questions. *Danforth* invalidated a Missouri statute that required the consent of the parents of a minor before the minor could get an abortion and required the consent of a married woman's husband before the married woman could obtain an abortion. The Court noted that the pregnant woman is the person most affected by the abortion decision and that, therefore, her decision must prevail. Nobody else may exercise an absolute veto over the abortion decision. Thus, *Danforth* made plain that the right recognized in *Roe* belonged to the pregnant woman and nobody else.

Needless to say, some persons who do not believe that the State of Texas should be able to make abortion a crime also think that parents ought to have a role to play in their minor daughter's abortions. Some might even think that husbands are not totally irrelevant to the abortion decision. Thus, by making plain the personal nature of the abortion right, *Danforth* began to sap from *Roe v. Wade* the support of some abortion moderates.

Danforth also played a significant role in beginning to define the nature of the abortion right. Obviously, a state may constitutionally require parental consent for a nonemergency appendectomy on a minor. It may not require parental consent for abortion on a minor. Only one thing can explain that difference: There is no constitutional right to an appendectomy. Indeed, in a 1977 case the Court stated in dictum that there is no constitutional right to any kind of health care.[58] This seems to suggest that the most obvious reading of *Roe* is the correct one: The constitutional right recognized by *Roe* is the right to an abortion, not simply the right to be free from criminal penalties for seeking, obtaining, or performing an abortion. That is, *Roe* and *Danforth* seemed to stand for the proposition that abortion is an affirmative right, something a woman is entitled to and can insist on receiving, subject to the second and third trimester restrictions permitted by *Roe v. Wade*.

This reading of *Roe* was very problematic. If there is an affirmative right to an abortion, then a public hospital must perform abortions regardless of its fiscal condition and the attitude of its staff. Indeed, the public hospital's staff would have to include persons willing to perform abortions. This is no fanciful law professor's nightmare. Lower court rulings did require public hospitals to perform abortions,[59] and the United States Court of Appeals for the Eighth Circuit refused to allow the City of St. Louis to staff its welfare clinic with physicians from St. Louis University Medical School because St. Louis University is a Catholic university whose physicians were conscientiously opposed to abortion.[60] This is the only example I know of in which a federal court has held that employment discrimination based on religion is not only constitutionally permitted, but constitutionally compelled.

The existence of an affirmative, personal right to an abortion also created practical problems for physicians. Suppose, for example, that a legally incompetent, mentally retarded woman sought an abortion to which her guardian refused to consent. What was a doctor at a public institution supposed to do? Before *Roe v. Wade* the answer was clear. An unconsented-to medical touching was a battery for which a physician would be liable. A guardian's consent was required to authorize a medical touching on an incompetent person. Without the guardian's consent, the touching was still a battery. Therefore, the physician would not perform the abortion because without the guardian's consent, s/he would be liable if s/he did.

After *Roe v. Wade* the law of battery remained the same. But given *Roe* and *Danforth*, the woman had a personal right to an abortion, which her parent or husband or guardian seemed unable to take from her. Therefore, refusing to do the abortion might expose the physician or his/her state institution to liability for depriving the woman of a civil right. In other words, the physician was now damned if s/he did, damned if s/he didn't. This prospect did not make physicians very happy, and the possibility of resolving it through more litigation is not an appealing prospect to most physicians.

Similarly, many persons believed that state institutions, which seemed to have to do abortions, also had to make whatever information a woman considered relevant to her abortion decision available to her. For example, the institution might have to provide amniocentesis to disclose the fetus's sex in order to permit abortion for sex choice. Needless to say, many persons besides committed right-to-life advocates are troubled by the notion of abortion for sex choice.

Importantly, none of these problems would have arisen from legislative reform, not even from total repeal of all criminal anti-abortion legislation. The absence of a statute that makes behavior a crime has no implications at all. It does not create any right to engage in the noncriminal behavior. No statute makes it a crime for me to own a watch. That does not mean the state of Indiana is obligated to give me one, or, for that matter, to teach me how to tell time.

By 1977 the implications of *Roe v. Wade* were beginning to become clear. Some of them were troubling, even to persons with a generally pro-choice point of view. As a practical matter, the likelihood that the Supreme Court would go as far as the logic of *Roe* seemed to suggest was very small, as anyone who thought about reality rather than ideology should have been able to predict. Thus, beginning in 1977, and in fits and starts, the Supreme Court has backed away from *Roe v. Wade*. It has done this by refusing to follow *Roe*'s implications and by backing away from the trimester analysis. Rejecting implications, of course, requires rejection of the principle that seems to lead to the implications. Thus, refusal to go where *Roe* leads undercuts the principled victory the reformers thought they had won. Retreat from trimesters opens the door to major regulation by the states, thus reducing the practical benefits the reformers thought they had gained. Doing all of this while refusing to overrule *Roe v. Wade* leaves *Roe* as a symbolic target for abortion foes to rally against and provides a constant goad to anti-abortion activity. For the supposedly victorious reformers this may be the worst of all possible worlds.

The Supreme Court acted quickly to dispel the notion that a woman has an affirmative right to an abortion. It reversed the Eighth Circuit's decision in the St. Louis welfare clinic case;[61] denied that state governments have an obligation to pay for abortions for indigent women, even if they pay for childbirth services;[62] and upheld the federal government's refusal to provide money to state Medicaid programs to pay for abortions.[63] Rather than a right to an abortion the Court now suggested that *Roe* protected an interest in decision making and in freedom from unduly burdensome restrictions on decision making.[64] As we have seen, *Roe*'s statement that the right of privacy is "broad enough to encompass a woman's *decision* whether or not to bear a child"[65] [emphasis added] invited this result. Nonetheless, a right to decide to terminate a pregnancy is not worth much to a woman who is unable to act on her decision.

According to the Court the inability to act, however, is not the state's fault. Failure to make money or facilities available is not an unduly burdensome restriction on decision making because the poor woman seeking an abortion had too little money to begin with. The refusal to fund does not impose any new roadblocks in her path to an abortion.[66] While it is true that funding childbirth, but not abortion, may make childbirth the more attractive option, that is all right. The Constitution permits states to adopt policies favoring childbirth over abortion.[67]

In fact, the Constitution apparently permits consideration of a wide range of policies (or state interests) besides those mentioned in *Roe*. The Court considered some of them, and backed off of its position that the abortion right is purely personal, in a series of decisions about minors who seek abortions.

In those cases the Supreme Court manifested its continuing confusion over the nature of the constitutional right at stake. Sometimes it referred to the right to choose an abortion,[68] sometimes the right to seek an abortion,[69] and, occasionally, the right to an abortion.[70] Given the enormous difference between seeking an abortion and getting one, this is quite confusing.

Hardly less confusing is the Court's specific response to the issue of abortion for minors. The Court has reaffirmed the unconstitutionality of parental consent requirements that it first struck down in *Danforth*.[71] However, it has upheld a parental consent requirement if the state provides the minor a satisfactory alternative to obtaining parental consent.[72] The alternative procedure may, but does not have to be a judicial hearing. It must be fast and provide anonymity for the minor. It must authorize the abortion *either* if the minor is mature enough to decide for herself *or* the abortion is in her best interests. The state may not insist on both maturity and best interests. It may not require the minor to seek parental consent before using the alternative procedure, but the decision maker may decide that parental consultation is in the minor's best interest and require it. The state may require the consent of both parents, but if only one consents, that consent should be given "great, if not dispositive, weight."[73] How helpful this will be to a pregnant minor (e.g., an impoverished, terrified, pregnant thirteen-year-old girl) is open to question.

Of course, states are not limited to choosing between parental noninvolvement and parental consent with a bypass. The Supreme Court has upheld a requirement that a minor's parents be "notified if possible" before an abortion is performed on her, at least if the minor is living with and dependent on her parents, is not emancipated, and has made no claim or showing with regard to her maturity or her relationship with her parents.[74] However, it has also held that requiring notice to both parents is unconstitutional, but that a provision for a judicial bypass in the event the two-parent notice requirement is enjoined saves the statutory scheme.[75] Finally, it has upheld a statute that prohibits an abortion on an unemancipated woman under eighteen unless (1) one parent consents in writing, or (2) the physician has given notice to one parent or a guardian, or (3) a court has given authority based on (a) maturity or (b) parental abuse of the minor or (c) a finding that notice would not be in the minor's best interest, or (4) the court has failed to act fast enough. This scheme is constitutional even though the procedures under it could take twenty-two days and even though the minor has to prove her maturity or best interests by clear and convincing evidence.[76] So much for clear, principled decision making.

The apparent confusion and lack of clarity in the abortions-for-minors cases goes beyond efforts to define the relevant right and to establish rules about which preconditions to abortions for minors are acceptable. In *Roe v. Wade* the Court quite plainly held that the abortion right (whatever it may be) is fundamental. That holding led to the conclusion that state infringements on the right are unconstitutional unless they are necessary to a compelling state interest. In the cases about minors, however, the Court moved away from the necessary to a compelling state interest standard. It applied a variety of different standards to restrictions on the abortion right, including whether the restriction was reasonably calculated to achieve the state's end.[77] That is the lowest level of scrutiny the Court applies to invasions of rights and is inconsistent with the idea that the abortion right is fundamental.

Additionally, the Court deviated from *Roe* by expanding the number of state interests that may be considered in deciding whether a particular intrusion into the abortion right is acceptable. The Court recognized as worthy of consideration the interest in family integrity, the interest in protecting adolescents, the interest in providing essential medical information (even in the first trimester), the interest in protecting potential life (even before viability), and the interest in full-term pregnancies.[78] Obviously, some of these interests exist regardless of the age of the woman seeking an abortion. Obviously, too, the interests in providing information, protecting potential life, and full-term pregnancies permit massive inroads into women's opportunities to obtain abortions.

A 1979 abortion for minors case makes clear the reason for the Court's backing away from *Roe* and for the Court's confused and inconsistent approach.

The Supreme Court understands, like everybody else except the most committed zealots, that abortion questions are hard. There is right on both sides of the controversy, and a principled, rights-based victory for one side is impossible. If the Justices did not understand that in 1973, at least four of them did by 1979.

Bellotti v. Baird[79] was the case that permitted a parental consent requirement if an acceptable parental bypass exists and that spelled out the requirements for the bypass. Justice Powell's plurality opinion poignantly illustrates the agonizing difficulty of trying to resolve questions about abortion. The opinion repeatedly states a vitally important proposition and then states its opposite as it waffles between values. Thus, the plurality writes,

> [A] State reasonably may determine that parental consultation often is desirable and in the best interest of the minor. It may further determine, as a general proposition, that such consultation is particularly desirable with respect to the abortion decision—one that for some people raises profound moral and religious concerns.[80]

But after a supporting quotation, the opinion says,

> But we are concerned here with a constitutional right to seek an abortion. The abortion decision differs in important ways from other decisions that may be made during minority. The need to preserve the constitutional right and the unique nature of the abortion decision, especially when made by a minor, require a State to act with particular sensitivity when it legislates to foster parental involvement in this matter.[81]

For another example compare these three sentences, which occur within one twelve-line portion of the opinion:

> In sum, there are few situations in which denying a minor the right to make an important decision will have consequences so grave and indelible.
> Yet, an abortion may not be the best choice for the minor.

> Nonetheless, the abortion decision is one that simply cannot be postponed, or it will be made by default with far-reaching consequences.[82]

Or, how about this in two consecutive paragraphs?

> [E]very minor must have the opportunity—if she so desires—to go directly to a court without first consulting or notifying her parents. If she satisfies the court that she is mature and well enough informed to make intelligently the abortion decision on her own, the court must authorize her to act without parental consultation or consent. If she fails to satisfy the court that she is competent to make this decision independently, she must be permitted to show that an abortion nevertheless would be in her best interests.

> There is, however, an important state interest in encouraging a family rather than a judicial resolution of a minor's abortion decision. . . . If, all things considered, the court determines that an abortion is in the minor's best interests, she is entitled to court authorization without any parental involvement. On the other

hand, the court may deny the abortion request of an immature minor in the absence of parental consultation if it concludes that her best interests would be served thereby, or the court may in such a case defer decision until there is parental consultation in which the court may participate.[83]

Abortion for minors, like abortion in general, is simply too hard a question for resolution at the level of principles and rights.

The problems of attempted constitutional resolution have dogged the Court in areas beyond consent for minors. In 1983 the Court decided a number of issues in *Akron v. Akron Center for Reproductive Health, Inc.*[84] In some ways *Akron* seemed to halt the slide away from *Roe*, while in other ways it continued it. The one thing it clearly continued was the movement away from clarity and principle.

In *Akron* the Supreme Court reaffirmed *Roe v. Wade*, but only, it noted, out of respect for *stare decisis*.[85] Still confused about the nature of the abortion right, the Court referred to it as the right to choose an abortion;[86] but it also stated that a woman has a right to effectuate her decision,[87] and once, the Court even referred to the constitutional right to obtain an abortion.[88]

The Court dealt even more confusingly with *Roe*'s trimester analysis. The majority said that it retained the trimester approach.[89] However, the boundaries between the trimesters became blurry. The first trimester ends at approximately 12 to 14 weeks.[90] As a scientific observation that most human pregnancies last between 36 and 42 weeks, that statement may be accurate, but the Supreme Court is not teaching science. It is making constitutional law. How can the constitutionality of a state action depend on whether it occurred during the first or second trimester of pregnancy if the boundary between the trimesters may occur approximately during a two-week period? As to the third trimester, it is not and never has been a true trimester. The final period of pregnancy for purposes of constitutional law has been fixed not by time but by viability, the potential ability of the fetus to survive outside the mother's womb, albeit with artificial aid. This "standard" varies from case to case depending on facts of maternal health, fetal development, genetics, environment, etc. It cannot be measured except by complicated tests. It is inherently ambiguous because it opens, but does not resolve, the question of whether viability is to be measured before the abortion or after it. And it is likely to change as technology for keeping ever more premature babies alive improves. How can matters of constitutional significance depend upon such a standard?

To make matters worse, the Supreme Court in *Akron* did not even apply the vague and ill-defined rules it purported to adopt. Under *Roe* the state may restrict abortions to the extent necessary to protect maternal health after the first trimester (approximately 12 to 14 weeks). The Court began to evaluate state requirements that abortions be performed in hospitals as early as the day it decided *Roe*. As noted, *Doe v. Bolton* invalidated a Georgia hospitalization requirement.[91] In *Akron* and two companion cases the Court addressed the issue again. It adopted a set of rules almost as complicated as its rules about abortions for minors. For present purposes, however, what matters is the *Akron* analysis.

The City of Akron required all second trimester abortions to be performed in a hospital. The Supreme Court invalidated that requirement. It held that a state may require some, but not all, second trimester abortions to be performed in a hospital. In the ten years since *Roe v. Wade*, changes in technology had made abortions outside of hospitals safe during the first few weeks of the second trimester (i.e., the first few weeks after approximately 12 to 14 weeks). Therefore, the city's requirement was not reasonably related to maternal health.[92] Presumably, as technology continues to change, the law will change with it. This is a very funny way to develop the meaning of the nation's basic charter. Also, obviously, it deviates from the clear trimester divisions adopted in *Roe*.

The Court also failed to make plain how safe a nonhospital abortion has to be to prevent the state from requiring that the abortion be performed in a hospital. It did, however, require state abortion regulations to comply with accepted medical practice.[93] How accepted medical practice became part of the United States Constitution one can only guess.

The Court's analysis of the hospital abortion requirement illustrates what is wrong with its trimester approach. One cannot make national, principled, rights-based law on the basis of rapidly changing, scientific facts. The Court is out of its depth in trying to deal with science. It is trying to do inconsistent things when it tries to decide cases one at a time based on their facts and to make claims for the principled basis of what it is doing. It is trying to give constitutional clout to common law decision making. It just cannot have it both ways.

Justice O'Connor in an important separate opinion in *Akron* attacked the trimester analysis head-on.[94] Unlike the majority, Justice O'Connor advocated rejection of the trimester analysis, noting that as scientific facts change, the system collapses on itself. Viability occurs earlier in pregnancy, while the need to act to protect maternal health occurs later. O'Connor is surely correct that rejecting the trimester approach would eliminate a great deal of arbitrary and trivialized constitutional decision making.

The problem is that it is not clear what to use in place of trimester analysis. Justice O'Connor herself argued that in deciding whether a state restriction on abortion is constitutional the Court should follow a two-step analysis. First, it should decide whether the regulation unduly burdens the right to seek an abortion. Then, if it does, the Court must decide whether the state has shown that its burden is necessary to a compelling interest. If the restriction is not a significant burden, the state only has to show that it is rationally related to a legitimate state purpose.[95]

Unfortunately, as Justice O'Connor herself has now recognized,[96] this approach made no sense. The decision that a burden is "undue" would seem to mean that it is unacceptable and that no state interest could justify it. Yet Justice O'Connor's approach in *Akron* would have allowed the state to justify even some undue burdens. The reason that possibility did not pose significant problems for Justice O'Connor was that she thought the only burdens that are undue are those that amount to "absolute obstacles"[97] or "severe limitations."[98] Other burdens are not undue and therefore are permissible as long as they are rational. As a practical matter, what all of this seemed to mean was that Justice O'Connor would vote to invalidate very few abortion restrictions. Her votes bear this out, and the *Akron* version of the undue burden test seriously erodes the power of women to obtain abortions.

Finally, the Supreme Court in *Akron* struck down the city's requirement that doctors obtain informed consent after providing specific information to the woman seeking an abortion.[99] The Court found that the informed consent requirement was designed to persuade, rather than to inform; that some of the required information was wrong or misleading; that some of it was not information but statements of a value choice; and that the requirement intruded on the doctor's discretion. Conceding that all of those observations are correct, and that all of them are undesirable, the question of what they have to do with the Constitution remains. The Court did not apply any of its own constitutional analysis from *Akron* or any of its other cases to explain why the requirements were unconstitutional. Thus, again, one wishing to criticize the Court for imposing its preferences has a much easier task than one seeking to defend it as operating on the basis of principle.

By the mid-1980s, then, nobody knew what the nature of the abortion right was; nobody knew what kind of showing was required to uphold a state intrusion on the right; nobody knew what all the relevant state interests were; the trimester framework was in disarray; and the Supreme Court's abortion jurisprudence was nothing more than a series of results in specific cases.

As the decade ended, the pendulum swung ever farther away from the position of the pro-choice movement and the apparent position of *Roe v. Wade*. One can easily attribute this to politics and the Reagan-Bush Court-packing plan, and no doubt the personnel on the Court affect the Court's positions. But if *Roe v. Wade* had been analytically sound, retreat from it would have been more difficult, even for conservative judges, and if it had been institutionally sound (that is, if it had been within the scope of what constitutional adjudication is good for), reasons to adhere to it might have appealed even to justices who were not committed to a woman's right to choose abortion.

Webster v. Reproductive Services, Inc.,[100] which was decided in 1989, very nearly undid the substance of *Roe v. Wade*. *Rust v. Sullivan*[101] in 1991 damaged free speech protection in a way that probably would not have occurred but for the reaction to *Roe v. Wade*.

Webster involved an attack on a Missouri abortion statute. Among other things the Supreme Court upheld provisions that prohibited public employees from performing or assisting in nonlifesaving abortions[102] and that prohibited the use of public facilities for such abortions.[103] Thus, the Court reaffirmed its rejection of the view that a woman has an affirmative right to an abortion. It also refused to decide whether the preamble to the Missouri statute, which stated that human life begins at conception, was unconstitutional because the preamble could be read as simply expressing the state's permissible value judgment that prefers childbirth to abortion, and the Court could not tell whether Missouri's courts would give it any greater weight.[104]

Most significantly, however, the Court considered the constitutionality of Missouri's statutory effort to protect fetuses. Section 188.029 of the Missouri statute provided,

> Before a physician performs an abortion on a woman he has reason to believe is carrying an unborn child of twenty or more weeks gestational age, the physician shall first determine if the unborn child is viable by using . . . that degree of care, skill, and proficiency commonly exercised by the ordinarily skillful, careful, and prudent physician. . . . In making this determination of viability, the physician shall perform or cause to be performed such medical examinations and tests as are necessary to make a finding of the gestational age, weight, and lung maturity of the unborn child and shall enter such findings and determination of viability in the medical record. . . . [105]

Five justices found the statute constitutional. For Justice Scalia that was easy. He simply favored overruling *Roe v. Wade.*[106] The other Justices, however, followed much more tortuous paths to their conclusions. Justice O'Connor and a plurality consisting of Chief Justice Rehnquist and Justices White and Kennedy first construed the statute. After construing it Justice O'Connor thought the statute did not conflict with *Roe v. Wade*; therefore, she found it constitutional. The plurality thought the statute did conflict with *Roe.* They resolved the conflict in the statute's favor.

The Court of Appeals had read the statute as requiring doctors to perform tests to find gestational age, fetal weight, and lung maturity.[107] Indeed, that certainly seems to be what the statute says. However, both Justice O'Connor and the plurality found this reading of the statute to be clear error. They read the statute to require those findings only when, in the physician's judgment, the tests would be useful[108] and, for Justice O'Connor, when performing them would also be prudent.[109] This construction may not comport with the ordinary use of language, but it makes good sense. It has the effect of leaving judgments about medical matters to doctors and of not asking doctors to use their judgment to do something their judgment says is inappropriate.

Previous cases had held that physicians, not the state, are the proper decision makers about whether a fetus is viable.[110] Justice O'Connor said that her construction of the statute left the viability question to doctors and, therefore, did not conflict with prior cases.[111] That view would leave *Roe* substantially intact. However, even in this moderate approach some weakening of *Roe v. Wade* occurred. The statute required testing of fetuses whom the physician believed to be at least twenty weeks old. Everyone agreed that no fetus could be viable until twenty-three or twenty-four weeks. However, everyone on the Court, including Justice Blackmun, the author and staunchest defender of *Roe v. Wade*, agreed that there may be a four-week margin of error in measuring gestational age and that the Constitution permits states to require actions before viability to protect their compelling interest in postviability potential fetal life.[112]

Obviously, performing viability tests on fetuses reasonably believed to be at least twenty weeks old increases the cost of second trimester abortions. Justice O'Connor nonetheless found that the testing requirement did not conflict with *Roe*. She applied the undue burden test and concluded that required twenty-week testing was not an undue burden because it did not increase costs of second trimester abortions too much.[113] How much is too much, and why the Supreme Court should play out the common law exercise of deciding, she did not say. Of course, Justice O'Connor thinks the Court should rethink the trimester analysis; therefore, finding an increased cost at the end of the second trimester excessive while upholding it a few weeks later would hardly have appealed to her.

In any event, Justice O'Connor's use of the undue burden test and her continued questioning of the trimester approach raised questions about her commitment to *Roe v. Wade*. The plurality attacked *Roe* more directly. The members of the plurality construed the Missouri statute the same way Justice O'Connor did. However they found the statute as construed did conflict with *Roe v. Wade*. The statute regulated the method of determining viability, something that *Roe* had remitted to doctors; and the statute raised the price of abortions. That conflict did not render the statute unconstitutional. Rather, it revealed that *Roe*'s adoption of the trimester framework was an error. Therefore, the plurality rejected the trimester framework while refraining from overruling *Roe*.

The plurality said that the trimester framework was both unsound in principle and unworkable in practice. This is because it does not speak in general principles; key elements of the analysis are not in the Constitution or anywhere else one might look for constitutional principles; the indeterminate boundaries of the inquiry lead to a complex web of rules more like regulations than constitutional doctrine; and the state's interest in potential life is compelling even before viability.[114] The arguments based on the nature of constitutional adjudication are telling. The Supreme Court hears very few cases, and therefore it cannot possibly provide the narrowly tuned supervision that a factually based analysis requires. Moreover, the impact of the Supreme Court's decisions is enormous. The explication of fundamental principles to govern the entire nation is the raison d'etre of constitutional adjudication. If the Supreme Court simply resolves cases on the basis of their facts, it is abdicating its special role while retaining its special power. This cannot be justified, especially given the counter-majoritarian nature of the Supreme Court. It is one thing to claim that certain principles are so fundamental that they should override the popular will. It is quite another to make that claim for factual determinations. The problem is exacerbated when the facts are rapidly changing and involve technical matters beyond the Justices' expertise. You just cannot make constitutional law one case at a time on the basis of rapidly changing, scientific facts.

Justice Blackmun offered two responses to this institutional attack. He noted that the Supreme Court frequently engages in such fact-based decision making.[115] Second, he noted that the Court is trying to balance individual rights against state interests; the resolution of such a balance can hardly be clear cut.[116]

These responses are not persuasive. The Supreme Court does engage in similar behavior elsewhere, and it almost always fails. Two conspicuous non-biomedical examples of the inability of constitutional adjudication to do a common law job are the Supreme Court's failed efforts to deal with the law of defamation[117] and of search and seizure.[118] At least the Constitution forces the Court to say something about search and seizure.[119] Why it gets itself into these situations when it does not have to is hard to understand.

As for Justice Blackmun's balancing argument, it simply misses the point. Of course, there are important interests to balance on both (or all) sides of the abortion controversy. That is why the Supreme Court should never have entered the field. The mediation between right and right that is needed here is too subtle to permit resolution by the meat cleaver of constitutional adjudication. If, on the other hand, the Court was right to enter the field, then its job was to provide principles that would permit others (legislators and lower courts) to balance the conflicting interests, not to try to do the balancing itself on the basis of the few cases that reach it.

Obviously, if these arguments are sound, many of them could be made, not just against *Roe*'s trimester analysis but against the recognition of the constitutional right involved in *Roe* as well. As with trimesters one looks in vain for references to privacy or abortion in the Constitution's text; the boundaries, even the nature, of the constitutional right are vague and indeterminate; and no principle that supports the right is readily apparent.

Justice Blackmun tried to remedy the lack of principle in his *Webster* dissent: "It is this general principle, the ' "moral fact that a person belongs to himself and not others nor to society as a whole" ' . . . that is found in the Constitution."[120] Unfortunately, this statement of principle sixteen years after *Roe v. Wade* came sixteen years too late to be useful. It also conflicts with *Roe*'s explicit rejection of a person's right to do whatever she wants with her body.[121] Most importantly, however, it is not a principle that even Justice Blackmun really supports. Immediately after announcing the principle of individualism quoted above, Justice Blackmun reaffirmed his support for regulating abortion after the first trimester to protect the mother's health.[122] Such regulation is directly at war with the notion that the person belongs to herself and not to society.

Thus, *Roe* remained as unprincipled in 1989 as it was in 1973. The growing recognition of the failure of principle among the Justices suggests grounds for real concern about the future of *Roe v. Wade.*

The plurality's assertion that the state's interest in the potential life of the fetus is compelling before viability is less persuasive than its arguments based on the nature of constitutional adjudication. Basically, the plurality simply states that the interest in potential life is compelling before viability because it sees no reason to say that the interest does not become compelling until after viability.[123] Justice Blackmun tries to offer reasons—(1) the viable fetus has more ability than a previable fetus to feel pain and pleasure and to react to its surroundings; and (2) the viability test is easy to apply.[124] The first reason, like the reason Justice Blackmun gave in *Roe*, simply describes what it means to be viable. It is no *reason* for the state's interest to become compelling. The suggestion that the standard is easy to apply is simply ludicrous. Who is to determine viability? When? How can we accommodate technological changes? Doesn't determination of viability require (or permit) some tests before viability? Isn't there a four-week margin of error in measuring gestational age? Simple, indeed! The war between Blackmun and the plurality here is simply a war of *ipse dixits.* Each side says it is right because it says so. Clearly, though, the plurality's rejection of the idea that the state's interest in potential life only becomes compelling at viability is a frontal assault on *Roe v. Wade.*

The plurality went even further by requiring a state's intrusion on the abortion right to be merely rationally related to a legitimate state end in order to be upheld.[125] That position challenges the view that the abortion right is fundamental, and it is therefore another deadly assault on *Roe v. Wade.*

Thus, after *Webster* little seemed to be left of *Roe.* Justice Scalia would overrule it. The plurality virtually did so. Justice O'Connor's approach weakened *Roe* almost to the point of uselessness. The principled, nationwide victory of 1973 seemed virtually to have disappeared by 1989. At least it seems fair to say that by 1989 nobody could predict with certainty the outcome of cases or the continued constitutional vitality of *Roe v. Wade.*

This uncertainty troubled some of the members of the Supreme Court. In 1992 a plurality of the Court, consisting of Justices O'Connor, Kennedy, and Souter, began their opinion in the Court's most recent major abortion case with a cri de coeur for certainty: "Liberty finds no refuge in a jurisprudence of doubt."[126]

Unfortunately, it proved easier for the plurality to issue a heartfelt plea for certainty than to provide it. In *Planned Parenthood v. Casey* the Court upheld three Pennsylvania abortion restrictions and struck down one. Seven Justices once again reaffirmed the permissibility of a state requirement of parental consent, with the alternative of a judicial bypass procedure, before a minor could obtain an abortion.[127] A five Justice majority, however, invalidated a requirement that except in certain circumstances the husband of a married woman be notified before the woman could obtain an abortion.[128] Seven Justices upheld an informed consent requirement as a prerequisite to abortion as long as the information that had to be provided was accurate, even if that information was designed to encourage the woman to carry her pregnancy to term.[129] Finally, seven Justices also upheld a twenty-four-hour waiting period as a prerequisite to abortion unless the wait would be dangerous to the mother's life or health.[130]

More important than the results, however, were the variety of approaches the members of the Court took to the abortion question in general and to the continuing validity of *Roe v. Wade*. In *Casey* only two Justices, Blackmun and Stevens, continued to express full support for *Roe v. Wade*.[131] Four Justices, Rehnquist, White, Scalia, and Thomas, continued to believe that *Roe* should be overruled.[132] Those four Justices denied the existence of a fundamental abortion right and would only invalidate abortion restrictions that are irrational.[133] In a rare joint opinion the remaining three Justices, O'Connor, Kennedy, and Souter, reaffirmed the "essential holding" of *Roe v. Wade*.[134]

The authors of the joint opinion said that the essential holding of *Roe v. Wade* contained three parts: (1) There is a right to abortion before viability without undue interference by the state; (2) the state may restrict abortions after viability as long as there are exceptions for pregnancies that threaten the mother's life or health; and (3) the state has a legitimate interest from the outset of pregnancy in the health of the mother and the life of the fetus.[135]

The position of the joint opinion, which seems likely ultimately to become the Supreme Court's dominant view, is quite remarkable. First, the joint opinion allows the state to override a woman's right to an abortion without showing that the state's intrusion is necessary to a compelling state interest. That means that according to the joint opinion the right to an abortion is no longer a fundamental right.[136] This retreat from *Roe v. Wade* is all the more remarkable because Justices Blackmun and Stevens joined this part of the joint opinion despite their claim to be reaffirming *Roe*. Thus, after *Casey* none of the nine members of the Court really supported the position that there is a fundamental right to abortion.

Second, the joint opinion raises more questions than it answers. Most importantly, (1) Why are only the three enumerated points the "essential holding" of *Roe*? (2) Why did the plurality reaffirm the essential holding? and (3) Why did they reaffirm *only* the essential holding?

The essential holding of *Roe v. Wade*, as defined by the joint opinion, does not include *Roe*'s trimester framework. Yet the trimester approach was central to *Roe*; indeed, it determined what restrictions on the abortion right were permissible, and when. Moreover, the trimester approach had been followed since *Roe* despite all the difficulty it had caused. Thus, trimester analysis could not be said to be nonessential either because the trimester part of *Roe* was mere dictum, or because it had faded away and was no longer taken seriously. Moreover, the trimester approach was no less essential than any other part of *Roe* merely because it was an implementation rule rather than the recognition of a right. Implementation is often the essence of constitutional decision making, as for example, in criminal procedure, where excluding illegally seized evidence from trials[137] and requiring police officers to tell detained persons their constitutional rights,[138] are ways in which the Supreme Court gives meaning to constitutional protections. In other areas, too, rules that protect rights, like rules that impose onerous proof burdens on public figures who sue critics for defamation,[139] are central to the Constitution in the sense that they are what define and limit constitutional rights.

In short, no good reason exists to dismiss the trimester framework from the "essential holding" of *Roe v. Wade*. That the trimester framework was unwise and unworkable may be good reasons to overrule the parts of *Roe* that depended upon it, but simply dismissing it as unessential is unsound and dangerous. That dismissive style of decision making makes it too easy for opponents of a rule simply to reject it without analysis, here weakening women's abortion rights, and elsewhere potentially imperiling other rights as well. Moreover, the approach is disrespectful of precedent, that is of the principle of *stare decisis*. That disrespect is especially difficult to understand in an opinion that rested much of its analysis on the importance of adhering to precedent.

The joint opinion explained its reasons for reaffirming the essential holding of *Roe v. Wade* on two quite different bases—one of substance and one of *stare decisis*. The *stare decisis* reasons apply to all parts of the essential holding (and might have been expected to apply to the now nonessential trimester analysis as well); different substantive reasons apply to each of the three parts of the essential holding.

In reaffirming the essential holding of *Roe v. Wade* out of respect for *stare decisis*, the authors of the joint opinion did not take the position that decisions should never be overruled. Indeed, their opinion would overrule some earlier decisions. Given that, the obvious question is why *stare decisis* precluded overruling the essential holding of *Roe*. The joint opinion answered that question in two different ways, first pointing to general reasons for following precedent, and then arguing that special prudential reasons counsel against overruling here.

In general, the joint opinion noted, courts could not function if they always had to consider everything anew.[140] Moreover, respect for precedent is part of the rule of law.[141] It is essential to judicial legitimacy. The Court's power lies in its legitimacy. Principle is essential to judicial decisions because the people must understand that judicial decisions are not simply grounded in political compromise.[142] This does not mean that the Court can never overrule one of its decisions, but it does mean that it must be especially careful about doing so. It must not overrule too often,[143] and it should be especially careful not to overrule a case that has resolved an intensely divisive controversy.[144] When the Court resolves such a controversy, it calls upon the people to accept a common mandate rooted in the Constitution. This imposes on the Court a special obligation to the opponents of the decision not to let them pay the price of their acceptance in vain.[145]

Regrettably, none of this is persuasive, and it certainly will not convince opponents of *Roe v. Wade* that the Court has done them a favor by refraining from overruling *Roe*. Of course, the courts cannot reconsider every issue anew each time it might arise. However, that does nothing to tell us which issues are to be reconsidered, or when.

Similarly, nobody would deny the importance of judicial legitimacy and the vital role of principle in constitutional adjudication. However, the argument from principle rings hollow in applying *stare decisis* to *Roe v. Wade*, an opinion that was principled neither with regard to substance nor in its perception of the judicial role. Where is the principle in adhering to the unprincipled?

Moreover, the entire history of the Supreme Court's abortion jurisprudence, including the decision in *Casey* itself, has been a history of compromise. That truth cannot be erased by pretending that it does not exist.

The argument that intensely divisive decisions should not be overruled is especially problematic. First, many issues before the Supreme Court are especially divisive. That is why they come before the Court. The joint opinion offers no guidance for determining which intensely divisive decisions are divisive enough to deserve special protection against being overruled. Moreover, *Roe v. Wade*, an unprincipled, non-text-based decision, might well be seen as promoting an intensely divisive controversy rather than resolving one. As Justice Scalia points out, *Roe* nourished divisiveness and precluded political compromise.[146] The promotion of controversy can hardly be a reason to retain a judicial decision.

Chief Justice Rehnquist adds further telling criticism of the joint opinion's reasoning. He notes that giving special protection to cases that resolve especially divisive controversies would mean that the Court could only overrule decisions that have not been criticized, an intensely silly notion,[147] and that the joint opinion's approach penalizes protest.[148] Moreover, to the extent that it is important to appear to be immune from political pressure, the Chief Justice rightly notes that affirming a decision, as well as overruling one, can be seen as bowing to such pressure.[149] Opponents of *Roe v. Wade* will not be grateful to the Court for maintaining *Roe* so that their disappointment will not have been in vain.

The joint opinion's general *stare decisis* reasons for affirming the essential holding of *Roe v. Wade* do not withstand analysis. However, the opinion also offers special prudential reasons to refrain from overruling in this instance. It argues that, given a general preference for following precedent, a court should be reluctant to overrule unless the existing rule has proved unworkable;[150] that courts should not overrule decisions upon which people have relied;[151] that they should not overrule unless support for the original decision was weak in legal principle;[152] and that they should not overrule unless the facts that underlay the original opinion have changed.[153] The joint opinion then applies these prudential considerations to *Roe*.

The opinion asserts *Roe* is not unworkable.[154] Unfortunately, the history of

Supreme Court abortion jurisprudence between *Roe* and *Casey*, Congressional and state political reactions, and failure to control anti-*Roe* zealots demonstrate the opinion is, in fact, unworkable, or, at least, that it has not been made to work yet. To the extent that there was anything workable about *Roe v. Wade* it might have been strict adherence to rigid trimester guidelines, measured by weeks of gestation. In *Casey*, though, the joint opinion abandons trimesters rather than trying to make them workable. In retaining the essential holding of *Roe* because it is not unworkable, the joint opinion may have rendered it so. The joint opinion's reliance argument is quite interesting. In general, the fact that people have relied on a decision is a reason to be reluctant to overrule it. The critical question is the factual one: Have people relied? In *Casey*, the joint opinion makes no effort to demonstrate specific acts of reliance by specific persons on the essential holding of *Roe v. Wade*. Rather, the opinion argues "that for two decades of economic and social developments, people have organized intimate relationships and made choices that define their views of themselves and their places in society, in reliance on the availability of abortion. . . . "[155] The availability of abortion has contributed significantly to women's equal participation in the life of the nation.[156]

Properly understood, this is not a reliance argument or an argument for *stare decisis*. The argument is that *Roe* was a good decision because it contributed to women's equality. That may be so, but it is a reason to affirm *Roe* on the merits, not out of respect for *stare decisis*. This argument will not persuade an opponent of *Roe v. Wade* who is also a judicial legitimist, committed to the idea of stability in law. Without a showing that women have become pregnant in reliance on the availability of abortion and that they could not change their behavior if *Roe* were overruled, there is simply no valid reliance argument against overruling *Roe v. Wade*.

The joint opinion next inquired into the weakness of support in legal theory for the original decision as yet another prudential factor relevant to the decision whether to overrule. Here the joint opinion concludes that theoretical legal support for *Roe v. Wade* was no weaker in 1992 than it was in 1973.[157] What a ringing endorsement! Surely, Justice Scalia is correct in asserting that some attention to the original weakness of the decision is relevant, as long as that factor is not dispositive by itself.[158]

Finally, the joint opinion inquired into whether the facts had changed between the decision in *Roe* and the date of *Casey*. It concluded that they had. Nonetheless, says the opinion, that is not sufficient reason to overrule *Roe*, because the factual change is not central enough. Viability now occurs earlier than it did in 1973. Nonetheless, whenever viability occurs it may continue to serve as the critical fact.[159]

This obviously makes no sense. A constitutional rule cannot depend upon a fact that is constantly changing and that will differ from place to place in the United States depending on available technology. This is all the more true when the reason that the fact is determinative is itself not clear. Indeed, the focus on the rapidly changing, scientific fact of viability was one of the fundamental errors in *Roe v. Wade*.

None of the joint opinion's *stare decisis* arguments in support of affirming the essential holding of *Roe v. Wade* is persuasive. However, the opinion also offered substantive reasons to affirm *Roe*.

On the merits, the joint opinion upheld the right to abortion before viability without undue interference by the state because the right to define one's concept of the existence and meaning of the universe and the mystery of human life is at the heart of the concept of liberty;[160] because the unique and intimate suffering experienced by women in pregnancy and childbirth requires that a woman's destiny be shaped by her own conception of her spiritual imperatives and her place in society;[161] and because if there is no right to have an abortion, the state could interfere in the opposite direction with the right to bear a child.[162] The opinion found these arguments supported by two lines of decisions—those supporting intimate relationships and decisions,[163] and those protecting personal autonomy and bodily integrity.[164] In a similar vein Justice Stevens also focused on bodily integrity and the freedom to decide matters of the highest personal and private nature,[165] and Justice Blackmun emphasized bodily integrity and the right to make decisions.[166]

The substantive arguments in support of affirming the essential holding of *Roe v. Wade* sound very attractive at first blush. Unfortunately, they will not withstand analysis. Cherishing the individual's view of the existence and meaning of the universe and the mystery of human life tells one nothing about whether the Constitution protects a right to abortion. Suppose a person believed deeply that a child does not become a human being until age three. Would that person have a constitutional right to kill children before they reached their third birthday? The suggestion is preposterous. But when one asks why the view that a person is not alive before viability should be respected, but the view that one is not alive until age three should be denigrated, the answer lies in the fact that the joint opinion's authors have decided without analysis or explanation that a fetus is not a living person. As Justice Scalia points out, they have begged the question of the fetus's status.[167]

Similarly, the joint opinion begs the question of the status of the fetus when it argues that rejecting the right to abortion would also amount to rejecting the right to bear a child. That is only true if one assumes that the fetus is not a person entitled to constitutional protection. If it is entitled to such protection, then it would make perfect sense to protect it by both prohibiting abortion and protecting bearing and giving birth to a child.

The joint opinion's argument based on the unique and intimate suffering of pregnant women is essentially an equal protection argument that the law should do what it can to put women into the same position as men. Unfortunately, the opinion fails to do the necessary equal protection analysis to decide whether there has been an equal protection violation. A person or group may not overturn a government action just because it falls especially heavily upon them. The difficult question, which the joint opinion made no effort to resolve, is whether the equal protection clause requires the law to compensate for factual differences by attempting to make everyone the same. That is, does "equal" mean "same"? That question is worth addressing, but it cannot be answered without considerable thought. Moreover, one cannot answer the question simply by defining a political or philosophical position for oneself. In other contexts, for example, women's groups who support *Casey* would bridle at the notion that equality requires that women and men be treated the same.

More interesting than the equality argument is the decision-making and bodily integrity argument that Justices Stevens and Blackmun, as well as the authors of the joint opinion, make. Here, a majority of the Supreme Court comes tantalizingly close to providing a principled rationale for the right to an abortion. Here, as Justice Blackmun did in *Webster*, a majority seems to be adopting autonomy as the principle that underlies the abortion right.

Unfortunately, the nature of the autonomy claim that the five Justices are making is not entirely clear. Some language suggests that what is at stake is individual freedom of choice. Elsewhere, however, autonomy seems to mean having one's bodily integrity let alone. These two quite different notions of autonomy can push in quite different directions, as we shall see when we explore the law about sterilizing mentally incompetent persons.[168]

Having one's bodily integrity protected does not seem to have much to do with whether states may prohibit abortions. It is the abortion that invades bodily integrity, and one could see the prohibition simply as an effort by the state to prevent some kinds of invasions of bodily integrity, just as the state prohibits murder and mayhem regardless of whether the victim consents. Thus, the autonomy claim here must be essentially a freedom of choice claim, an assertion that a woman must have the freedom to choose whether to reproduce.

As a freedom of choice claim, the autonomy rationale has two problems. One is that none of the members of the Supreme Court really believes it. The Court still allows restrictions on the abortion right to protect maternal health. Once that enormous inroad on maternal autonomy is conceded, not much is left of autonomy as a persuasive basis for a constitutional right. More importantly, the freedom of choice point once again begs the question of the fetus's status. The woman's power to choose cannot prevail over the fetus without deciding that the fetus has no claim to a similar autonomy, a similar power of choice. Somebody has to explain why the fetus should not be protected until it is able to make choices.

The free choice-autonomy focus assumes that decisions affect one person and that we can figure out who that person is. This assumption is likely to prove dangerous, not only for fetuses but also for other groups who are in danger of being treated as nonpersons—groups like persons with disabilities and persons in a persistent vegetative state. As attractive as it may be to persons with one point of view on the abortion issue to assume the fetus's lack of personhood, the failure to justify, rather than simply assume that position, creates enormous difficulty.

Finally, the joint opinion offered reasons for reaffirming the power of the state to restrict abortions after viability, and it reaffirmed the view that the state has a legitimate interest from the outset in the health of the mother and the life of the fetus. The opinion supported the state's power to restrict abortions after viability for three reasons: (1) After viability the fetus has a reasonable possibility of life outside the womb so that this "second life" can be a fair and reasonable object of state protection that overrides the right of the mother.[169] (2) No other line is more workable than viability.[170] (3) The viability line is fair to women; a woman who waits until viability to obtain an abortion has consented to state intervention.[171]

These reasons are no more satisfactory than the reasons the opinion gave for reaffirming the mother's abortion right. The fetus's ability to survive outside the womb remains a definition, not a reason to do anything. The viability line has proved over two decades to be singularly unworkable, and, as the opinion concedes, the time of viability is changing. The joint opinion characterized the fact that the concept is changing as creating tolerable imprecision,[172] but, as we have seen, it is just this kind of imprecision that is intolerable in constitutional adjudication. The fairness argument is particularly outrageous. Suppose a woman is poor and was not able to save enough money for her abortion until the fetus became viable; suppose she lives far from a place where she can obtain an abortion; suppose she truly agonized over her decision and did not fully define her own concept of existence, the meaning of the universe, and the mystery of life until viability. In what sense can a woman in any of those situations be deemed to have consented to state intervention?

As to the state's legitimate interest from the outset of the pregnancy in the health of the mother and the life of the fetus, the joint opinion reaffirms those interests, but it gives no substantive reasons for doing so.[173]

The substantive reasons to reaffirm what the joint opinion treats as the essential holding of *Roe v. Wade* are exceptionally weak, as the authors of the opinion seem to recognize. The weakness of their substantive reasons may account, in part, for their emphasis on *stare decisis*. Moreover, the authors' hearts do not appear really to be in supporting *Roe* on the merits; often throughout their opinion the authors talk about the need to reaffirm *Roe*, whatever their own views on the merits[174]—hardly a ringing endorsement! Finally, as we noted at the beginning of this discussion, the results that the joint opinion reached in *Casey* supported the state on three out of four issues, including two that changed state law to favor the state over a pregnant woman.

In conclusion, then, the position of women and those who support the right to abortion seems no more secure after *Casey* than it did after *Webster*, and the constitutional law of abortion remains an unintelligible and unprincipled quagmire.

A final disturbing effect of *Roe v. Wade* is the impact that decision has had on other aspects of American life and law. The broad scope of constitutional adjudication and the Court's failure to articulate a rationale or describe boundaries for the right of privacy invited litigants to claim that a variety of behaviors are protected by that right. Those efforts had mixed results. As we shall discuss later,[175] the Supreme Court of New Jersey held that if the right of privacy is broad enough to encompass the abortion decision, it must also be broad enough to encompass a decision to reject life-saving medical care.[176] The United States Supreme Court has come close to taking the same view[177] despite the rather obvious differences between being forced to carry a child to term, give birth, and acquire a lifelong set of obligations and relationships on the one hand and being forced to accept treatment that may restore one to full and unfettered life on the other. Conversely, the Court has rejected the argument that the right of privacy includes a right to commit sodomy, even for consenting adults.[178] All of this is simply further illustration of the unprincipled nature of *Roe v. Wade* and its failure to provide the kind of guidance we should be able to expect from a constitutional decision by the Supreme Court.

Unfortunately, in its retreat from *Roe v. Wade* the Court may be doing damage to constitutional rights it would leave unscathed if cases about them had arisen outside the abortion context. In *Rust v. Sullivan*,[179] the Court upheld regulations that the Secretary of Health and Human Services promulgated under Title X of the Public Health Service Act.[180] Title X provides federal funding for family planning services and empowers the Secretary to promulgate regulations governing grants and contracts under the Act. The statute provides, "None of the funds appropriated under this subchapter shall be used in programs where abortion is a method of family planning."[181] Reversing a long and consistent approach to the statute, the Secretary enacted new regulations in 1988.[182] The regulations prohibit Title X projects from providing both counseling and referrals for "abortion as a method of family planning."[183] They prohibit engaging in activities that "encourage, promote or advocate abortion as a method of family planning."[184] And they require the projects to keep abortion activities "physically and financially separate" from other activities.[185]

When recipients of Title X funds challenged the regulations, the Court first decided that the regulations were based on a permissible interpretation of the statute.[186] It then upheld the regulations' constitutionality. The recipients argued that the regulations violated the First Amendment protection for freedom of speech by preventing them from discussing abortion. The Court characterized the prohibitions as simply preventing grantees from engaging in activities outside the project's scope. Projects were funded to do pre-conception counseling. Therefore, discussing abortion on project time was using money for something Congress had not enacted: "[W]hen the government appropriates public funds to establish a program it is entitled to define the limits of that program."[187] Besides, grant recipients remain free to discuss abortion outside the grant project.[188]

The Court did admit that government funding plus freedom to speak outside the scope of the project is not always enough to justify government control over the content of speech. For example, it might not suffice in a university setting.[189] If it does not suffice there, why does it suffice in the doctor-patient context? The Supreme Court said it did not have to answer that question because the Title X regulations "do not significantly impinge upon the doctor-patient relationship."[190] This, of course, is nonsense. By limiting a doctor's ability to communicate about one of the two options available to a patient, the regulations remove the value of the doctor's judgment and expertise from the relationship. More importantly, though, this approach to the regulations now means that future recipients of federal funds run the risk of being silenced about their viewpoints on any number of significant issues as long as they may speak about them elsewhere and the Supreme Court finds the restrictions insignificant or otherwise acceptable. Thus, *Rust v. Sullivan* has given the government an effective new tool for stifling dissent. It is hard to believe the Court would have permitted such inroads on free expression if it were not trying to undo the work it had done in *Roe v. Wade*.

Roe v. Wade, then, far from providing the total, principled victory that pro-choice advocates had sought, simply introduced chaos into the law. In the long run it gave abortion reformers freedom from criminal penalties, which they had been achieving legislatively anyway. It led to disrespect for law and reinforced the view that law is nothing more than the personal preferences of those in power. It made abortion law unintelligible and invited constant legislative efforts to avoid *Roe v. Wade* and constant litigation to expand it. It contributed to litigation, but not to sound results in areas of law besides abortion, and it caused the Court to take dangerous positions regarding clear fundamental rights.

Moreover, *Roe v. Wade* galvanized the opposition to abortion. While giving pro-choice advocates much less than it promised, it gave pro-life advocates a symbol to rally against. The Supreme Court *seemed* to have chosen one side in an intense moral controversy. By finding that women had a "right" with regard to abortion, it implied that those who opposed abortion were somehow wrong—wrong to protect what they saw as human life, wrong to support their view of morality. The Court turned mediation between right and right into a choice between right and wrong. That leads to a fight. As Professor Schneider has observed in another context,

> [W]hen interests are described as 'rights,' accommodation is impeded. Defining an interest as a right masks the nature and complexity of what is actually at stake; defining an interest as a right makes accommodation seem arbitrary, since we lack a hierarchy of rights to help us choose between them; and defining an interest as a right makes accommodation seem to be the breaching of a right or the defining away of a right and thus, a moral and political wrong.[191]

The pro-choice advocates' mistake was insisting on a right to an abortion. Their apparent victory in 1973 led to the prohibition of federal funding for abortion; state refusals to fund abortion; efforts, many successful, in every state to restrict abortion; constant litigation; the creation of restrictions that did not exist before; violence against abortion clinics; and lawlessness in the streets. All of this is in addition to the general confusion and disrespect noted above and the absurd specter of one-issue voting on abortion in a country faced with worldwide military and economic challenges, environmental degradation, poverty, homelessness, a crisis in health care, drugs, violence and renascent racism. Proponents of constitutional abortion reform made a terrible mistake.

The mistake was a mistake at the time they made it. Attention to institutional competencies should have alerted everyone to the futility of constitutional abortion reform before it was undertaken. As explained in chapter 1, constitutional adjudication is law (1) made by judges (2) who get their information from lawyers. It involves (3) the national imposition of solutions, is (4) sweeping in its impact, and is (5) difficult to change. It is made through (6) case by case adjudication, and (7) real, existing disputes serve as vehicles for lawmaking. The abortion issue is characterized by (a) inadequate information, which is based in part on rapidly changing, scientific facts; (b) an intense, deep, and broad conflict of moral values; (c) unforeseeable ramifications, as one is hard put to know whether dying, sodomy, sterilization, surrogate motherhood, and goodness knows what else are "like" abortion; (d) the absence of even a *plausible* constitutional text in which to ground a decision; (e) a lack of relationship to the structure and function of government; and (f) the availability of a meaningful route to reform other than constitutional adjudication. The failure of constitutional abortion reform can hardly be a surprise.

We have already seen the inability of judges informed by lawyers to cope with scientific facts. We have seen that sweeping, national decisions cannot be based on rapidly changing facts. This is especially so when decisions are difficult to change.

Constitutional adjudication is supposed to represent the official statement of the principles by which we live. How can it do that in an area beset by as much legitimate moral disagreement as abortion? When constitutional law chooses between right and right, it makes one side wrong. The issues in abortion law are too subtle to accommodate such an extreme approach.

The lack of even a *plausible* textual basis for an abortion decision exacerbates the problem of ruling in the face of conflict. The Supreme Court has no rock of legitimacy to cling to, and a losing partisan can well say, "Why should I believe you? You have power on your side, but nothing more." This is a critical point that serves to distinguish abortion from other areas of intense conflict. School desegregation in the 1950s was as controversial as abortion in the 1970s (although one may doubt the *moral* nature of the opposition). But the post–Civil War amendments were designed *explicitly* to free black persons from slavery and to assure them equal status with whites. Thus, the Court had not only the moral high ground but plausible text in which to root its famous 1954 school desegregation opinion.[192]

The suggestion that we need a plausible text is not a claim for strict interpretation. "Plausible" does not mean "literal." The Constitution must be able to grow and change with the nation, but that does not mean it ceases to exist. The framers of the Fourteenth Amendment did not intend to prohibit school desegregation, but the Supreme Court in 1954 could reasonably decide that the prohibition was essential to accomplish the goals of the Fourteenth Amendment, and the words could be applied without linguistic torture. On the other hand, nothing in the text of the Constitution, the structure it tried to create, or the mischiefs it reacted against has anything remotely to do with abortion. Therefore, the Court invites disrespect for law when it pretends to be applying the Constitution so far from even a most generous, liberal reading.

Having once let the privacy-abortion genie out of the bottle, who can put it back? If the Supreme Court makes up a right, persons will try to bring their activities within it. If the right is not based in any principle or text, the only basis for deciding whether to include or exclude behavior is arbitrariness—death is in, sodomy is out. This in turn reinforces disrespect for the law and confusion in it. All of these problems are exacerbated by the case by case resolution of issues, which deprives the law of any hope of certainty. Abortion is either fundamentally important, or it is not. Treating it as a matter of constitutional law suggests that it is. Deciding every case on its particular facts suggests that it is not.

Finally there was no need for the Supreme Court to decide anything about abortion. We need a Supreme Court to decide the kind of governmental structure issues that arise in a federal, balanced powers government. What is for the states? What for the federal government? What are the proper roles of Congress and the executive? What limits does our system place on police and the courts? If government enters a field (like education), what rules must it follow? What individual liberties are necessary for a democratic system to work? Those are the kinds of questions the Constitution is about and the Supreme Court is for. Abortion has nothing to do with any of this. Moreover, the legislatures were reforming abortion law on their own. Maybe a scenario could arise where everyone would agree that some reform was essential to correct a hideous abuse but where no organ of reform was available. If so, maybe the Supreme Court should properly act as court of last resort even if reasons not to act are present. In abortion, however, the legislative reform movement was highly successful. The Supreme Court did not need to intervene.

The story of abortion reform is the story of a Pyhrric victory. Thinking big ultimately led to the downfall of the apparently victorious reformers and did other harm as well. If reformers had considered institutional competencies before 1973, and if they had been wise, they would not have pursued constitutional reform. As other issues posed by the intersections of biology, medicine, and values arise, let us hope that we can learn from the abortion experience.

THREE

Sterilization
The Big Advantage of Thinking Small

Law's response to issues about whether and under what circumstances mentally incompetent persons may be sterilized presents an interesting contrast to the law's response to abortion. Here constitutional law and legislation have given way to statutory repeal and common law adjudication. The law has moved from thinking big to thinking small, with results that are quite attractive.

By definition, a legally incompetent person is incapable of consenting to sterilization. Therefore, someone else must authorize the procedure if it is to be done. In the United States two different kinds of situations have arisen. First is what might be called truly involuntary sterilization, sterilization by the state for the state's benefit—either eugenic or punitive—without regard to the wishes of the person being sterilized and with, at most, a secondary and after-the-fact concern for that person's welfare. Second is sterilization at the behest of a parent or guardian of an incompetent person—usually a girl or woman—ostensibly for that person's benefit, and with the parent or guardian consenting for the ward according to the ward's best interests as in the case of any other medical procedure. Here the law does care about the subject's consent; it simply recognizes her incapacity and substitutes someone to consent on her behalf.

Truly involuntary sterilization flourished in this country during the first third of the twentieth century. At various times as many as thirty-two states statutorily authorized the sterilization of those thought to be "unfit"—the "feebleminded," the insane, epileptics, paupers, and drunkards—primarily for eugenic reasons.[1] Occasionally statutes authorized sterilization as an additional punishment for crime, over and above fines and imprisonment.[2]

Only one Supreme Court decision, *Buck v. Bell*,[3] has directly confronted the question of whether truly involuntary sterilization is constitutional. A Virginia statute authorized the sterilization under some circumstances of "mental defectives" resident at the State Colony for Epileptics and Feeble Minded. Carrie Buck, the feebleminded daughter of a feebleminded mother, was a resident of the Colony. Ms. Buck had a daughter, who was also believed (albeit erroneously) to be feebleminded. The Superintendent of the Colony sought Ms.

Buck's sterilization. Virginia courts authorized the operation, and Ms. Buck obtained review in the United States Supreme Court. In 1927 that Court affirmed the judgment that ordered sterilization. In one of his most notorious opinions, Justice Holmes upheld the Virginia statute on an essentially public health rationale. He wrote,

> We have seen more than once that the public welfare may call upon the best citizens for their lives. It would be strange if it could not call upon those who already sap the strength of the State for these lesser sacrifices, often not felt to be such by those concerned, in order to prevent our being swamped with incompetence. It is better for all the world, if instead of waiting to execute degenerate offspring for crime, or to let them starve for their imbecility, society can prevent those who are manifestly unfit from continuing their kind. The principle that sustains compulsory vaccination is broad enough to cover cutting the Fallopian tubes. . . . Three generations of imbeciles are enough.[4]

The Court dismissed out of hand Ms. Buck's claim that the statute deprived her of the equal protection of the laws because it applied only to institutionalized persons. Such an argument, wrote Holmes, "is the usual last resort of constitutional arguments. . . . "[5]

Last resort or not, the argument prevailed fifteen years later. An Oklahoma statute called for the sterilization of some but not all repeat criminal offenders. The Oklahoma Attorney General sought to use the statute's authority to obtain the sterilization of Mr. Skinner, a "three time loser," who was a robber and chicken thief. Noting that the statute permitted the sterilization of persons convicted of larceny, but not of embezzlement, the Court held the statute unconstitutional as violating the equal protection clause of the Fourteenth Amendment. The distinctions between larceny and embezzlement are arcane and of human origin. There is no reason to believe they are reflected in the laws of genetics. Therefore, the state could not provide such drastically different treatment for the two kinds of criminals.[6]

The equal protection approach permitted the Court to strike down the statute without questioning *Buck v. Bell* or confronting the basic question of the constitutionality of compulsory sterilization. Unfortunately, however, the Court's language went far beyond what was needed to reach its result. The Court noted that sterilization "involves one of the basic civil rights of man"[7] and that, therefore, the statutory classification scheme must be subjected to "strict scrutiny,"[8] a scrutiny it could not withstand.

No one can doubt that the freedom to procreate is an important interest. Nonetheless, labeling the interest a "right" has the same effect here as calling a woman's interest in being free not to procreate a right. It elevates the interest to a level of importance that seems to subordinate other interests, often with adverse results. Thus, the interest in procreation may conflict with other personal interests, including the important interests in freedom from confinement and in *not* procreating. *Skinner*'s elevation of the interest in procreation to the status of a "right" made it difficult to accommodate those other interests. The problem arose in the context of sterilization cases brought by parents or guardians on behalf of their wards.

Courts have long recognized that sterilization is an extreme course of action and that parents or guardians may have a conflict of interest with their children or wards. After all, the life of the parent of a mentally retarded teenage girl will be much easier if the parent need not fear that the daughter may become pregnant. Courts must be vigilant to protect such girls from being sterilized for their parents' benefit rather than their own.

Accordingly, the courts have consistently held that parental or guardian consent is insufficient to authorize the sterilization of a child or other incompetent person.[9] One seeking the sterilization of another person must first obtain a court order. However, until recently such orders were virtually impossible to obtain.

Recognizing that the power to sterilize is "awesome," and having been told that procreation is a right, courts typically took the position that they lacked jurisdiction to authorize sterilization unless a statute specifically granted them that power.[10] Most state statutes only authorized the sterilization of persons confined in state institutions. Thus, the only way to obtain the sterilization of an incompetent person was to have her confined. Given the overcrowded condition of most state facilities for retarded persons, that was often impossible. In cases where it was possible, the incompetent person lost her general freedom along with her freedom to procreate. Thus, no matter how beneficial sterilization might be to an individual, she could not obtain it, at least without being incarcerated.

In 1978 a federal court in Connecticut considered the constitutionality of a typical state system that authorized sterilization only for residents of state institutions.[11] The court found that system denied the equal protection of the laws to three severely mentally and physically handicapped girls because the state lacked a valid reason to deny them the *benefit* of sterilization, which it accorded to institutionalized persons. Reading between the lines, it seems likely that the same court would also have invalidated the statute if it had been challenged by inmates of state institutions who were exposed to the *detriment* of sterilization that their noninstitutionalized counterparts were spared. If so, then either sterilization or nonsterilization of retarded persons would be permissible as long as persons inside and outside of institutions were treated the same.

A 1974 federal case[12] and *Roe v. Wade*[13] combined to shift the balance in the direction of nonsterilization. Congress had authorized the expenditure of certain monies for family planning. The Department of Health, Education and Welfare authorized the expenditure of some of those funds for the sterilization of incompetent persons if certain procedural safeguards were employed. A federal court in the District of Columbia held that the DHEW regulations exceeded the Department's statutory authority. Federal family planning money could not be used to sterilize incompetent persons.[14]

Theoretically, Congress could have passed a new statute that authorized sterilization. Realistically, however, such a statute would probably have been held unconstitutional. The District of Columbia Court hinted broadly that it would invalidate a sterilization statute. It focused on the statute's requirement of voluntariness and noted,

> [T]he term voluntary . . . assumes an exercise of free will and clearly precludes the existence of coercion or force. . . . And its use in the statutory and decisional law, at least when important human rights are at stake, entails a requirement that the individual have at his disposal the information necessary to make his decision and the mental competence to appreciate the significance of that information. . . .
>
> No person who is mentally incompetent can meet these standards, nor can the consent of a representative, however sufficient under state law, impute voluntariness to the individual actually undergoing irreversible sterilization.[15]

The court recognized that it was not making a constitutional decision about whether Congress could fund sterilization of incompetent persons, but it noted that the intent to fund such sterilization "will not be lightly assumed in light of the fundamental interests at stake. . . . Involuntary sterilization . . . invades rather than compliments [*sic*] the right to procreate."[16]

Roe v. Wade and the early post-*Roe* abortion cases seemed to support the view that sterilization of incompetent persons was unconstitutional. *Roe* cited *Buck v. Bell* without apparent disapproval.[17] Nonetheless, it is hard to see how the right of privacy, which is broad enough to encompass a woman's decision whether to terminate her pregnancy, could fail to be broad enough to encompass a person's decision not to be sterilized. Thus, the right of privacy seems to reinforce the right to procreate, which was first recognized in *Skinner*. As *Danforth v. Planned Parenthood*[18] seemed to make clear, that right belongs to individuals and may not be waived for them by persons purporting to act on their behalf. If that is so, then incompetent persons cannot be sterilized. They lack the ability to consent on their own, and nobody else can consent for them.

Thus, in the mid-1970s sterilization of mentally incompetent persons at the request of their parents or guardians seemed unavailable. If *Buck v. Bell* was still good law, states could sterilize persons for reasons that seemed important to the states. Private persons, however, could not obtain sterilization of their children or wards. Therefore, persons (mostly women) who would really benefit from sterilization, for example, by being able to live an unrestricted life in the community, were denied that benefit. "Rights talk"[19] led to the need to deprive women of all of their freedom, including the actual freedom to procreate, in order to preserve their biological ability and theoretical right to procreate. This made no sense.

Fortunately, however, the "lesser" institutions of government, the legislatures and state courts, have largely remedied the problem. Arguably, the Constitution still permits states to sterilize persons for eugenic or punitive reasons. In fact, however, all but eight states have now repealed their compulsory sterilization statutes,[20] and truly involuntary sterilization no longer is practiced in the United States.

Sterilization by parent or guardian consent, on the other hand, is now available, but difficult to obtain. The fundamental recognitions that sterilization is an extreme course of action and that parents and guardians cannot be trusted to act in the best interests of their children and wards remain valid. Nonetheless, the courts have increasingly begun to recognize that in the sterilization area, as in others, the courts themselves are capable of protecting defenseless persons, and that what protects a person best will depend on the facts of each case.

Thus, in 1980, when the Supreme Court of Washington confronted a petition to authorize sterilization of an incompetent woman who was not institutionalized, the court found that its general jurisdiction authorized it to act. It recognized the extreme nature of sterilization and the strong interest in being free to procreate. It also recognized, however, that sometimes sterilization may be the best option for a person. Therefore, the court held that in some circumstances an incompetent person may be sterilized, but it created extremely rigorous procedural requirements that proponents of sterilization had to meet before a court could authorize a particular sterilization. The court adopted a "heavy presumption" against sterilization. The proponent could only overcome the presumption by proving with clear and convincing evidence that sterilization is in the retarded person's best interest. There must be a hearing in which the incompetent person is represented. The court must receive advice from independent experts based on medical, psychological, and social examination of the incompetent person. To the extent possible the court must consider the incompetent person's views. The court must consider her age, educability and potential as a parent as well as "the degree to which sterilization is . . . the last and best resort for the individual." Specifically, the judge must find (1) that the incompetent person is incapable of making her own decision about sterilization, (2) that she is unlikely to become capable, (3) that she is physically capable of procreation (4) that she is likely to engage in sexual activity, and (5) that she is permanently incapable of caring for a child, even with help. In addition there must be no alternative to sterilization: (1) All less drastic measures are unworkable; (2) sterilization involves the least invasion of the person's body; and (3) there is no reason to expect development of reversible sterilization, less drastic contraceptive measures, or a treatment for the person's disability.[21]

These showings are almost impossible to make. Some even require sterilization proponents to prove a negative. There will be no abusive mass sterilizations of incompetent Washingtonians. Nonetheless, in the rare instances in which sterilization truly is a benefit, the possibility of receiving that benefit is left open.

Since 1980 the Washington approach has increasingly been adopted throughout the United States.[22] Thus, by focusing on interests and the facts of particular cases courts have been able to offer the benefits of sterilization to incompetent persons without exposing them to the risk of imposition.

The most thoughtful opposition to this trend is found in a dissenting opinion to a 1985 California sterilization case.[23] California differed from other states in that rather than remaining silent about whether mentally incompetent persons could be sterilized, the California legislature had specifically prohibited their sterilization. The parents of Valerie N., a woman with Down's syndrome, sought permission to have their daughter sterilized. The probate court agreed with the parents that sterilization was safe and would improve Valerie's quality of life. Nonetheless, the court decided that it lacked jurisdiction and could not authorize Valerie's sterilization because of the statutory prohibition. The parents appealed.

Because the statute plainly precluded sterilization, the California Supreme Court could not authorize the procedure without holding the statute unconstitutional. It could, however, prohibit sterilization without deciding whether the statute was valid. In fact, the court did refuse to authorize Valerie's sterilization because the parents had failed to produce enough evidence in the probate court to justify sterilizing her. Therefore, the court did not have to reach the constitutional question. However, as we saw in the abortion setting, judicial restraint is out of fashion. The California court confronted the constitutional issue head-on.

The majority of the court thought that what was at stake in the case was Valerie's interest in living the fullest and most rewarding life possible, her right to personal growth and development, her right to develop to her maximum economic, intellectual, and social level.[24] To serve those ends the court focused on Valerie's right to choose not to bear children and to implement that choice.[25] Of course, the court recognized that Valerie lacked the capacity to make a choice, but it overcame that problem by finding that she had a right to have someone else make the decision for her.[26] The court characterized Valerie's rights as fundamental.[27] That meant that state infringements were invalid unless they were necessary to a compelling state interest. The state had an important interest in protecting Valerie's right to procreate, but prohibiting her sterilization was not necessary to serve the state's interest because it could be adequately served in a less restrictive way—the adoption of Washington-style procedural requirements to protect persons like Valerie from abusive sterilization.[28] Since the statute infringed upon a fundamental right and was not necessary to accomplish a compelling state end, the statute was unconstitutional.

Chief Justice Bird dissented.[29] She saw the case in a radically different way. To Chief Justice Bird, the protected constitutional right in Valerie's case was the right to procreate.[30] That right, she argued, is unrelated to choice, which is impossible for Valerie anyway.[31] Rather than a choice-based right Bird saw the right to procreate as a primal right, rooted in notions of bodily (rather than intellectual) autonomy.[32] It is not a freedom *to* choose whether to procreate, but rather a freedom *from* bodily invasion. This right is fundamental.[33] The state's interest in protecting Valerie's liberty, growth, and development is important, but no one has shown that allowing Valerie to be sterilized is necessary to serve that interest.[34] Therefore, allowing sterilization would be unconstitutional, and the statute prohibiting it is valid.

It is hard to imagine more widely divergent views than those of the majority and Chief Justice Bird. What the majority sees as the personal right at stake, Bird sees as the state interest. What Bird sees as the right, the majority sees as the state interest. The majority's view of rights is choice-based and consequentialist. Chief Justice Bird's view is essentialist and deontological. Whose view is right?

The disagreement between Bird and the majority shows once again the futility of basing legal arguments on the existence of rights when the rights lack an apparent source, are not universally shared, and are not necessary to prevent the state from running roughshod over people.

Chief Justice Bird's view has a deep and intuitive appeal. It also offers the advantage of not having to talk about making a choice in a case in which the principal cannot choose, and it saves us from the fiction that a surrogate's choice is the same as the choice of the person affected.

Yet, at bottom, Chief Justice Bird's approach is unsatisfying. What are we doing for Valerie by respecting her primal right to procreate if we then lock her away to be sure she does not procreate, or if the procreation experience is a frightening and awful one for her? How can we justify making Valerie suffer for Justice Bird's ideals?

Is not the sensible approach (1) to recognize that there is much to be said on both sides of the question; (2) to resolve cases of legislative silence as the Washington court did, resolving one case at a time in order to do the least damage possible; but (3) to resolve cases where the legislature disagrees with that approach by upholding its statutes? In other words, the *Valerie N.* majority reached the right result for a case in which there is no statute, but it is not so clearly the right result as to justify imposing it if the popularly elected legislature disagrees. There is a wide gulf between believing one is right and being so sure of one's rightness that it is acceptable to impose the "right" view on everybody.

In any event, despite its unnecessary constitutional decision making, the California Supreme Court reached a result that is consistent with the national trend. That trend is now well established. States do not sterilize people for the state's benefit anymore. Parents and guardians may not effectively consent to the sterilization of their children or wards, but state courts can authorize such sterilizations, and will do so, in the rare instances in which sterilization is truly the best alternative for the incompetent person and in which rigorous procedural safeguards make inappropriate sterilizations extremely unlikely to occur. This is not as exciting as deciding that people have a right to be sterilized or a right not to be sterilized, but it has a better chance than either rights approach of reaching right results.

FOUR

Alternative Reproductive Techniques

Although the national obsession with abortion often obscures the fact, most people want to have children. Often, however, male or female infertility precludes conception or carrying a pregnancy to term. In addition, persons who lack partners of the opposite sex and persons who are at risk for having children with genetic diseases or environmentally caused birth defects may wish to reproduce. Of course, they will want their children to be healthy. Three techniques—artificial insemination, surrogate motherhood, and in vitro fertilization—can provide assistance to such persons.

ARTIFICIAL INSEMINATION

Artificial insemination has been used in human beings since at least the beginning of the twentieth century. While statistics about artificial insemination are probably unreliable, they suggest that about 65,000 children are born annually in the United States through use of the technique.[1]

Artificial insemination is technically quite simple: a man ejaculates into a container and the ejaculate is inserted into a woman's vagina by syringe. If the process occurs around the time of ovulation, the chances for achieving pregnancy are good.

Obviously, any man can provide semen for artificial insemination. Standard terminology, which developed when uses outside of marriage seemed unlikely, spoke of two kinds of artificial insemination—artificial insemination by husband (AIH), in which a husband's semen was used to inseminate his wife, and artificial insemination by donor (AID), in which a third party provided the semen.

AIH may be used for cases in which sexual intercourse, but not procreation, is difficult or impossible, or when pooling the husband's sperm is desirable because of reduced fertility or for use after exposure to mutagens or even after death. In AIH the husband is both the social and the biological father of the child. Therefore, AIH has not troubled the law, although a few old cases did consider whether a wife's submission to AIH precluded her from obtaining an annulment of her marriage for lack of consummation,[2] and one can easily imagine complicated inheritance cases when AIH occurs after a husband's death.

AID has typically been used in cases of male infertility when married couples have sought to have a child that is biologically half their own. The technique is also useful for reducing the risk of genetic disease. For example, if both husband and wife carry the gene for a recessive disease like sickle-cell anemia, Tay-Sachs disease, or phenylketonuria, they can reduce their chance of having a child with the disease from 25 percent to virtually zero by using semen provided by a noncarrier male. Outside of marriage AID provides a way for women without mates, including lesbians, to have children. Gay men can only utilize the technique by finding a surrogate mother to bear the child.

Artificial insemination by donor is inaptly named. The semen provider typically sells his semen; no donation is involved.

Recent studies suggest that physicians who perform AID do little genetic or other testing of potential "donors."[3] Cases involving transmission of genetic diseases and infectious diseases, especially AIDS, seem certain to arise.

To date, however, legal questions have concerned social and financial relationships among husbands, wives, children, semen providers, unmarried women, and those women's companions. The early cases arose in the context of divorce. They were common law cases in the sense that no statutes about AID existed, although general legislation establishing grounds for divorce and regulating custody, child support, etc., did exist.

The earliest cases involved husbands seeking divorces. Before the days of no-fault divorce a person seeking to terminate a marriage had to establish the existence of grounds to do so. One fault-based ground was adultery. If a woman had a baby despite long separation from her husband, the husband's divorce suit premised on adultery seemed strong. At least two women, however, defended against their husbands' claims by asserting that they had conceived their children through AID. In a Canadian case the court simply disbelieved the woman and granted the divorce.[4] In *MacLennan v. MacLennan*,[5] a Scottish case, however, the court actually addressed the question of whether AID of a married woman without her husband's consent is adultery. The opinion, which Lord Wheatley seems to have written with his tongue lodged firmly in his cheek, is a caricature of common law reasoning despite the facts that Scotland is not a common law jurisdiction and that the problem only arose because a statute provided limited grounds for divorce. A critic of common law method could have a field day with *MacLennan v. MacLennan*.

Lord Wheatley immediately recognized that he was facing a case of first impression. No matter—the way to decide the case was to define adultery by looking to previously decided cases and learned treatises and then to decide whether nonconsensual AID fit within the definition. Of course, Lord Wheatley recognized that the earlier cases and treatises had not considered this question. Nonetheless, he said, the court could extract basic principles from them. The basic principle he extracted is that adultery involves sexual intercourse. Sexual intercourse, in turn, requires penetration of the female organ by the male organ. Given contraception and infertility, it does not require impregnation or even the possibility of impregnation. The essence of the offense is not the introduction of an alien seed into the bloodline, but rather the introduction of an "alien and unlawful sexual organ."[6] AID does not require penetration. Therefore, it does not involve sexual intercourse and cannot be adultery.

Lord Wheatley may not have been happy with this conclusion. He believed that AID without the husband's consent is "a grave and heinous breach of the contract of marriage."[7] Nonetheless, a rule is a rule, and if science has created a situation the law does not provide for, it is the legislature's job to create a new statutory category, not the court's job to fit the new situation into the old one.[8]

Near the end of his opinion Lord Wheatley did allow himself to consider the consequences of holding nonconsensual AID to be adultery.[9] A court would have to decide who the other adulterer was: the donor? the physician? What if the woman did the procedure herself? What if the physician were a woman? Could a male physician's wife divorce her husband on the ground of his adultery because he performed the technique? If the donor were the adulterer, and if he were dead at the time of insemination, would the inseminated woman be guilty of necrophilia?

All of this is highly amusing, but not very helpful. If the common law had to work as it did in *MacLennan*, it really would be ill suited to resolving biosocial problems. In fact, however, a good common law judge would never approach a case the way Lord Wheatley approached *MacLennan*.

A good American common law judge would ask what is at stake in the case. Two possibilities exist: The case is either about whether Mr. MacLennan should get his divorce or about whether to encourage or discourage AID without a husband's consent. If such AID really is a grave and heinous breach of the marriage contract, it should be discouraged and the divorce should be granted. Given that outlook, the judge would then consider why the legislature would have made adultery grounds for divorce. Marriage contemplates *both* sexual and reproductive exclusivity. Adultery sacrifices one or both of those. AID without consent sacrifices reproductive exclusivity and therefore should provide grounds for divorce if one wants to make the statute maximally effective in attacking the mischief at which it is aimed. Therefore, *for purposes of divorce* AID without the husband's consent is adultery.

The problems Lord Wheatley raised about who the other adulterer is do not have to be resolved. No other person is necessary to provide a divorce to the MacLennans. If a male doctor's wife sues him for divorce because he performed the technique, she will lose. She has suffered no affront to her interest in sexual or reproductive exclusivity with her husband. If a donor's wife sued him, however, she might prevail. The main point, however, is that none of these questions has to be resolved. The genius of the common law is that it solves one case at a time. The MacLennans do not need a general definition of adultery. They only need to know whether Mr. MacLennan will get his divorce. Lord Wheatley answered that question incorrectly. Luckily his mistake did not matter. Mrs. MacLennan failed to prove she underwent AID. Therefore, birth of the child proved conventional adultery, and Mr. MacLennan finally got his divorce.[10]

By the end of the twentieth century no-fault divorce has become the norm in the United States. Therefore, the question of whether AID is adultery is no longer a significant legal question.

What matters now is what the effect of AID is on family social and economic relationships. A number of cases have explored the question of what relationship a husband who consented to AID of his wife bears to the resulting child. For example, after divorce must the husband support the child? May he gain custody or visitation rights? Can he prevent another man from adopting the child? Can a child inherit from the husband if the husband dies intestate?

The early cases discussed the question of whether a child born of consensual AID is the legitimate child of its mother and her husband.[11] If so, then the answers to all the questions are the same as for conventionally conceived children of a marriage. The courts showed great reluctance to label the children of AID legitimate. One famous case held that they were illegitimate.[12] Nonetheless, every case reached the same conclusion that would be reached in a case involving the clearly legitimate child of a married couple.[13] Thus, the husband must support the child; he is entitled to visitation; no other man may adopt the child without his consent; etc.

These results seem clearly to be correct from every point of view. They give the child the social and financial benefits of having two parents. They reduce the risk that the state will end up supporting the child. They discourage thoughtless use of AID by making plain the serious legal consequences that attach to it. They avoid the gratuitous cruelty to husbands that would result from cutting them off from children they probably love, while making the husbands (like all fathers) bear the burdens of parenthood as well as receive its benefits. They protect women from being unfairly left to bear the entire burden of raising children their husbands agreed to have. They do not impose obligations on service providers (doctors) or persons who had and suggested no intention of entering into long-term relationships (donors). In short, the decisions reach the right results from the point of view of husbands, wives, children, doctors, donors (and their families), and the state.

If the decisions are so plainly right, one might well ask why the courts do not now simply say that children of consensual AID are legitimate or, alternatively, why legislatures do not adopt statutes to that effect. The best reasons for a court not to make such a statement are that doing so is neither necessary nor authoritative and that it may cause a court problems it cannot foresee. A legislature can act authoritatively, but it faces the same concerns of necessity and foresight that a court does plus the added problem of drafting language that will achieve its purpose without doing things it does not want to do. Some examples should make the points clear.

A California sperm bank accepts sperm only from Nobel prizewinners and uses it to inseminate "superior" women in order to produce "superior" children.[14] A court may disapprove of this form of "positive eugenics," but as long as the legislature has not outlawed the practice, the court cannot forbid it. It can, however, make the sperm supply dry up by requiring one of the Nobel laureates to support a child conceived with his sperm. Such an approach, which discourages conduct but does not require the expense and effort of outright prohibition, is quite attractive. If, however, the state supreme court had held that children of consensual AID are the legitimate offspring of their mother and her husband, or that they are not the children of the donor, the court that wanted to discourage positive eugenics would have a problem. Either it would be bound by the earlier decision, which surely would not have contemplated the Nobel sperm bank problem, or it could avoid that result by distinguishing the prior case. It could say the first case is not binding in the present context because it did not involve a Nobel sperm bank. The new rule would be that children of consensual AID are the legitimate children of their mothers and their mothers' husbands, and not the children of sperm donors except when the sperm donors are Nobel prizewinners (and in any other cases we decide to create exceptions for in the future). In other words, either the court would be bound to reach a decision it did not want to reach or its clear rule about legitimacy would disappear.

The same problem would arise in cases of unmarried women. Either the donor would be free of parental responsibility because donors aren't legal fathers or he would not be, in which event the clear rule is for an ever-contracting universe of cases and not so clear after all. The courts' actual solution to these problems is much more satisfactory.

In *C.M. v. C.C.*[15] a couple was dating and (apparently) planned to marry. The woman wanted a child before marriage but did not want to engage in sexual intercourse before marriage (!). Unable to find a doctor to accommodate them, the couple performed AID unaided, and the woman became pregnant. During the pregnancy the couple split up. After the child was born the man faithfully paid child support and sought to visit the child. The woman denied visitation. The New Jersey court held that for visitation purposes this donor was the child's father, entitled to visit. This seems clearly the right result, but it is a result the court could not have reached if it had had a rule that donors cannot be fathers, unless it had started eroding the rule.

At bottom the only objection to the courts' actions discussed so far is that they do not clearly resolve all issues of paternity once and for all. As suggested, courts are unlikely to be able to provide such an all-purpose solution. Can legislatures do a better job?

Over the years a number of legislatures have tried. For example, Georgia adopted a statute that "irrebuttably presumed" children conceived by married women through AID to be legitimate "if both spouses have consented in writing."[16] Suppose they consent orally. A well-established canon of statutory construction says that the expression of one thing is the negation of another. In other words, if consent is not written, the child is illegitimate. Yet surely it makes no sense to treat a child as illegitimate because of a clerical error.

An alternative reading would say that the statute only dealt with cases of written consent. Oral consent cases are left open for the courts to decide. That approach will probably avoid the absurdity of negative implication, but it also eliminates the across-the-board certainty the legislation was meant to provide. A Kansas court dealt with a statute similar to the Georgia one in just that way.[17] It avoided an absurd result, but the statute was an obstacle to be overcome, not an aid to sound decision making.

The Georgia statute provides that only licensed physicians may perform AID.[18] Anyone else performing the technique is guilty of a felony and is to be imprisoned for one to five years. What about the woman who performs the technique on herself? It is hard to believe that the Georgia legislature intended to make her a felon, but that is what it has done, and a similar statute in Oregon has been construed to make it a misdemeanor for a woman to perform artificial insemination on herself.[19]

The Georgia statute provides that a doctor who obtains the necessary written consent,

> shall be relieved of civil liability to the husband and wife or to any child conceived by artificial insemination for the result or results of said artificial insemination, provided, that the written authorization . . . shall not relieve any physician or surgeon from any civil liability arising from his or her own negligent administration or performance of artificial insemination.[20]

What does this provision mean? Suppose a doctor who has obtained written consent to perform AID uses sperm from a donor of a different race than the consenting couple. Is he immune from liability? Or is he not immune because he was negligent? Or is he immune because even if he was negligent his negligence was not in the "administration or performance of artificial insemination"?

Alternatively, suppose a doctor writes a provision exempting himself from liability for negligent administration or performance into the consent form. Is the provision valid? Does the statute prohibit such a term as contrary to public policy, or does it merely resolve cases in which the consent document is silent on the point?

The Georgia statute comes no closer to resolving issues once and for all than does the common law. Along the way it creates new problems and poses roadblocks to sensible resolutions of questions. Obviously this legislation is no improvement over the common law.

Other state statutes have problems similar to Georgia's. Even a model statute proposed by the Commissioners on Uniform State Laws created terrible problems. The Commissioners are not popularly elected and are very distinguished lawyers, judges, and law professors. If anybody can draft a good statute, it should be they.

Section 5 of the Uniform Parentage Act[21] sought to achieve the end that everyone seems to agree is sound—treating consensual AID children as legitimate. The statute provided,

> (a) If, under the supervision of a licensed physician and with the consent of her husband, a wife is inseminated artificially with semen donated by a man not her husband, the husband is treated in law as if he were the natural father of a child thereby conceived. . . .

> (b) The donor of semen . . . is treated in law as if he were not the natural father of a child thereby conceived.

Under this statute suppose a husband opposes a support obligation to the child, or suppose the husband's parents oppose the child's claim to inherit from the husband. May they show that the husband and/or wife paid for the semen? After all, the statute only applies when semen is "donated." If payment is relevant, does it render the statute inapplicable? Does it make the child illegitimate by negative implication, or simply leave the issue unresolved?

Even if the semen was donated does the statute make the child legitimate and entitled to inherit? What does it mean when it says the husband is treated as the father of the child, without saying anything about how the child is to be treated?

Under subsection (b) what happens when a married woman acts as a surrogate mother? The man who provided the semen, and who presumably wants the child, is now the donor, specifically prohibited by the statute from being treated as the father of the child. If the surrogate's husband consented, he is presumably to be treated as the father. Surely, this is not what the drafters had in mind.

Legislation, even when drafted by experts freed of political constraints, is not as likely to achieve certainty and comprehensiveness in fact as it is in theory. It also creates problems of its own. In an area like AID where the courts seem to be doing a good job of solving problems despite their inability to always explain what they have done in generalizable terms, pursuing legislative solutions seems unwise.

The Commissioners on Uniform State Laws have now taken a second crack at the AID question. In addition to the Uniform Parentage Act of 1973 the Commissioners drafted the Uniform Status of Children of Assisted Conception Act (USCACA)[22] in 1988. That Act, which has been adopted in two states,[23] corrects some of the problems with the Uniform Parentage Act, which is in force in eighteen states.[24] For example, USCACA defines "donor" to include an individual who produces sperm for assisted conception, regardless of whether payment is made. The Act declares the husband of a married woman to be an AID child's father unless a court finds he did not consent to the AID.

Section 4 of the Act provides, "A donor is not a parent of a child conceived through assisted conception." This removes flexibility from the courts if they encounter a Nobel laureate sperm bank or other social experiment they wish to discourage. More importantly, though, it leaves a child conceived through AID of an unmarried woman fatherless even if the donor is willing to serve as father to the child. The father in *C. M. v. C. C.* would have neither visitation rights nor support obligations under USCACA, although it is hard to see why not. Here the statute provides certainty at the expense of child support and a father figure for a child, protection of both mother and state from financial burdens, and even a chance to decide that in some circumstances treating a donor as a father may make sense. No overwhelming social problem required such a certain solution.

The Act also (perhaps inadvertently) takes a strange position in the case of lesbians who become pregnant through AID. If the woman's lover seeks some sort of parental rights in the child, the statute is silent about whether she can prevail. It excludes the child's biological father, the donor, from any such rights. Legislative action answers one question and leaves the other open, allowing courts to adjudicate half of the social issue posed.

Without legislation courts are doing fine on their own. For example, in *Jhordan C. v. Mary K.*,[25] a California case, a donor and a mother's female friend each sought parental rights in the child. Under the Uniform Parentage Act, which was in effect in California, the donor would have been precluded from paternity if he had provided his semen to a doctor to use for the insemination. Since no doctor had been involved, the statute did not apply. Deciding the case at common law the court entered a declaration of the donor's paternity and provided him with visitation rights. It examined the facts of the case and found for the donor because (1) he was the biological father, (2) he was being legally forced to pay support, (3) the mother had sought an increase in his support obligation (4) he acted like a father by setting up a trust fund for the baby, buying baby furniture, taking baby pictures, and visiting the child regularly, (5) the mother let him do those things, and (6) there was a conflict in the evidence about the nature of the agreement between the mother and the donor. In other words, no good reason existed to deny social fatherhood to this particular biological father. As to Victoria, the mother's friend, the court refused to declare her the child's de facto parent, but it guaranteed her rights of visitation too.

If either the UPA or USCACA had applied, the donor would have been legally excluded from the child's life. Victoria would have been no better off than under the court's order. In other words, the statutes would have failed to resolve all issues and would have resolved the ones they did resolve incorrectly.

Similarly, in Oregon the legislature enacted a statute to legitimate AID offspring of married women whose husbands had consented to the use of AID.[26] The statute did not define the term "donor," but it provided that neither the donor nor a resulting child would have any rights, obligations, or interests vis-à-vis the other. The statute also made it a misdemeanor for anyone other than a physician to perform artificial insemination. Kevin, in Oregon, provided semen to Linden, who used it to inseminate herself. The parties disagreed about what, if anything, they had agreed to about Kevin's ongoing relationship with the intended child. In Kevin's filiation proceeding after the child was born, the court had to deal with a statute whose terms applied to a situation the legislature obviously had not contemplated. It decided that Kevin was a "donor" under the statute. Therefore, he had no rights in relation to the child. However, if the parties really had agreed that Kevin was to have an ongoing relationship with the child, as he contended, then the court said it would be unconstitutional to apply the statute to deny Kevin's relationship.[27] Thus, the statute solved nothing. It forced the court to construe an undefined term and then to decide that the statute as construed could not be applied to one of two possible views of the facts. Sound social policy probably demands that known donors who seek the rights of fatherhood should have those rights in some cases, but not in others. The common law courts are much more likely to reach the right result in particular cases without disturbing implications for others if the legislatures refrain from becoming involved.

None of this should be a big surprise. Society is unsure what it thinks about lesbian motherhood in particular and unwed motherhood in general. In the light of that uncertainty, resolution by legislation is premature, especially because the problem occurs so infrequently that no case can be made that some answer is needed regardless of whether it is right or wrong.

The common law method is ideal for resolving issues like those posed by AID. Common law's greatest weakness, its inability to control conduct, is insignificant where, as with AID, conduct control is not a major need. The social problem is small, and no need exists for a speedy or comprehensive solution. Society's values are unclear, so that any effort to achieve certainty would be premature. The issues raised are the kinds of issues courts are used to dealing with and for which large bodies of relevant analogy are available for courts to draw on. Sound results do not require the ability to understand scientific facts.

The question remains whether AID law has important lessons to teach about dealing with surrogate motherhood.

SURROGATE MOTHERHOOD

In its simplest form surrogate motherhood involves artificial insemination of a woman, who is called the surrogate, with semen from a known man in the expectation that the surrogate will conceive, carry the child to term, give birth, and surrender the baby and her rights in it to the man who provided the semen. A more complicated version involves in vitro fertilization followed by embryo transplant into a woman who carries the pregnancy, gives birth, and surrenders parental rights. In simple surrogacy the surrogate is the genetic and gestational mother of the child. In in vitro fertilization surrogacy, she may well not be the genetic mother.

Simple surrogacy is useful when a married woman is infertile or unable to carry a pregnancy. The technique, which is technologically the same as artificial insemination, offers that woman and her husband the same kinds of benefits that AID offers couples in which the husband is infertile. The assumption is that the surrogate will surrender the baby to its father and his wife and that the wife will adopt the baby or, at least, act as its mother. Of course, the technique can also be used to provide single men or gay couples with babies or to allow women to avoid the risk, discomfort, and inconvenience of pregnancy. Professor Martha Field reported that as of 1986 there had been 500 surrogate births in the United States, 495 of them without dispute or difficulty.[28]

Of course, disputes and difficulties are easy to imagine. The surrogate may not want to surrender the child; the father and his wife may not want to accept it; the surrogate may decide to seek an abortion; she may refuse prenatal medical care or otherwise act differently than the father and his wife wish; etc.

Whether the common law can deal adequately with surrogate motherhood depends on assessing the needs for rapid resolution of the issues surrogacy poses and for conduct control in an area in which values are in flux, the narrow issues involve the kinds of status questions courts are used to resolving, and the scientific facts are easy to understand.

Surrogate motherhood does not seem a very good candidate for legislative treatment. Its social impact may be dramatic, but it is very small both in terms of the number of times surrogacy is used and the likelihood of something going wrong. A busy legislator confronted with a list of social problems that includes surrogacy might well be forgiven, or even praised, for saying, "First things first." Moreover, courts can deal well with surrogacy issues, which require no sophisticated scientific knowledge and which involve child custody and parental obligation questions, the type of questions courts deal with all the time.

Why then is there a push for legislation to regulate or even prohibit surrogate motherhood? Two major and a few minor concerns convince some observers that legislation is necessary.

First some persons see surrogacy as baby selling, which should be prohibited.[29] At most this concern suggests prohibiting paid surrogacy, not surrogacy performed for free by a relative or friend. Baby selling is opposed because it is an affront to people's sensibilities; because it is thought to threaten the creation of a slave race of babies; because it takes from a desperate woman her most precious possession, her child; and because it encourages the breakup of the family unit.

To the extent that the affront to sensibilities reflects more than a reaction to the other three reasons, it must indicate a general disgust at making a human being into a commodity. That affront exists in surrogate motherhood, although the baby is hardly to be treated as a commodity in the whole sense. Nobody envisions resale, lease, or most of the other attributes of personal property. The commodity notion is probably rooted in the long discredited idea that a child was its father's chattel. Modern parental rights are not property rights. One can recognize the concern for sensibilities without going overboard in responding to it.

The concerns about a slave race of babies and breaking up families obviously do not apply to surrogate motherhood. Women are not being encouraged to have the maximum number of children to serve as slaves; a very few babies are being created to be raised as family members. Similarly, surrogacy does not resemble the pre–Civil War evil of separating slave siblings by selling them to different masters. It is giving custody of a child, who either has no siblings, or none who know it, to one of its parents rather than the other. Finally, the argument against baby selling because it deprives a desperate woman of her child is also misplaced here. In a common sense view of what constitutes baby selling, a woman in terrible need of money might be persuaded to part with her child. In surrogacy, however, the transaction occurs before conception, when the surrogate has no child to love. The argument from desperation is not really an argument about baby selling but a separate suggested reason to outlaw surrogate motherhood.

The second major set of concerns about surrogacy focuses on the practice's impact on women.[30] They suggest that surrogate motherhood imposes on women both economically and psychologically and that it demeans women by treating them as a thing, a uterus for hire, to be used like an incubator. These concerns are harder to deal with than those about baby selling.

The economic argument is straightforward: Rich women will not serve as surrogates, and only rich persons will be able to hire surrogates. Thus, if allowed, surrogate motherhood will be an instance of rich persons imposing on poor women to do something the rich would not do themselves. Again, of course, this argument only applies to surrogacy for a fee.

In the absence of data one can only imagine the demographics of surrogate motherhood. It does seem reasonable to believe that rich women will not choose to become surrogates. I think it is also unlikely that impoverished women will become surrogates. Persons seeking a surrogate mother for their child will have all the prejudices and beliefs about why people are impoverished that other people have. They will avoid truly impoverished potential mothers for their children in favor of college students who need some money and lower middle-class women seeking to supplement their incomes. Some wealth discrepancy will exist between surrogates and those who seek them, but it is not likely to be extreme.

Is the wealth discrepancy that exists a valid reason to prohibit paid surrogacy? The suggestion that it is seems oddly out of keeping with the entire economic system of the United States. People work in order to get money. The greater their need for money, the more things they will do to earn it. Most upper middle-class persons are willing to work as lawyers, physicians, educators, or business executives. They are not willing to serve as domestics, and indeed, many of them seek to hire persons to clean their homes. No one suggests that poor persons should be prohibited from earning a living as housecleaners because they would be unwilling to do the same work if they were rich.

Surrogate motherhood, moreover, offers relatively poor women two advantages that menial but less controversial work does not—advancement and fulfillment. A surrogate mother can earn between ten and fifty thousand dollars for her nine months of pregnancy in addition to whatever she may earn at a conventional job. Menial labor does not pay that well. For some women surrogacy may be the route out of poverty. Who are we to deny them that escape?

In addition, some few persons (law professors, for example) are blessed with jobs that provide personal fulfillment as well as a livelihood. Most are not. Surely, some women would find it more fulfilling to carry a child for a couple than to clean that couple's house. Is it not arrogant to deny the possibility of such fulfillment and to preclude anyone from experiencing it?

To the extent that the concern about exploitation is not about the receipt of any fee but a fear that the fee may be too low, legislation could impose a minimum fee requirement for valid surrogacy contracts. Doing so, however, would be unwise, unnecessary and inefficacious. It would be unwise because any figure selected would be arbitrary and would fail to take into account the personal situations of the surrogate and the persons she contracted with, and because any figure chosen would rapidly become outdated, thus requiring the already overworked legislature to waste time amending the statute every few years. Legislation is unnecessary because the common law doctrine of unconscionability already exists to preclude the enforcement of grossly unfair contracts. A statute would also be inefficacious because it would leave open the question courts must grapple with now—who gets the baby if the contract is not enforced? Arguments to prohibit or regulate surrogacy based on financial exploitation are unsound.

The exploitation of women argument, however, is not entirely economic. Critics of surrogacy also suggest that it involves psychological exploitation as well.[31] The suggestion is that a woman entering into a surrogacy contract cannot anticipate what her feelings will be after she has lived with the pregnancy and its hormonal changes for nine months, and that holding her to her bargain would be to take unfair advantage of her inability to make a truly informed, comprehending decision. Again, while this may be true of some women, it seems extreme to attribute it to all. Moreover, the vast majority of surrogacy transactions go off without a hitch, which suggests that generalization from a few sad cases is probably not warranted. Finally, this argument about women is itself demeaning and condescending. Professor Judith Younger made the point quite eloquently:

According to [this argument] . . . , a biological mother is linked by an overpowering bond to her young. Her consent to give up a child is, by definition, uninformed or "irrelevant," it is "well beyond normal human capabilities" for such a woman to part "with her newly born infant without a struggle," she may be expected to do anything—even endanger her baby—to prevent herself from being separated from it. She is, thus, a poor, driven, irrational creature who needs protection from herself and from others. It is, therefore, right to excuse her from her promises, to prevent her from engaging in certain conduct like having children for infertile couples, and to keep her out of other paying jobs as well—in [one writer's] . . . view, those of wet nurse, nanny, prostitute, egg donor, or womb renter. I have spent a good deal of my professional career fighting against the proposition that women are such slaves to their biological destinies, unable to act as rationally as men, and in need of special "protections." I am suspicious of people who and laws which would prevent women from earning money. I subscribe to the view that whatever one's work and whatever job one undertakes ought to be done responsibly and carefully with a sense of professionalism. Professionals complete the tasks they begin even if it is easier or more pleasant not to. That . . . is what the law should expect of both women and men. [footnotes omitted][32]

This argument seems decisive also against the claim that surrogacy demeans women by treating them as mere objects for gestating babies. A more plausible view is that surrogacy treats women as free moral agents who are able to make rational choices about what to do with their physical potential. Prohibiting surrogacy to protect women *from* imposition deprives them of the freedom *to* make decisions and act on them.

Thus, the major concerns about surrogacy that lead to calls for its prohibition turn out to be unpersuasive. Less important concerns that may lead some to seek the conduct control that only legislation can provide may also exist. To some it may seem desirable to control the conduct of the surrogate to prevent fraud, abortion, or inadequate care of the fetus. None of these concerns would justify prohibiting surrogacy. If fraud is a concern, tort suits, theft laws, and escrow accounts are all available to deal with it. A surrogate mother may have a constitutional right to abort the fetus, but even if she does not have that right, banning surrogacy because an occasional surrogate mother might seek an abortion would be an extreme overreaction. Similarly, the extent to which women must protect their fetuses is an evolving issue in pregnancy law in general.[33] To prohibit all women from being surrogate mothers because some might do a bad job would be as ridiculous as banning all motherhood because some pregnant women drink alcohol or smoke. The law can determine on a case by case basis how much relevance, if any, prenatal care clauses in surrogacy contracts have to the question of pregnant women's obligations.

No need for legislation to ban surrogacy exists. In addition, a ban, if enforced by criminal penalties, would be an inappropriate use of the criminal sanction. It would involve criminalizing conduct that is not almost universally condemned as immoral and that may not cause harm to anyone. It may be wasting the criminal sanction on trivia. It may be unenforceable, and it would surely create a crime tariff as surrogacy brokers are driven underground. Finally, a criminal ban would force us to decide who should be punished. Surely nobody seriously wants to incarcerate the surrogate mothers or the men who desperately want babies, and even those who would like to imprison doctors who perform abortions would not want to imprison doctors who pursue new methods to provide life. That leaves only the brokers; nobody loves a middle man, so perhaps some would be willing or even eager to incarcerate surrogacy brokers. In these days of overcrowded prisons when many murderers, rapists, thieves, and drug peddlers clamor for prison space, however, this hardly seems a wise use of limited resources.

How then should surrogate motherhood, not involving in vitro fertilization, be dealt with? Artificial insemination law offers a model. AID law responded to a small number of difficult problems in an area that is not characterized by moral consensus, that does not require scientific sophistication to resolve disputes, and where the need for conduct control is slight, through common law adjudication. Surrogate motherhood raises the same kind of problems and should be dealt with the same way. Case-by-case, fact-centered dispute resolution offers the best hope for protecting children, preventing women from being either exploited or treated as irrational objects, and offering relief to infertile women and their husbands without committing the law to an extreme position and without committing the state's resources to a wasteful enforcement effort.

The disputes that are most likely to arise in the surrogate motherhood setting will involve surrogate mothers who decide not to surrender the child after it is born. That is what happened in the famous *Baby M.* case in New Jersey.[34] In that case the New Jersey Supreme Court held that surrogate motherhood contracts are void; it refused to terminate the parental rights of Mary Beth Whitehead, the surrogate mother; but it awarded custody of the child to David Stern, the father, while ordering consideration of whether Ms. Whitehead should be granted visitation. As with the AID cases, the court's result was sensible even though it said some less than sensible things en route to that result and even though it made a mistake in its treatment of the contract issue.

The court held that the contract was void because it conflicted with New Jersey law and public policy.[35] It expressed concerns about economic exploitation[36] and imposition on women[37] and the fact that the contract assigned custody without regard to the best interests of the child.[38] As suggested earlier, the exploitation and imposition arguments seem an insufficient basis to reject surrogacy. The best interest of the child argument requires consideration.

The child's best interest is the usual criterion for assigning child custody.[39] However, that does not answer the question of whether courts are better suited than parents to decide what is in the child's best interest, especially when the decision is made before the parents are fighting with each other. AID "contracts" also assign custody without regard to the best interests of the child, yet the courts do not invalidate them.[40] What can explain the different treatment of surrogacy? In New Jersey a statute specifically authorized AID, but was silent about surrogacy. The court, therefore, was able to read a negative implication into the AID statute and take it as disapproving of surrogacy. Suppose, however, that no such statute had existed. Should AID and surrogacy contracts, neither of which considers the best interests of the child, be treated differently?

The most obvious difference between AID and surrogacy is irrelevant to the best interests of the child. A sperm donor devotes a few minutes to the child's creation; a surrogate mother carries the pregnancy and experiences its discomfort for nine months, and then undergoes childbirth. However, none of that helps decide whether the best interests of the *child* require treating surrogacy and AID differently.

Focusing on the best interests of the child only in the surrogate motherhood context could be seen as an example of discrimination against women. AID helps infertile men to experience fatherhood. Surrogate motherhood uses the same technology to allow infertile women to experience motherhood. Focusing on the best interests of the child in surrogacy but not AID facilitates sperm selling and fatherhood for men while impeding ovum selling, womb use, and motherhood for women. It is one thing not to reduce women to breeding machines. It is quite another to handicap their desires for reproduction.

Treating surrogacy contracts as void can have other adverse effects on women. A void contract is a contract without legal effect. It cannot be enforced by anybody. Thus, a surrogate mother who wants to fulfill her agreement, but who is confronted with a contracting father who wants to renege, cannot rely on the void contract to force the father to accept the child or even to pay the agreed upon fee. Surely that is a perverse result to reach from a decision to protect women by treating surrogacy contracts as void.

The perverse result could be avoided, as it has been in other states,[41] by treating the contract as voidable rather than void. A voidable contract is enforceable against the party in the stronger bargaining position but may be disclaimed by the party in need of protection. If one believes that women need an escape hatch from surrogate motherhood agreements, then treating the agreements as voidable by the woman provides that protection without providing a similar escape hatch for undeserving fathers. This is another example of the wisdom of avoiding extreme legal positions because one feels strongly about the merits. Here, as almost everywhere, the low level, moderate response is more likely to be successful.

Even so, the question of whether surrogacy contracts are void or voidable is something of a tempest in a teapot. If the contract is not to be enforced against the woman, the question of who gets custody of the child remains to be resolved. In the simple surrogacy situations that we are considering, both the surrogate mother and the contracting father are biological parents of the child. Each has a strong claim to custody. How are their competing claims to be resolved?

In battles for children courts may consider terminating one parent's parental rights. That extreme action, which deprives a parent of any legal interest in a child, is taken only when the parent is unfit.[42] While one party to a surrogacy arrangement may be an unfit parent, that is not a likely scenario. Here, as in other custody battles, neither parent is likely to be unfit. The usual approach in such cases is to determine custody according to the best interests of the child.[43] A parent who loses custody has not been labeled a bad parent, and he or she typically retains both rights (visitation) and obligations (support) to the child. Moreover, noncustodial parents may reopen the custody question if circumstances change.

Even if the failure to advert to the best interests of the child is an inappropriate basis for invalidating surrogacy contracts, it is a sound basis for resolving custody disputes. It focuses the law's concern on the one person who certainly needs the law's protection and who could not possibly have done anything wrong—the baby. It requires deciding one case at a time, and by accepting evidence of everything that is relevant to the baby's interests, it maximizes the chance of reaching sound results in each case. It avoids stigmatization, and it protects some interests of whoever loses the case. That is the best that a system run by fallible human beings can do.

The New Jersey Supreme Court applied the best interests of the child test to decide the custody issue in the *Baby M.* case.[44] It considered evidence about the life situations of both Ms. Whitehead and the Sterns as well as expert information about the parties' psychological conditions. It decided that the child's best interests required placing her with the Sterns. The Sterns' family life was stable; their financial and employment situations were secure. They were committed to the baby's education and well suited to nurture and protect Baby M. while encouraging her wholesome, independent psychological growth and development. They were open to professional psychological and counseling assistance.[45] On the other hand, the evidence suggested that Ms. Whitehead was in an unhappy marriage and financially insecure. She perceived herself as omniscient and omnipotent; she was dishonest, rejected professional help, and was not committed to the baby's education.[46] While many opponents of surrogate motherhood have criticized the expert testimony in the *Baby M.* case[47] or disagreed with the case's outcome,[48] it is hard to believe that a child would be better off with the Ms. Whitehead depicted by the evidence than with the Sterns.

The real question is whether the best interests of the child test is wrong because it fails to accord significant weight to the interests of the mother. The test is the one ordinarily used in all child custody disputes. Where the debate is between two parents, rather than between a parent and the state, little would be gained by attempting to weigh the comparative grief of mothers and fathers and to reduce concern for the baby in order to serve intuitions about parental need.

Two features of the best interest approach require further comment. First, as the court noted in *Baby M.*,[49] stability is usually in an infant's best interest; therefore, whoever has the child until the time of the custody hearing has an advantage because that person can argue that stability suggests leaving the child where it is. If one believes that fathers have an advantage in surrogacy custody fights because they are usually richer than mothers and will usually be in good marriages and able to show a strong desire for the child, then one could even out the playing field by placing temporary custody with the mother. The *Baby M.* court required that approach for future cases.[50] An alternative approach would be to determine temporary custody through a very speedy process that made a tentative best interest judgment based on readily available facts and then to expedite the permanent custody proceeding.

Second, the best interest analysis controls the custody issue but not the question of visitation.[51] The parent's interests, as well as the child's, are relevant to visitation.[52] This virtually assures that whoever fails to obtain custody will receive the right to visit the child.

If *Baby M.* is indicative of what a common law approach to simple surrogate motherhood would do, then how satisfied ought one to be with this approach? The *Baby M.* approach does not prohibit surrogacy, but it discourages it by leaving potential fathers and surrogates in positions of uncertainty and by providing a custody-visitation solution that will not be wholly satisfactory to either one. One will lose custody; the other will have an unwanted influence regularly present in their child's life. It takes care of the child as well as normal child custody law does. This seems the right balance to strike. It does for the child what can be done, while slowing down and discouraging a practice that troubles many people, without foreclosing the option for those who want it enough to run the risks. It reduces the costs of mistakes by reducing their number and their reach. That is as much as a legal system of limited abilities and resources can do.

The common law can also deal adequately with other issues that are likely to arise out of the practice of surrogate motherhood. For example, as noted before, any practice that involves impregnation through the asexual insertion of semen from a man into a woman who is not his wife creates some risk to the health of the woman and to any child she conceives. If either one is injured, the question of who is to bear responsibility for the injury arises. This is precisely the kind of question that is the daily fare of common law courts, and there is no reason to doubt their ability to deal with it. Adapting old remedies to new circumstances is a traditional common law strength.

One case involving alleged injury to a surrogate mother and her baby has already been resolved.[53] Noel Keane, a Michigan attorney, is a leading surrogacy broker. A deal Keane put together in 1982 went sour when the surrogate mother gave birth to a baby who suffered from cytomegalic inclusion disease, which caused microcephaly, hearing loss, mental retardation, and neuromuscular disorders. The man who had contracted for the surrogate's services refused to accept the child. Paternity testing resolved the question of his obligation by revealing that the child was the offspring of the surrogate mother and her husband. However, the child's condition was caused by his mother's exposure to and contraction of cytomegalovirus (CMV), allegedly from the contracting male. The mother sued Keane and several doctors, alleging their negligence in failing to protect her from CMV. They denied responsibility. The United States Court of Appeals for the Sixth Circuit resolved the case in favor of the plaintiff. It reviewed the facts of the case and found that Keane and the other defendants had a special relationship to the mother based on their participation in the surrogacy program and their use of the mother in that program. That special relationship imposed an obligation on them to make reasonable efforts to protect her health, and if she could prove that they failed to do so, she was entitled to compensation from them.

All of this is perfectly conventional common law torts. People are liable to those they negligently injure as long as they owed a duty to behave reasonably toward the injured person. One has no such duty to act affirmatively to protect strangers, but does owe a duty to those with whom one is in a special relationship. Which relationships are special enough to impose a duty is a question of policy. Those who voluntarily undertake to deal with another for their own profit have a duty to treat the other person reasonably. That was the situation here. In addition, normal ideas about spreading the costs of accidents suggest that the mother's costs should be placed upon those who were both best situated to avoid her losses and best placed to spread them through insurance. Finally, the Sixth Circuit ruling encourages surrogacy brokers and doctors to be careful; it may discourage some from entering the business at all. Both of those results are sound when dealing with a new activity that society is not yet ready to welcome with open arms and that can be dangerous. Again, the common law is working just fine.

Whether the common law is adequate to deal with issues posed by surrogate motherhood that involves in vitro fertilization requires examination of in vitro fertilization and the full range of legal issues it poses.

IN VITRO FERTILIZATION

In vitro fertilization is a technique that involves fertilizing an ovum outside of a woman's body and transplanting the resulting embryo into a woman to carry the child to term. The woman who gestates the child may or may not be the woman who provided the ovum, and any man may be the sperm provider. Where a husband's sperm is used to fertilize his wife's ovum and the wife bears the child, the social, if not the technological situation is nearly identical to conventional reproduction. The only problems that are likely to arise involve negligence in performing the technique and the question of what to do with any unused embryos. Additional vexing issues of personal legal relationships arise when a third party is involved as provider of sperm, ovum, or womb. An additional set of problems exists because in vitro fertilization is still an experimental technique.

The in vitro fertilization situation that is most like simple surrogate motherhood is that in which a married man's semen is used to fertilize an ovum provided by someone other than his wife; the embryo is implanted into the body of the ovum provider; and the ovum provider carries the pregnancy to term. No reason exists to treat the parties to that kind of arrangement differently than parties to a simple surrogacy contract. The fertilization and embryo transplant do not change the best interests of the child. One would expect fees paid to in vitro surrogates to be higher than those paid to other surrogate mothers because of the experimental, invasive nature of the impregnation.

More troubling are situations in which the woman who carries the pregnancy (the gestational mother) is not the woman who provided the ovum (the genetic mother). Three possibilities exist: The sperm provider (genetic father) may be married to the genetic mother, the gestational mother, or neither.

The presence of two mothers, one gestational and one genetic, forces us to consider how far we are willing to push reliance on the best interests of the child and whether the common law is adequate to make that decision. In simple surrogacy cases it was fairly easy to resolve disputes between two biological parents by focusing on the well-being of the child. Does the same principle hold when a third party seeks parental rights and custody against one or even both genetic parents? More importantly, how is the law to figure out the answer to that question?

Normally, when we say that custody is to be determined according to the best interests of the child, what we mean is that the child will be placed in whichever of two parental environments will be better for him. The law does not make a global search and place a child with whoever would be the best parent in the world. A stranger may not have his claim for custody considered simply by asserting that his custody would be best for the child. Is a gestational or genetic mother to be treated like a stranger, like a mother, or in some other way?

Recently the law has begun to recognize that persons other than biological parents may raise claims to custody and visitation. Grandparents' and step-parents' claims are sometimes recognized,[54] as, less frequently, are those of "psychological parents."[55] Moreover, we have already seen that husbands whose wives are artificially inseminated with donor sperm are routinely treated as the fathers of the resulting children.

Those examples demonstrate that the law has already deviated from a simple biological determinism in deciding who is to be treated as a parent. Therefore, no insuperable obstacle exists to considering the claim of either a gestational or a genetic mother. The gestational mother lacks the characteristics of other third parties who are recognized as parents, but she has another characteristic that they lack. The genetic mother is similar to an AID "donor," except that in many cases she will have entered into the surrogacy agreement intending to serve the social role of mother to the resulting child.

Most third parties whose custody and visitation claims are considered are persons who have established a social (as opposed to a biological) relationship with the child. The child has lived with them, they have nurtured the child, supported it financially, etc. Usually some bonds of affection exist between the child and the third party, and severing the relationship would be cruel to both. Doing so would further injure the child by creating instability in his life.

None of this is true when the third party is the gestational mother and the decision is being made soon after the child's birth. No social relationship between gestational mother and child exists. However, a physical relationship exists, and while the child may know nothing of the relationship, the gestational mother, through the experience of pregnancy and childbirth, may have developed a psychological relationship that involves deep affection for the child. Cutting her out of the child's life may be cruel to her.

The argument for the gestational mother is essentially the same as that for surrogate mothers generally. However, conventional surrogates have a two-fold biological tie to the child, genetic and gestational. Should the absence of a genetic tie prevent consideration of a gestational mother's claims? To the extent that biology determines parenthood, one could argue that genetics is the part of biology that counts. Fathers are genetic parents, never gestational ones; yet their interests count as much as mothers' interests in normal custody-visitation disputes. However, rather than being persuasive, this crabbed view of biological parenthood can be taken as illustrating the inadequacy of a biological test. The consequences of a determination of parenthood are entirely social, psychological, and economic. Therefore, even if some biological relationship to a child is enough to justify considering a person's claim to parenthood, the precise nature of the biological connection should not be enough to resolve the question.

No good reason exists to refuse to consider a gestational mother's claim. As with other surrogates, however, no good reason exists to always find in her favor. Again, what is best for the child should always be the question, both because asking that question protects the innocent and because a common law best interests analysis slows down a movement society is unsure about without prohibition or the costs of regulation.

The same arguments apply to genetic mothers who are not gestational mothers. Like AID donors, they may be viewed as legitimate parties to the dispute if they were not anonymous at the time they provided the ovum. The legitimacy of their interests, however, does not mean that their interests should always prevail. The gestational mother's legitimate interests still deserve consideration too.

A California gestational surrogacy case[56] pitted the married couple who provided both the sperm and egg to produce a child they intended to raise against the woman who bore the child. The state Supreme Court found that the genetic mother was the child's legal mother by focusing on the intent of the parties at the time they entered into the surrogacy contract. This seems the wrong approach because, as the dissenting judge pointed out, an intention-based analysis will always lead to the genetic parents prevailing over the surrogate without regard to her interests or consideration of what is best for the child. The best interests approach is more sensitive both to factual nuance and to child welfare. Moreover, the intent of the parties approach sacrifices the advantage that the best interests approach preserves through the uncertainty of its outcomes—the advantage of slowing down the growth of surrogacy to give society time to think through its position about this still new technology.

The greatest danger of continuing to expand the reach of the common law best interests approach to consider the claims of gestational or genetic mothers is that, unchecked, doing so could give "the butcher, the baker, the candle stick maker"[57] a claim to the custody of other persons' children. However, that problem is avoided if playing a role in the child's birth other than as a health care, legal, or brokerage services provider is a condition of being allowed to assert a claim. No more than six claimants could possibly exist—a husband, his wife, a sperm provider, an egg provider, a gestational mother, and her husband.

Given the availability and feasibility of common law techniques to resolve the questions of relationships that arise from the practice of in vitro fertilization, would it, nonetheless, be wise to attempt to regulate these matters by legislation? The California gestational surrogacy case arose in a state that has adopted the Uniform Parentage Act. Not surprisingly, the Act did nothing to help resolve the case. Both women had claims to be treated as the child's "mother" under the statute. Therefore, both the majority and the dissent had to search for some nonstatutory basis to resolve the competing claims.

As with artificial insemination, the Commissioners on Uniform State Laws have tried to provide a more up-to-date statutory solution to surrogacy problems. Again they have failed. USCACA is designed to be "a child oriented act,"[58] to "effect the security and well being" of the children of assisted reproduction.[59] That goal is the same as the one advocated here and by those common law courts that apply the best interests of the child approach. Therefore, adopting USCACA would merely restate a position that can and often does represent existing common law. In other words, one does not need a statutory solution unless one is in a state, like California, that follows a rule other than the best interests of the child and one is convinced that the opposing rule is intolerable. Moreover, adopting USCACA, or any statute, would hinder the courts' ability to use what may be their greatest strength—flexibility and the ability to paint with a fine brush. Determining relationships in advance for all cases will inevitably fail to consider factors that will be relevant to the real life well-being of real children.

Despite their expressed concern for children the drafters of USCACA wrote their statute in terms of the status and behavior of parents. They also failed to recommend a solution to the issues of either simple or in vitro surrogacy, offering instead two alternative versions of USCACA. (How the goals of achieving *uniform* state laws are advanced by recommending alternative statutory approaches is not clear. A statutory imperative, rather than a uniformity one, seems to be at work here.)

In one version of USCACA surrogacy agreements are void, and the gestational mother is the child's mother. This seems a particularly perverse across-the-board resolution because, as we have just seen, some argument is necessary to make the case that the gestational mother deserves *any* consideration when she is opposing the claims of both genetic parents. Certainly there is no reason to believe that gestational mothers will always be better mothers than genetic ones.

The other version of USCACA authorizes surrogate motherhood contracts if they are approved by a court. If the agreement is not approved before conception, the surrogate again is the mother. This is subject to the objections just made to the first option. In addition, this approach penalizes the child and the intended parents because a lawyer failed to get a court order fast enough. That makes no sense. If a court does approve the agreement in time, then the intended parents are the parents unless they, the surrogate, her husband, or the court has terminated the agreement. In that event the surrogate is the mother. This approach does not provide enough certainty to justify resort to legislation. It also has the failing the *Baby M.* contract had. It fails to take the best interests of the child into account.

USCACA demonstrates the failure of the legislative approach. It fails to serve the policies its own drafters support; it fails to provide certainty; it leads to results that are likely to be wrong or even perverse; and it does all of this without having yet been subjected to the political process, which will exacerbate the difficulties. None of this is necessary in the absence of a major public problem, some consensus about how to solve it, and a vacuum left by the common law courts.

Embryos and Experiments

In vitro fertilization raises two additional problems. First, the technique often involves the fertilization of multiple ova. Typically, some of the resulting embryos are not implanted. What is to be done with them? Second, in vitro fertilization may still be considered an experimental technique. What types of regulation should guide its development?

The multiple embryo problem has been played out dramatically in a small number of cases. In the most important, a Tennessee couple divorced and litigated the "custody" of seven unused embryos. Mary Sue Davis sought control of the embryos so that she could donate them to someone else for implantation. Junior Davis objected to having genetic fatherhood thus thrust upon him. After the trial court awarded custody to Mary Sue[60] and the Appellate court awarded control to Junior,[61] the case made its way to the Tennessee Supreme Court.

That court recognized that the embryos (or, technically, preembryos) could not be treated either as persons, entitled to a determination of what was in their best interests, or as property, to be divided like any other marital property.[62] That finding was important because if the preembryos were persons, they would have been entitled to legal protection and could not have been destroyed. The trial court had held that the preembryos are persons, but that finding seems clearly erroneous as the adoption of one competing religious view, which has been consistently rejected by every member of the United States Supreme Court.

Next the Tennessee court provided a lengthy disquisition on the right of privacy, which it decided exists under the Tennessee constitution.[63] That discussion was unnecessary to the disposition of the case because ultimately, the court simply recognized that both the ex-husband and ex-wife had interests in the preembryos and that the court had to decide whose interests were more important.[64] In this case it decided that the burden of unwanted fatherhood was greater than the burden of not being allowed to give the preembryos away;[65] Junior prevailed. For the future the court said that disputes about the disposition of preembryos should be decided according to the preferences of the progenitors. If they cannot agree, or if their wishes cannot be ascertained, then any previous agreement between them should be carried out. If there is no agreement, then the interests of the parties should be weighed. Normally, the party wishing to avoid procreation should prevail, at least if the other party has a reasonable chance to achieve parenthood by some other means.[66]

This seems quite sensible. It leaves decision making to the most affected persons when that is feasible; it encourages them to try to reach agreement; it encourages them to think in advance about what they will want to do if an undesired contingency should arise; but it does not hold them to their preexisting agreement if it no longer represents their wishes. When all else fails, the courts will decide the cases by weighing competing interests, not ignoring either party's needs. Usually, it will not force parenthood on someone, but, wisely, the court leaves open the possibility that facts may sometimes exist which would make that the best thing to do. This is common law decision making at its best, and the decision in *Davis v. Davis* should provide some assurance that the common law courts can do their job. Unfortunately, the court filled its opinion with unnecessary constitutional discussion, thereby planting the seeds of future controversy. A truly excellent decision would have said only what was necessary to resolve the case, and stopped.

The other cases about embryo disposition also suggest that no need for legislation exists. Two disputes between genetic parents and infertility programs both recognized that the parents' interests are dominant. One awarded the parents damages for the unauthorized destruction of embryos,[67] and the other required a fertility clinic to deliver an embryo to the couple whose sperm and ovum created it.[68] Only an Australian case[69] is truly problematic. An American couple died in a plane crash, leaving unused frozen embryos in an Australian fertility clinic. The couple died intestate, and the question arose of whether the embryos had or, if born, could develop an interest in their estate. That question was sensibly answered in the negative. Unfortunately, however, nobody has been able to decide what should be done with the embryos. They remain at the clinic and presumably will do so until they lose their potential to develop into infants.

In a similar case that involved sperm and potential artificial insemination, rather than embryos and in vitro fertilization, the disputed sperm has been allocated.[70] A California lawyer with two adult children deposited fifteen vials of his sperm in a sperm bank. He attempted to transfer the sperm by will or gift to his girlfriend shortly before he committed suicide. His children opposed the transfer. After an appellate court held that the vials of sperm could be transferred by will and that California's public policy does not prohibit either postmortem artificial insemination or artificial insemination of unmarried women, a trial court ordered the vials distributed according to an agreement for the distribution of the rest of the lawyer's estate.[71] Under that agreement the girlfriend was to receive 20 percent of the estate's assets. Therefore, she received three of the fifteen vials of sperm.

One state has adopted a statute to govern the embryo disposition issue. Louisiana requires that disposition be made in the best interests of the embryo and that fetuses be made available for adoptive implantation.[72] As the adoption of one side of a legitimate moral controversy and the imposition of an inflexible result, the Louisiana statute is unsound. Given the very small number of cases and their successful resolution by the courts, it is also unnecessary.

Legislation is necessary, however, to regulate one set of issues about in vitro fertilization. In vitro fertilization is a new and imperfect technique. Developing and improving it requires experimentation on human subjects and the products of human reproduction. Safety cannot be adequately assured for the subjects of the research by after-the-fact determinations about whether specific injured persons should be compensated. Conduct control in advance is necessary. In addition, research will benefit greatly from the expenditure of federal research dollars. As there is insufficient money to go around, not all research can or should be funded. It is appropriate for the popularly elected branch of government to determine how public resources ought to be spent or to remit that decision to a government agency with scientific expertise. Thus, the conduct control and resource allocation issues in experimentation make it an appropriate subject for legislative or legislative/administrative oversight. In fact, legislation and administrative regulations do exist to govern research in general, research with human subjects in particular, and, even more specifically, research involving pregnant women, fetuses, and in vitro fertilization. We shall defer consideration of the relevant statutes and regulations until our discussion in chapter 7 of the regulation of research.

FIVE

The New Genetics

Perhaps the most exciting ongoing developments in biology and medicine are those in the field of human genetics. James Watson and Francis Crick discovered the double helix structure of DNA, the basic building block of life, in 1953.[1] In the forty years since that time genetic counseling has become an established part of medical practice, prenatal diagnosis has become commonplace, mass screening for certain genetic diseases has become ubiquitous, presymptomatic diagnosis of some genetic diseases has become available, and genetic research proceeds apace. Genes from different organisms can be recombined to create new, genetically engineered life forms, and scientists around the world are busily engaged in developing a map of the entire human genome.

All of these developments have enormous importance for human health. Genetic disease is responsible for 20 percent of infant deaths and is the leading cause of death in the 1- to 4-year-old age group. Genetic disorders account for 25–30 percent of acute care hospital admissions of persons under 18 and about 13 percent of adult admissions.[2] Moreover, scientists are increasingly learning that there is a significant genetic component in many conditions that people seldom think of as genetic—conditions as diverse as cancer, heart disease, schizophrenia, and alcoholism.[3] New and emerging genetic knowledge permits individuals to practice preventive medicine through avoiding conception or birth of persons with genetic diseases and by altering their own lifestyles to reduce their risks of contracting conditions to which they are predisposed. Genetic advances increasingly hold out the promise of genetic therapy and even cures for some conditions.

The same growth in genetics that offers such promise also poses difficult ethical and legal dilemmas for society. As we recognize the extent to which our genes affect our lives, the risk of adopting a fatalistic genetic determinism that represses individualism and eschews responsibility arises. The history of Nazi Germany and of the eugenic movement in the United States illustrate the inappropriate uses to which genetic information may be put. On a more mundane level avoidance of genetic disease obviously raises issues of abortion and sterilization; genetic advances pose significant threats to privacy and the risk of discrimination; and the availability of genetic counseling, prenatal diagnosis, and genetic therapy raise issues about how to cope with failures to provide those services properly.

WRONGFUL BIRTH AND WRONGFUL LIFE

The first legal problems to arise out of modern medical genetics were, not surprisingly, malpractice problems. As genetic counseling and prenatal diagnosis became available, some persons claimed that they had been injured through the receipt of negligently delivered genetic services or the negligent failure to provide any services at all. These would have been unremarkable medical malpractice claims were it not for the unusual nature of the alleged injuries. In most malpractice cases a patient claims that a doctor negligently hurt the patient's body or prevented the patient from recovering from what ailed him. In the genetic cases, however, parents who had a baby with a genetic disease did not claim that the physician or other health professional caused the disease, but, rather, asserted that the professional deprived them of accurate information that would have led them to refrain from having the baby in the first place. A second, and even more striking claim, was that the counselor had inflicted the injury of being born on the baby, who, presumably, would have been better off never to have lived. Courts and commentators now generally call the cases that litigate the parents' claims "wrongful birth" cases and those that consider the baby's claim "wrongful life" cases.

Wrongful birth and wrongful life cases can be evaluated in two quite different ways. They can be seen as virtually unique cases that raise fundamental moral questions, or they can be thought of as ordinary tort cases.

One who sees the cases as special would take seriously the labels the courts have attached to the claims and ask in what circumstances it is appropriate to consider a birth or a life "wrongful." Should a parent ever be compensated for having a child? Should a person ever be compensated for being born? Since the alternative to the birth of a child with a defect is often an abortion, how can the law compensate a person for being denied the information that would have led to aborting a pregnancy? And how can we make judgments about which lives deviate so disastrously from "normal" that a parent must be paid for having an "abnormal" child or the child must be paid for the wrong of having a life? If a child would have been better off never having been born, then would it now also be better off dead? Should we compensate the child for the "wrong" of refusing to kill it?

Alternatively, one can consider wrongful birth and life claims without addressing any of those questions. Wrongful birth and life claims, like most tort claims, simply assert that one person has inflicted unwanted expense upon another. Under our system a person who inflicts unwanted expense upon another must provide compensation, at least if he behaved negligently. The purposes of providing compensation are to return the injured person to the status quo, to deter negligent behavior, and to utilize insurance to spread the costs of accidents throughout society. This approach does not require us to say that some lives are not worth living. It requires only a finding of negligence by the professional and a showing that the negligence did cause expense by bringing into the world a baby who otherwise would not have been born and who has special medical or other needs.

The legal system has no tools for resolving the kind of moral questions posited by the first approach. It does have tools for resolving questions about tort liability and hundreds of years of experience in doing so. Occasionally legislatures have attempted to impose one moral view (typically a view about abortion) on the questions of wrongful birth and life, and some courts have lost their way in the fog of trying to solve the insoluble; but for the most part the legal system has dealt quite modestly and quite sensibly with wrongful birth and life cases through the common law tort system.

Some state legislatures have prohibited tort claims based on the allegation that but for the defendant's negligence someone would have obtained an abortion.[4] Obviously, their statutes are simply more salvos in the ongoing abortion wars and do nothing to contribute to solving the social and economic problems of caring for seriously ill children with genetic diseases. They also leave open, even in the states that have adopted them, the problem of how to resolve wrongful birth and life cases involving claims that parents, if properly informed, would have refrained from conceiving in the first place.

Judicial approaches have generally been more sensible. Most courts have recognized that parents who can prove negligence and causation can recover for wrongful birth.[5] That decision makes perfect sense. To reach the opposite conclusion would be to give genetic practitioners immunity against their own negligence, an immunity that no other group in our society enjoys. It would also leave the families of children with genetic diseases without support for the enormous medical and other expenses they are likely to incur. This would treat victims of genetic negligence worse than the victims of any other kind of negligence and would run counter to the general social policy of minimizing the costs of accidents by deterring accident-causing behavior and spreading the costs of those accidents that occur. Thus, the decision to compensate the parents is easy to justify. The harder questions are what kinds of losses parents should be compensated for and how great their compensation should be.

Parents in a wrongful birth case will typically claim two kinds of losses, financial and emotional. All courts that recognize the validity of the wrongful birth claim agree that the parents may recover for their economic loss.[6] Any other decision would be absurd because it would overlook the goals of spreading losses and putting persons in as good a position as they would have been in if the defendant had not been negligent.

The proper way to measure economic loss is less clear. One approach would award the parents the entire cost of raising the child.[7] The rationale for that approach is that if the defendant had not been negligent, the parents would not have had the child, and, therefore, would not have incurred any expenses for raising him. While logically sound, this approach has not commended itself to most courts. It is an extremely expensive approach, which may impede the growth of an important health care service. Moreover, by carrying a pregnancy to term a mother has indicated her willingness to undertake the costs of raising a normal child. Therefore, most courts have thought that it is sufficient to award parents only the special costs associated with their child's genetic disease, rather than all the costs of raising the child.[8] This seems the more sensible approach because it provides resources for the child's medical and other needs while remaining sensitive to the needs of the genetic services profession and to the consumers who benefit from it. In any event, however, the choice between the two measures of economic harm is the kind of dispute about which reasonable persons can disagree and as to which uniformity among the states is unimportant. All that matters is that the law in each state be clear so that professionals can insure themselves adequately, but not excessively, and so that insurers can set their rates intelligently.

Whether parents should be compensated for their emotional distress at having a child with a genetic disease is a more difficult question. On the one hand, nobody can doubt the severity of the suffering of a parent who experiences the birth of a seriously handicapped child or watches his child suffer, and perhaps die, from a genetic disease. On the other, however, money hardly seems an appropriate balm for that kind of emotional suffering. Moreover, unlike economic loss, emotional loss is intangible, and little is accomplished by spreading it through the community. In a sense, if the law puts a dollar value on emotional distress, the law creates a loss for the community to bear. That is not true of economic loss, which exists in dollar terms regardless of whether the law recognizes it. Emotional distress is also inherently unmeasurable, which means that the awards of sympathetic juries will be controlled only by the jurors' imaginations. Thus, the risk of awarding damages for emotional distress is that the awards will unduly cripple the provision of genetic services.

The arguments about awarding damages for emotional distress in wrongful birth cases are the same as those about awarding damages for intangible losses in general. No widespread agreement about the proper approach exists. Thus, the "progressive" view is to be ever more liberal in awarding damages for emotional distress[9] at the same time that damages for pain and suffering and noneconomic losses in general are being severely criticized and, increasingly, capped.[10] In the wrongful birth cases the courts have been of two minds.

Some courts have recognized the reality of the parents' suffering and have awarded them damages for emotional distress.[11] Others have refused to do so.[12] Unfortunately, the rationale of the leading cases that have refused recovery has been so absurd that a danger exists that other courts will simply reject that result out of hand without working through the more serious arguments for rejecting compensation.

The New York courts are hostile to emotional distress claims in all contexts. In cases about parents who see their children run over by negligently driven vehicles, those courts have adopted the so-called bystander rule: A person who is exposed to the risk of physical injury and fears for his own safety may be compensated for his emotional distress if a close relative is injured by whatever frightened the observer; however, if the observer was not in personal peril or did not fear for himself, then he is a mere bystander who cannot recover for the emotional distress of seeing his loved one injured.[13] The New York courts have applied this questionable rule to wrongful birth cases. In a case brought by the mother of a child with Tay-Sachs disease against her obstetrician, the Court of Appeals held that if any injury was inflicted, the injury was to the child; the mother was merely a bystander at the birth of her child and, therefore, was precluded from recovering for her emotional distress.[14] This view of the birth process does not seem likely to commend itself to other courts. Nonetheless, the wisdom of compensating parents in wrongful birth suits for emotional distress remains an open question. State by state resolution seems most likely to lead to results that make sense given the different economic conditions and medical resources of the different states. Until one approach seems clearly the best, no reason exists to freeze developments by enacting statutes.

Wrongful life cases, lawsuits brought on behalf of children rather than their parents, have proved difficult for the courts because the courts have had problems separating straightforward tort problems, with which they can deal, from metaphysical concepts they are unequipped to handle. Until 1982 every court that considered the issue of wrongful life denied the child compensation.[15] The courts reasoned (1) that life is always a good, so that a person cannot be said to have suffered an injury from having been born alive, and (2) that damages cannot be measured in a wrongful life context. The purpose of damages is to put a person back into the position in which he would have been if the defendant had not been negligent. Here, however, the person would not have been born if the defendant had not been negligent, and no way exists to compare the value of the child's life in his impaired condition with the "utter void of nonexistence."[16]

Neither of those arguments seems sound. In the first place, Americans have overwhelmingly rejected the view that life is always a good. Beginning with the *Quinlan* case in 1976,[17] both courts and legislatures have taken the position that in some cases a person has a right to die, or at least a right to be allowed to die, because for that person continued life is a burden rather than a benefit. Second, arguments about the inability to measure damages are merely makeweights. Courts routinely award damages for injuries that cannot be measured. Damages for pain and suffering and for emotional distress are the leading examples. The difficulty of measuring damages is simply an after-the-fact rationalization for a decision to deny compensation that has been made on some other ground.

The inadequacy of the standard arguments for denying wrongful life claims does not mean those claims should be granted. Two better reasons to deny the claims exist. First, in many cases the awards will be duplicative and unduly burden the genetic services profession while providing a windfall to parents. Second, granting recovery may force the courts into metaphysical seas they cannot navigate by forcing them to decide which children should be allowed to recover.

Many genetic diseases are incompatible with long life. Therefore, a baby born with such a disease will not receive much benefit from an award of compensation to him. Instead, after his early death, the award will pass through the baby's estate to his heirs, that is, his parents. However, as we have seen, the parents have their own lawsuit for compensation for their economic and, often, their emotional losses. Therefore, the practical effect of awarding damages to the infant is to compensate the parents twice. Doing that burdens the genetic services profession and raises the costs of genetic services for no good reason.

Of course, some genetic diseases are compatible with long life. The argument just made does not apply to them. However, recognizing a claim for the predictably long-lived while rejecting it for the predictably short-lived would require making dramatically new law. Doing so would be very difficult and possibly unconstitutional. A very strong case for wrongful life claims would have to be made to justify such extraordinary efforts.

The second problem with granting a wrongful life claim is that if such a claim exists, courts will have to decide which children can successfully assert it. Making that decision is likely to force courts to consider the very kinds of ultimate moral questions for which they are unequipped. How can a court decide which children would be better off never to have lived? If the decision cannot be made, then the courts ought not to create a situation in which they will have to make it.

Rejecting the validity of a claim for wrongful life thus seems attractive on practical grounds. Nonetheless, the rejection may work some real hardships. Suppose, for example, that the parents of an affected child squander their wrongful birth award or flee the jurisdiction, leaving the child behind, or die and leave most of their estate to someone other than the child. In those circumstances who is to bear the burden of supporting and providing for the special needs of the child? Impressed by those concerns, a small number of courts has now recognized that the child does have his own claim to recovery.[18] However, each of those courts has been careful to provide that economic costs of caring for the child be awarded *once*, to the parents *or* the child, not both, in order to avoid the double recovery problem. The courts have also denied the child's claim for compensation for noneconomic losses to compensate for the pain, suffering, emotional loss, and indignity of being born with a handicap. Awarding partial recovery in that way is illogical (the child either has a claim or he doesn't), but it makes wonderful practical sense. It assures support for the child and his special needs while keeping the costs of genetic services relatively low and avoiding windfalls to parents.

Even this sensible approach does not answer the question of which children should receive compensation. However, with a limited, solely economic approach, the answer seems clear: Any child who has special medical or educational expenses that a professional negligently failed to warn the parents about early enough to have enabled them to make a practical decision about whether to have the child should be compensated for those special expenses. That answer does not require any consideration, much less decision, about whether some lives are not worth living.

Obviously, recognizing that wrongful birth or life claims may exist does not resolve the question of whether any particular claim will be successful. In order to prevail the plaintiff must prove that the health care professional acted negligently and that the negligent behavior caused the harm.

Usually, proving negligence will require a plaintiff in a medical malpractice case to prove that the defendant deviated from the professional standard of care. In a rapidly growing area such as medical genetics, no accepted standard of care may exist. In that event, experts will testify for each side about what kind of care was reasonable, given the state of knowledge and practice and the patient's condition and family history. Then a jury will decide whether the particular professional's behavior was good enough. This is typical of what happens in malpractice litigation and is not affected by the genetic nature of the claim.

However, genetic cases will often be slightly atypical. Genetic medicine is still largely talking medicine. That is, it involves exchanging information more often than it involves doing procedures or prescribing medication. Often the plaintiff's claim will be that the professional failed to tell somebody something. Therefore, genetic negligence cases may look more like informed consent cases—the other category of talking malpractice cases—than like more typical malpractice claims.

Physicians are required to inform patients about risks and side effects of proposed medical treatment and to obtain the patient's voluntary consent to provide the treatment after the patient has been informed. If the patient was not adequately informed, and if a risk he should have been told about materializes, then the doctor will be liable to the patient for failing to obtain informed consent. Often the question in informed consent cases is how much information a doctor is required to tell a patient. Two different standards have emerged. A physician either must tell a patient what a reasonable physician would disclose,[19] or he must provide all material information,[20] that is, the amount of information that a reasonable patient would need in order to make an informed decision whether to accept the proposed treatment. In the genetic disease context the analogous question is how many genetic possibilities and genetic tests must the practitioner tell the patient about. The answer will be determined either by the standards of a reasonable practitioner or the needs of a reasonable patient, depending on the law of the state where the claim arises. The profession-centered approach is better if one wishes to keep the price of genetic services down. The materiality approach is better if one wants to maximize loss spreading and increase patient control. Under either approach, juries, acting one case at a time, will make the ultimate decisions about how much has to be revealed. Thus, genetic counselors will not be able to ascertain with assurance what information they are required to convey. However, the law seems to have adopted a strong preference for patient control of the medical decision-making process. This suggests that counselors should err in the direction of over-, rather than underinforming patients.

The most interesting case that has arisen so far occurred in Minnesota. In *Pratt v. University of Minnesota Affiliated Hospitals and Clinics*,[21] parents sought genetic counseling to ascertain whether birth defects suffered by their third child were likely to recur in future children. Defendant physicians diagnosed the child's condition as sporadic and advised the parents that they were not at increased risk for having another affected child. However, the defendants were not able to rule out the possibility that the child suffered from an autosomal recessive condition, which, if it existed, would have a 25 percent recurrence risk. They did not inform the parents of that possibility. The parents, believing they bore no special risks, conceived a fourth child. That child was born with birth defects similar to those of his brother. Finally, both boys were diagnosed as having an autosomal recessive condition. The parents sued the doctors who made the initial diagnosis and failed to warn them of the risk of a recessive condition. By the time the case reached the appellate courts, the parents had dropped their contention that the original diagnosis was negligently made. However, they alleged that the doctors were negligent in failing to disclose the possibility that the child had a recessive condition.

After the doctors prevailed in the trial court, the parents appealed. The intermediate appellate court ruled in their favor, holding that information must be disclosed if the defendants knew or should have known that the parents would attach significance to it.[22] The Minnesota Supreme Court disagreed.[23] It held in favor of the doctors because requiring them to disclose the information would, in essence, require them to tell the parents that their diagnosis might be wrong; there would be no logical stopping point to such a requirement.

Which court reached the right result depends on which goals one wants to pursue. Clearly, the Supreme Court's approach is better in terms of fostering the availability of affordable genetic services and imposing liability only on persons whose behavior was truly blameworthy. The Court of Appeals' approach is better from the standpoints of cost spreading, placing costs on those who could more efficiently have avoided them, and satisfying the expectations of those who seek genetic counseling. This is precisely the kind of value conflict that is resolved daily in all American common law tort litigation. Nothing about the genetic basis of the parents' claim suggests a need for a new or different approach.

Finally, in order to prevail in a wrongful birth or life suit a plaintiff must prove that the defendant's negligence caused his harm. That is, he must prove that if the correct information had been provided, the child would not have been born. This is difficult to do because there will seldom be any evidence other than the parents' testimony about what they would have done if they had been properly informed.

In informed consent cases courts have followed three different approaches to this causation problem. They have either let the jury decide whether to believe the patient's claim that he would have refused consent if properly informed;[24] adopted a presumption that a properly informed patient would not have consented;[25] or adopted an objective standard under which the question becomes whether a reasonable patient would have consented if properly informed.[26] The same three approaches are available in the genetic context. The first lets juries exercise their common sense; the second virtually guarantees that patients will win; and the third, which virtually ensures a defendant's victory in the informed consent context, here is likely to lead to results similar to those a jury would reach under the first approach.

As the law of wrongful birth and wrongful life has developed so far, it is characterized by uncertainty and common sense. The precise standards to which genetic service providers will be held, what acts will be deemed to be negligent, and what test of causation the courts will apply are all uncertain. This is similar to the situation in any area of law governed by a negligence standard. Nobody can say in advance which of the infinite possible acts in an infinity of possible circumstances will be negligent. While most persons would like somebody to tell them precisely what they must do or avoid, the realities of life do not permit such certainty. Juries, ordinary members of the community, acting with guidance from experts, make those decisions in myriad cases. They are no less able to make them here than anywhere else.

To the extent that the law can actually take positions regarding wrongful birth and life, the courts have behaved very sensibly so far. They have provided compensation for clearly legitimate injuries while being careful not to unduly handicap an emerging branch of medicine and not to overcompensate injured patients. They have reached sound results, even if they have not always said sound things. Only those legislatures that have cut off all possibility of legitimate compensation, deterrence, and loss shifting because of their inability to break free from their fixation on abortion have played a negative role in the development of the emerging law of wrongful birth and wrongful life.

THE GENETIC CHALLENGE

Wrongful birth and wrongful life claims can be handled like any other tort claims despite their apparent novelty. Other issues posed by advances in genetics are more problematic because they challenge in fundamental ways many of our assumptions about people, relationships, and law.

First, genetic information is different from other kinds of medical information. Most medical information about a person can be learned from an examination of that person alone. Also, except for the risk of contagion and the impact of a patient's suffering on those who love or are dependent on him, most information about a person's health tells us nothing about anybody else's health. Genetic information, however, is different. Learning about one person's genetic makeup often requires learning about someone else, and gaining genetic information about one person inevitably reveals information about others. These characteristics of genetic information require us to rethink our traditional view that information about a person belongs to that person alone and may not be shared with others without the affected person's consent.

Second, genetics poses special social challenges because it suggests that persons have less free will than American ideology and law assume. This poses the twin risks that society will adopt legal positions that make no sense because they ignore biological determinism, and that it will adopt repressive and/or eugenic legal positions based on an overstated sense of that determinism. The genetic challenge is to reconceptualize the nature of humanness to take account of new insights without losing the incalculable benefits of a liberal, humane society.

Genetic Information

Genetic information is family information. People seek genetic advice because of concerns about conditions that exist in their family; once learned, the information is relevant to many members and potential members of the family (and perhaps even to others); and often the family's cooperation must be enlisted to learn useful information.

Several types of situations arise quite often: The diagnosis of a child with a genetic disease reveals information about the child's parents and the parents' relatives that may be relevant to those persons' reproductive decision making; the diagnosis of a person with a genetic disease reveals information about that person's relatives that may be relevant to their own health; genetic testing to diagnose or confirm the diagnosis of a condition may reveal that a woman's husband is not the parent of her child. Each of these situations challenges traditional notions of doctor-patient confidentiality and raises questions about the obligations of the genetic professional.

Suppose a boy is diagnosed as having hemophilia, or suppose a person is diagnosed as having hereditary polyposis of the colon. Hemophilia is an X-linked disease. That means that only males are affected by the disease and only females can transmit the gene for it. If a woman is a carrier of the hemophilia gene, then each of her sons has a 50 percent chance of having the disease. If a boy has hemophilia, then his mother is a carrier of the hemophilia gene. Each of her sisters has a 50 percent chance of being a carrier; each of her nieces has a 25 percent chance of being a carrier; and so forth. Knowledge about their possible carrier status and its implications may be highly relevant to those women. It may cause them to refrain from conceiving, or it may lead them to receive prenatal diagnosis of their fetus's sex and to abort male fetuses.

Hereditary polyposis of the colon is a condition in which the affected person develops many precancerous polyps in the colon. If diagnosed early, the condition can be monitored and treated. If no timely diagnosis is made, the condition will lead to colon cancer, which is often fatal. Hereditary polyposis is an autosomal dominant disease. That means that if a person has the disease, 50 percent of his or her offspring will inherit it. Therefore, if a person is affected, one of that person's parents had the condition. Each of the affected person's siblings has a 50 percent chance of being affected; each nephew and niece, a 25 percent chance; and so forth. Relatives at risk have a strong interest in learning about their risk so that they can be monitored to avoid cancer.

Should a physician or other genetic health professional try to find and warn the relatives of either the boy with hemophilia or the person with hereditary polyposis of the colon? How is the conflict between the patient's interest in confidentiality and the relatives' interests in informed reproductive decision making or their own health to be resolved?

Common law precedents exist that permit one to work through these problems and come to a conclusion. However, the precedents point in different directions. Reasonable persons evaluating them could reach opposite conclusions. Therefore, this may be an area in which a legislative solution would be appropriate, especially if lawmakers think it is important to encourage genetic professionals to act one way or the other.

At common law a physician owes his patient a duty to maintain in confidence information learned about the patient during the doctor-patient relationship.[27] Neither a physician, nor anybody else, owes strangers, persons with whom he or she has no preexisting relationship, an obligation to take affirmative steps to help them.[28] This suggests that in both the hemophilia case and the hereditary polyposis case the professional should maintain the patient's confidence and not attempt to find or warn relatives. Breaching confidence will make the professional liable to the patient. Keeping it will not lead to liability to anyone. This solution will commend itself to persons who value individual liberty and privacy more highly than the avoidance of suffering.

Persons who have the opposite value preference, however, can argue that traditional rules suggest that the professional should breach confidentiality and disclose. The law has long recognized that doctors not only may, but must breach patient confidentiality when the public interest supervenes, that is when some public interest is more important than the patient's interest in confidentiality.[29] Moreover, the rule that there is no duty to help strangers has little to recommend it. It is an affront to human decency that is at odds with conventional notions of morality.[30] The law retains the rule not because it is sound, but because formulating an alternative may be too difficult and may not accomplish much anyway.

Adopting a duty to aid would present serious line drawing problems. How is one to ascertain which of the hundreds of persons who pass by an automobile accident ought to go to the aid of the victims? In what circumstances would the duty to aid exist? Moreover, the existence of a duty to aid may not promote many rescues because often people fail to act out of fear, or even psychological paralysis, conditions that are not likely to be affected by the law. Finally, imposing a duty may not accomplish much loss spreading, because failure-to-rescue insurance does not exist and is unlikely to be developed because of the actuarial difficulties involved in predicting a person's exposure to potential rescue situations.

Thus, the law retains the unattractive rule that one need not help others for practical reasons. Given the unattractiveness of the rule, however, the courts look closely at real situations to see whether the reasons for the rule are present. When the reasons are not present, the courts create exceptions to the rule. Not surprisingly, numerous exceptions to the no-duty-to-rescue rule exist.[31]

In the genetic disease context, the reasons for the no-duty rule do not exist. Lines are easy to draw. One doctor or one small group of professionals is the only candidate for liability. The behavior involved is planned professional behavior, quite different from confronting a sudden disaster that may make one freeze in terror. Finally, malpractice insurance exists to spread the losses caused by failing to warn.

In analogous situations courts have imposed duties to breach confidentiality and warn persons at risk. Thus, a psychotherapist must make reasonable efforts to warn a person the psychotherapist's patient said he was going to kill.[32] This is true even though psychotherapists overpredict violence from their patients and despite the argument that the rule will actually increase violence by discouraging dangerous persons from seeking psychotherapy or from telling the truth to their therapists.

In the genetic disease setting one could argue that the predictive value of genetic information is much greater than that of psychological information. There is an important public interest in avoiding colon cancer and in giving persons who wish to avoid the birth of children with a genetic disease the chance to do so. The reasons for the no-duty rule do not exist. Therefore, there should be an exception to the ordinary rules, and genetic professionals should breach confidentiality and attempt to warn relatives at risk.

If the law adopts that position, a geneticist will not be liable to a patient for disclosing a confidence and will be liable for harm his negligent failure to warn causes to the patient's relatives. Of course, the professional will only be liable for injuries he *negligently* causes. A jury will have to decide how great an effort to locate relatives is required and which conditions require any effort at all. For example, even if there is a duty, the law would be unlikely to require someone to provide useless information to somebody: There is no reason to tell a child-less octogenarian that his sister has Huntington's Disease.

Thus, it is possible to resolve the duty to warn problem through the common law. However, that approach does not seem optimal here. The common law is at its least effective when it tries to control people's conduct. After all, fact-specific rulings made after a person has acted are relatively useless as a guide to future behavior. Where planned, professional behavior, rather than acciden-tal slips or errors of judgment, is involved, the law can expect to influence behavior if it acts prospectively and states its position clearly. In the warning to relatives setting, the law's primary goal is to control conduct. The legislature can decide as a matter of public policy whether it wants to make professionals respect confidentiality or avoid suffering. The professionals can do either one. They simply need to be told which goal to pursue. A legislature could even treat the hemophilia and hereditary polyposis cases differently if it wanted to. It could impose a duty to warn when a living person's health is at risk, but not when the warning is only relevant to reproductive decision making.

Unfortunately, the latter possibility illustrates two problems with the legis-lative approach. First, like any legislation related to birth, this area can be turned into part of the debate about abortion. Second, even though the legis-lature can act fairly specifically here, some room for doubt will always remain. Information about hemophilia may be relevant to the health of a living person as well as for reproductive decision making. Moreover, no sensible statute will require a geneticist to take every possible step to find every relative who may be at risk for any genetic disease. Some limit to the duty is necessary. The most probable rule would require the professional to make reasonable efforts to lo-cate and warn relatives of reasonably important matters. That will leave the professionals at the mercy of the jury's 20/20 hindsight, just as adopting a common law duty would.

Obviously, this is an area in which the law cannot contribute very much. The geneticist should try to persuade each patient to cooperate in locating and warning relatives. Friendly persuasion is likely to prove more useful than legal rules. Whatever position the law ultimately adopts should be viewed as the fall-back position, to be followed when all else has failed, and not as the pri-mary vehicle for getting people to do the right thing. If this is true with regard to the patient's relatives, it is even more clearly true when the question is whether to warn someone other than a relative about the patient's genetic makeup. The law cannot be expected to sort out the respective weights of confidentiality and truth telling between fiances, potential fiances, one-night lovers, etc.

In disclosure to relatives and potential mate cases, the proper course of con-duct for the patient, if not the professional, is clear. The patient should disclose.

However, the law does little to solve the real problems that confront genetic counselors in these situations. The subsidiary role of law is even plainer when real question exists about what the right thing to do is.

One of the most frequent dilemmas confronting genetic counselors is what to do when they discover that a man is not the father of his wife's child. Often the information is highly relevant to the couple's reproductive decision making, which may be what brought them to the counselor in the first place.

For example, suppose a child is diagnosed as having an autosomal recessive disease such as cystic fibrosis or sickle-cell anemia. The child can only inherit that kind of disease if both parents are carriers of the defective gene. If tests reveal that the husband is not a carrier, then the geneticist knows that the husband is not the child's father. That means the couple can have further children without fear of the condition recurring. The husband needs to know that information for his future reproductive planning. Some husbands would also want to know it in case a question about their obligation to support the child or some similar issue were to arise. On the other hand, providing the information to the husband could hurt him deeply and could destroy what may have been a very good relationship with the child. As far as the wife is concerned, she too needs the information for reproductive planning. However, it may be very important to her that the information not be revealed to her husband. Revelation may lead to divorce and/or abuse and may render her a single parent. The impact of revelation on the child may also be very bad, removing an existing source of affection and support that a sick child sorely needs.

What is the clinician to do, and how useful is the law likely to be in providing guidance? Unaffected by the law, most professionals will try to maximize the useful effects of the information while minimizing its risks. They will divulge the truth to the wife alone, or they will explain the test results as indicative of a new mutation in the baby, a possible, but wildly improbable explanation. In ethical terms these approaches have much to recommend them. They serve the ethical principle of nonmaleficence, which is enshrined in the widely accepted medical dictum, "First, do no harm." Nonetheless, they are not self-evidently correct even from an ethical point of view. They violate the ethical obligation to tell the truth, and, by doing so, they deprive the husband of some of his autonomy. They also enlist the wife in an ongoing scheme of deception and pass the professional's ethical dilemma off onto the wife, who is unlikely to be very well equipped to deal with it.

Faced with a difficult practical problem and with conflicting ethical principles for its resolution, professionals may turn to the law for guidance. They won't find much.

The husband is one of the geneticist's patients. Therefore, the geneticist owes him a duty to report accurately about his medical status, at least regarding the very condition about which the patient consulted the professional. Alternatively, the husband could be seen as having contracted to receive accurate genetic information from the practitioner.

The problem is that the wife and child are the geneticist's patients too. Therefore, the geneticist owes them an obligation of confidentiality. The family nature of genetic information thus impales practitioners on the horns of a dilemma.

In this difficult situation disclosing the truth to the husband is probably the legally safer course of action for the professional to follow. Modern medical law consistently requires professionals to shift decision making power to patients after providing them with the information they need to make decisions.[33] Moreover, it is almost inconceivable that the law would impose an obligation to lie or even to mislead by silence. Failure to inform the husband will probably lead to liability to him for any damage the failure caused him, for example, inappropriately incurred child support expenditures, lost reproductive opportunities, and emotional distress. On the other hand, disclosure is unlikely to lead to liability to the wife. Invasion of privacy by disclosing embarrassing, but true, private facts, only gives rise to a valid claim if the facts are truly private and the disclosure is truly public.[34] Here, the information involves the husband so that it may not be private vis-à-vis the wife. Even if it is private, however, the disclosure to one person, the husband, is not enough to qualify as a public disclosure. Other theories have also been used to impose liability on physicians who disclose confidential information about patients,[35] but none of them has ever been used when the disclosure was to the patient's spouse in a case where the information was about the spouse as well as the patient.

Thus, if a professional were to predict the likelihood of liability from disclosure and from nondisclosure, disclosing the truth to the husband seems less likely to result in liability than lying or withholding the truth. This rather uncertain guess about potential legal obligations is not likely to provide much help or comfort to a genetic counselor who is truly torn about whether to tell the husband the truth. It will have even less effect if the counselor thinks that if he withholds the truth, the husband is unlikely to learn it and sue.

The law could resolve the dilemma definitively by adopting a statutory obligation to disclose or a statutory prohibition against doing so. It has imposed duties to disclose in other areas. For example, physicians must report cases of venereal disease,[36] child abuse,[37] gunshot wounds,[38] and other conditions.[39] Indeed, even the common law makes clear a doctor's obligation to warn when public safety is at stake.[40] Thus, for example, if presymptomatic diagnosis revealed that an airline pilot would develop Huntington's disease, the geneticist would have a clear duty to inform the patient's employer early enough to protect the traveling public. In nonpaternity cases, however, uncertainty about what the better course of action is makes imposition of a clear obligation undesirable. Such an obligation would give legal protection to genetic counselors who complied with it, but it would remove their opportunity to exercise professional judgment; it would preclude the possibility of doing different things in different cases depending on the facts; and it would always subjugate the legitimate concerns on one side of the disclosure/nondisclosure problem.

This seems to be an area in which the law's ability to contribute to a sound resolution is severely limited. Probably the best course of action (i.e., the one that will lead to the largest number of satisfactory results) is to remit decision making to the professionals and to refuse to impose liability on them either for disclosing or for failing to disclose the truth about nonpaternity. In other words, genetic professionals should be permitted, but not required, to disclose the truth to husbands. All the law has to do to permit that outcome is to deviate from the predicted course discussed above by refusing to impose liability on a professional who fails to tell a husband the truth. This approach, which results in no liability to anybody, not only maximizes the benefits to be obtained from allowing professionals to use their discretion, it also has the beneficial side effect of avoiding an increase in the costs of genetic services for a benefit that is by no means clear. Legal modesty in the face of a conundrum posed by biomedical advance seems the most socially sound approach.

The peculiarities of genetic information pose at least three additional problems. First, prenatal diagnosis reveals the sex of fetuses who are being diagnosed. Second, techniques for diagnosing particular genetic conditions often reveal that the person tested has some condition other than the one(s) the clinician was looking for; sometimes the significance of those conditions is unclear. Third, obtaining useful genetic information often requires performing tests on persons other than those who are seeking the information, including persons who may prefer not to be tested.

Even the simplest prenatal diagnostic test, amniocentesis followed by chromosome analysis to look for chromosomal anomalies such as Down's syndrome, reveals the sex of the fetus. Two questions arise: Is a woman who has no medical indication for amniocentesis entitled to receive the procedure so that she can learn her fetus's sex in order to abort a child of the unwanted sex? Should or must a physician who performs prenatal diagnosis for a medical indication reveal the fetus's sex to the mother if the clinician believes the mother will abort a fetus of the unpreferred sex?

As is so often the case, the problems here are inextricably intertwined with the abortion controversy. In the three or four years immediately following *Roe v. Wade*, when the Supreme Court seemed to take seriously the idea that a woman has an affirmative constitutional right to an abortion, it seemed likely that women were entitled to any information they considered relevant to their decision whether to terminate a pregnancy. That is plainly no longer the case. Even state-supported hospitals do not have to perform abortions and do not have to make available information that will help women decide whether to seek an abortion.[41] Thus, no professional is obligated to perform prenatal diagnosis for sex choice. As usual, however, the fact that the law has provided an answer to a question does little to solve practical dilemmas.

Sophisticated women who want to choose the sex of their offspring can often tender some plausible medical reason for prenatal diagnosis—perhaps advanced maternal age (over 35, or even 33) or simply relief of anxiety over an unspecific risk of birth defects—in order to obtain the information they really want, the sex of the fetus. Thus, the hard question for physicians is under what circumstances to perform prenatal diagnosis and whether to reveal the fetus's sex after ostensibly testing for some other reason. Of course, a physician who approves of abortion for sex choice or who believes that a woman should be able to obtain an abortion for any reason is free to learn and reveal the fetus's sex.

No physician is obligated to accept anyone as a patient.[42] Thus, a physician can be careful to inform would-be patients that their first consultation is to decide whether the doctor will accept the person as a patient. If the doctor believes the woman wants to learn her fetus's sex in order to obtain a sex-choice abortion, the doctor may refuse to accept her as a patient.

If a doctor-patient relationship already exists, the doctor is in only a slightly more difficult position. No patient may require a doctor to perform a procedure that is not medically indicated.[43] Thus, for example, a patient with a sore throat may not require a physician to perform an MRI to look for a brain tumor. Therefore, if no medical indication for prenatal diagnosis exists, a doctor need not perform it. The only risk the doctor will face is the possibility that a jury will second-guess the decision about medical indications in a wrongful birth or wrongful life suit if a baby is born with a defect that the requested prenatal diagnosis would have revealed. The hardest question arises when the doctor has performed prenatal diagnosis and the mother demands to know the fetus's sex. If the doctor has great foresight and is willing to engage in potentially unpleasant negotiations with the patient before doing the diagnostic procedure, the problem can be solved by contract. That is, the parties can agree in advance that the doctor will not provide information about the fetus's sex. However, many doctors may fail to think of this approach or may be unwilling to use it. Thus, the question becomes, what are they to do in the absence of an agreement?

Remarkably little law exists about patients' entitlement to personal medical information. Nonetheless, it seems clear that patients are entitled to information about their own condition that is relevant to making a medical decision about themselves.[44] Is information about a fetus's sex such information? Once again the answer one gives will probably depend on one's views about abortion, and once again the constitutionalization of the abortion question has failed to provide an answer.

If a physician wants to make a decision that provides the least threat of legal liability, he should tell the woman what she wants to know. Failing to do so could lead to litigation about whether the disclosure was required. Disclosure, on the other hand, cannot lead to liability to anybody unless one envisions a massive legal change to increase the entitlements of fathers or unborn children. Realistically, however, legal liability from either approach seems unlikely. Moreover, making clinical decisions based on guesses about possible liability will not commend itself to many clinicians, and this approach does little to help conscientious doctors decide what to do. Once again, the law does not seem a very useful tool for resolving a difficult ethical dilemma. Even the use of the extreme approach of constitutional adjudication has not solved the problem. Patients and professionals must accommodate themselves to the fact that they must look somewhere other than the law for answers about how to proceed.

The problems are similar when genetic testing reveals the presence of a condition of uncertain significance other than the condition(s) for which testing was performed. The classic example involves trying to learn whether a fetus has Down's syndrome and discovering instead that the fetus is a male with an extra Y chromosome. Normal males have one X and one Y chromosome. So-called XYY males, males with two Y chromosomes, tend to be taller than most males.[45] Some evidence suggests that they are statistically overrepresented in prison populations and may be more disposed than other persons to commit crimes.[46] This evidence has been severely criticized,[47] and any predisposition to criminality among XYY males is surely unproved.[48]

Should a physician tell a woman that her fetus is an XYY male? Doing so may lead the woman to terminate an otherwise desired pregnancy, with all the trauma and guilt that entails. If the woman does not obtain an abortion, the information may affect the way she behaves toward her son. If a mother acts as if she expects her son to become a criminal, she may turn the murky data about XYY males into a self-fulfilling prophesy. On the other hand, withholding the information will lead to the birth of a child who may, in fact, become dangerous. Failure to disclose may foist off on a woman a son she would prefer not to have, and may, if the data is right, saddle the community with a criminal.

If one takes the law's frequently stated preference for patient autonomy and distaste for paternalism at face value, the doctor should disclose the fetus's XYY status to his mother. Again, it is hard to imagine incurring liability for doing so. Whether that is the "right" thing to do, however, is not so clear.

Disclosure may protect the mother's decision-making autonomy, but it does so at considerable cost. It injures the mother and the fetus and may do damage to the child if it is allowed to be born. Moreover, the protection of autonomy is hardly perfect because the mother will have to make a decision based on scientific data that is unclear and may be wrong. The data provides a weak reed on which to base a procreative decision. What sense does it make, then, for the law to dictate one outcome or the other? Would requiring disclosure mean that a doctor must disclose all scientific data, however unreliable, if some reasonable person might rely on it? Surely that would make no sense. No one would advocate presenting every bit of alleged scientific support for quack cures, for example. Thus, the apparent requirement that the doctor inform a mother that her fetus is an XYY male may be unsound. Obviously, a requirement that the doctor not reveal would be equally unsound. The doctor must decide the best course of action in each particular case based on the facts about the patient and her situation and on the doctor's (ideally) well-informed ethical analysis. Law cannot tell us what is right in the face of unclear science and competing ethical norms.

All of the information issues discussed so far have involved questions about whether and to whom to disclose information. Another kind of genetic information problem also exists.

Increasingly, geneticists are able to diagnose asymptomatic persons as having a gene mutation that predisposes them to a genetic condition or that indicates that they have the condition. For example, Huntington's disease is an autosomal dominant disease; if either of a person's parents has the disease, the person has a 50 percent chance of having it too. Typically the disease does not manifest itself until mid-life, after most persons have finished procreating. When it does become manifest, HD is a very serious disease, characterized by increasingly uncontrollable movements, progressive dementia, and, eventually, death. Now, geneticists can often determine whether an asymptomatic person at 50 percent risk for HD will develop the disease. The information that one will or will not develop a progressive, serious, fatal genetic disease is obviously very important information to have. Until quite recently, however, testing could not be performed on one person alone. Using a technique called linkage analysis, many of the subject's relatives also had to be tested in order to make a diagnosis. What was a clinician to do if a patient requested presymptomatic testing and a relative who was essential to the process refused to participate? This problem, which technology has solved, by now permitting testing only of the person at risk for HD, will present itself over and over again as more and more diseases become susceptible to presymptomatic diagnosis through linkage studies.

In these cases the family nature of genetic information bedevils both law and ethics. As we have seen, American law does not require a person to be a good Samaritan. American law does, however, require a person to act to provide reasonable assistance to those with whom one has a preexisting relationship. Close family relationships often impose obligations. Thus, it would not be a very big stretch for the law to require even moderately distant relatives such as aunts or uncles and their nieces or nephews to act reasonably toward each other. The real problem is determining what reasonable behavior requires.

Ordinarily, the law takes the position that permitting physical intrusion into one's body is more than can be asked in the name of reasonableness.[49] Even a parent probably would not be forced to "donate" an organ to a child or held liable for failing to do so. However, providing a small blood sample for genetic analysis is a much smaller intrusion on the unwilling participant. And while forced participation obviously injures the autonomy of the relative, allowing that person not to participate deprives the patient of the opportunity to obtain information needed to make an autonomous decision. The shared genetic heritage of relatives binds them together in ways that make a simple focus on autonomy relatively unhelpful for solving problems.

Deciding how to proceed requires one to be cautious about the use of language. Clearly, no one would seriously consider adopting a rule that purported to "force" one person to be tested for another's benefit. Arresting unwilling

Limits

relatives, restraining them, and forcibly withdrawing their blood is not a serious option. Nor would it make any sense for the law to impose criminal sanctions on a person who refused to participate in genetic testing. Doing so could not begin to meet the criteria for use of the criminal sanction discussed in chapter 2. When one talks about whether a relative has a duty to participate in genetic testing for the benefit of another, what one is asking is whether the uncooperative relative can be held liable to the person who wants the test.

Viewed that way, different answers to the question in different states and different circumstances are acceptable. One state's highest court might think that making further inroads on the no-duty-to-be-a-good-Samaritan rule would be unsound; that insurance to pay for the costs of liability is unlikely to be available; that the desire of the noncooperating relative not to learn his own diagnosis deserves respect and is so strong that a legal liability rule is unlikely to change his behavior; and that any costs incurred because of his refusal to participate should not be spread throughout the community. Such a court would refuse to impose liability. Another state's court might think that the policies of reducing genetic disease and facilitating lifestyle planning are more important than allowing persons to remain ignorant; that the fear of legal liability will influence some persons to change their behavior; that family-centered rather than individual-centered decision making is necessary to gain maximum benefit from genetic advances; and that the law should adopt morally sound positions by recognizing, whenever possible, obligations like the one to be a good Samaritan. That court would impose liability on a relative who refused to participate in genetic testing, at least under some circumstances.

Different persons will have different preferences about which of the two outlined approaches to adopt. However, neither approach is so hideous that the possibility of its adoption should be precluded. Even uncertainty about which rule will be adopted does no harm. Indeed, uncertainty may do some good if it encourages a reluctant relative to participate voluntarily in genetic testing. Thus, the best course of action for the law is to do nothing until a dispute arises and then to deal with it through the common law of torts. That approach will do no harm. Any more proactive approach may.

Genetic Determinism

Even the difficulties posed for the law by the familial nature of genetic information pale when compared to the challenges presented by the new view of humanness that genetics offers. Our law is based on the assumption that human beings are autonomous moral agents, free to make decisions and act on them, and appropriately held to account when their decisions are inimical to the declared public good.

Today, however, developments in genetics challenge this traditional view and reopen the nature-nurture and free will-determinism debates. The Human Genome Project is the most ambitious biological research initiative ever undertaken. It has been compared to the Manhattan Project in physics, and its implications and ramifications could be even more far-reaching. The HGP is an effort to locate every human gene and to create a map of the entire genetic makeup of human beings.[50] In addition to the advance in understanding that this effort offers, it holds out the promise of enormous benefit for humanity— earlier and surer diagnosis of genetic diseases, diagnosis of ever more genetic diseases, recognition of the genetic component of many diseases and conditions not usually thought of as genetic, and, increasingly, genetic therapy.

However, as we learn that there is a genetic component involved in ever more aspects of human behavior and in ever more human conditions, the temptation to leap to the conclusion that all human conditions and events are predetermined and that individual choice is an illusion will become increasingly strong. To some extent recognition of our limitations is desirable. It should instill in human beings a degree of appropriate modesty, and it will permit us to adopt governing norms of behavior that are increasingly realistic.

However, it is easy to get carried away by visions of genetic determinism— to believe that more is predestined than is in fact the case, to become immodest about the possibility that the deterministic views of a moment may turn out to be incorrect, and to use genetic determinism both to justify existing social inequities and future discriminatory practices. One need only remember the horrors perpetrated in the name of a false genetics in Nazi Germany and the eugenic excesses of early twentieth-century America to eschew hubris in our response to genetic advance. Can the legal system respond to and take advantage of significant new understandings offered by modern genetics while protecting individuals and society from the dangers of excessive reliance on inadequate, and perhaps dangerous, science?

Genetic discoveries increasingly demonstrate that different persons are at different degrees of risk for developing certain illnesses or handicapping conditions. For example, some persons are genetically predisposed to develop certain cancers[51] or alcoholism.[52] Society can respond to this information in a number of different ways.

Society could view genetic predispositions as irrelevancies and treat all persons who experience illnesses or conditions alike. Alternatively, it could view persons with genetic predispositions as victims. Nobody chooses his genetic makeup. To the extent that one person's biological inheritance puts him at risk for developing a condition others are less likely to experience, that person has been unfairly exposed to suffering. A just society may have an obligation to create a level playing field by providing special benefits to such a person. Quite a different perspective would see persons with genetic predispositions as having special obligations to attempt to avoid the conditions to which they are predisposed. On this view persons who are more likely than others to develop lung cancer would have an obligation to refrain from smoking and to reject employment around known carcinogens.

Obviously, quite different legal consequences follow from the adoption of these different perspectives on genetic predispositions. The victimization view, for example, would lead to imposing requirements on other persons to make the environment safe for the predisposed and to compensate persons who develop the conditions for which they are at risk. The special obligation view, on the other hand, would close certain occupations to persons with genetic predispositions and would deny them ordinary social and private insurance benefits if they engage in behavior that activates their predisposition. Fundamentally different views of individual responsibility underlie these approaches.

Normally, law reflects a society's fundamental values. Thus, it may be too early to adopt any law about genetic predispositions because we know so little about them, and our knowledge is so new, that our society has not yet developed values for the modern genetic age. Certainly, any far-reaching legal response, such as constitutional adjudication or federal legislation, about social questions posed by genetic developments would be inappropriate. Resolutions of social questions will depend on an understanding of rapidly changing scientific facts, which neither judges nor legislators are likely to possess. National imposition of values in an area in which values are in flux cannot be successful, and it is premature to cut off experimentation by the states in the name of a possibly unnecessary uniformity.

Some persons, however, especially those who distrust our ability to deal responsibly with genetic information, will take a very different view. They will argue that our society's values are well established and that social questions posed by developments in genetics simply require applying existing values (and legal protections) in new contexts. American constitutional values recognize the dignity and autonomy of each individual and enshrine the principle of equal treatment for all. Applied consistently, this approach will be harsh and unyielding in some settings, gentle and humane in others. It will refuse to consider genetic determinism as a defense to charges of criminal behavior, preferring to state as an ideological fact that each person is responsible for his own behavior. On the other hand, it will refuse to allow persons to be excluded from opportunities because of their genetic predispositions because all persons are to be treated alike; different treatment based on an immutable characteristic is discrimination.

This latter approach is deeply flawed. Whether values adopted when people had one view of reality remain valid when reality changes is the question modern genetics forces us to address. Simply asserting that our values are established begs that question. It also overstates the extent to which our values have been clear even in simpler times, and it ignores the complexity of working out the results required even by apparently firmly held values. Finally, it leads to a constellation of conclusions that its proponents would probably reject, thus reminding us in a practical way of the limits of ideology.

Genetics, like machinery, is here to stay. Modern Luddites can attempt to wish it away, but they will be no more successful than their cousins of an earlier day. As an ethical matter we may insist that all persons are of equal value, but as a factual matter all persons are not the same. Human diversity is a fact. The question of which factual differences among persons may be taken into account in which ways is a difficult and troubling one. To ignore it as our ability to recognize more kinds of differences grows is to insist on maintaining a law and ethics that are out of touch with reality, frozen in an earlier age. If the law did not respond to new factual understandings and allow values to evolve, our country would still be characterized by the enslavement of an entire race and the subjugation of one sex by the other. What basis is there for believing that the rejection of those legal positions has completed the development of an ethically refined society? Evolution of ethics and of law cannot be frozen at one historical moment. We must confront the questions posed by modern genetics if we are to avoid an increasing dissonance between our law and ethics on the one hand and reality on the other, or, worse, the imposition of new rules upon us by those who may not care to engage in ethical analysis before they impose their will.

In any event, social values and the direction they push have never been all that clear anyway. For example, while we have insisted on an ideology of individual responsibility, we have always recognized that some persons lack the ability to act responsibly, and we have always made exceptions for them. Thus, the insanity defense, which excuses persons for their crimes if they were "insane" at the time they acted, is firmly entrenched.[53] The problem has always been in figuring out which persons qualify as insane. If mental incapacity can remove a person from the fold of morally and legally responsible agents, no apparent reason exists why genetic incapacity should not do the same. The ideology of individual responsibility has been and will continue to be tempered by reality.

Finally, few persons are willing to adopt an ideology and follow it wherever it leads. For example, recognizing genetic incapacity as a defense to crime may be logically inconsistent with refusing to recognize genetic variation as an acceptable ground for distinguishing among persons with regard to the jobs they may hold. Nonetheless, many persons may be willing to accept the one conclusion but not the other. Logic is only one of many criteria for determining sound policy. Moreover, logical conclusions always flow from premises. If one were to start from a premise of humanitarianism rather than a premise of individual responsibility, then considering genetic incapacity as a defense to criminal liability but not as a job exclusion would be perfectly logical. The point is that where one starts determines where one ends up. With regard to the relevance of genetics the proper starting point is unclear. Therefore, adopting far-reaching laws to deal with new genetic insights would be premature.

The question remains what use to make of existing laws that were adopted with little or no attention to modern genetics but that could be interpreted to apply to genetic conditions. For example, the insanity defense, as it exists, can be applied to excuse persons with some genetic conditions from criminal liability, and the Americans with Disabilities Act[54] could be applied to protect persons with some genetic conditions from differential treatment.[55]

Obviously, sound decisions about how the law should deal with genetic information require that lawmakers pay attention to genetics. If nongenetic cases or statutes reach sound results when applied in genetic contexts, that will simply be good luck. Yet I have argued that adopting specific laws related to genetic predispositions would be premature. What possibilities does that leave open?

Pregenetic laws exist. Lawyers who did not attempt to use those laws on behalf of their clients would be underserving those clients. Therefore, we can expect that the applicability of existing laws such as the ADA will be argued vigorously. Courts should respond to these arguments with caution, construing existing law narrowly and applying it in the genetic predisposition context only when doing so is well nigh unavoidable. That approach will accomplish two goals: (1) It will resolve existing disputes without taking far-reaching and premature steps. The courts will not be paralyzed, but they will be walking in place. (2) It will highlight the issues posed by the new genetics and foster the kind of public debate that is necessary to advance us to the point at which adopting more far-reaching laws may no longer be premature. Applying existing laws more generously would also highlight the new problems, but by taking bolder steps into the future it would be more likely than narrow approaches to make far-reaching mistakes and to goad the legislature into premature action.

Developments in genetics really are outstripping the legal system's ability to keep pace. In such a situation, sound legal decision making requires us to remember that law is for centuries. Short term lags are tolerable. Quick fixes never work. The costs of pausing to catch our collective breath will almost surely be less than the costs of acting precipitously out of ignorance, good intentions, and fear.

SIX

Death and Dying

At the same time that developments in biology and medicine have forced us to rethink questions about birth, reproduction, and the nature of humanness, they have also demanded a rethinking of our ideas about death and the process of dying. Respirators, heart-lung machines, and the ability to provide long-term nutrition and hydration to those who cannot eat, drink, or even swallow, have allowed us to prolong human life long past the point where it would have ended mere decades ago and long past the point at which many persons have lost the will to live. Organ transplant technology has provided a demand for human body parts, which the dying seem well situated to satisfy in part. The rising cost of medical care, especially at the end of life, has alerted us to what we trade for short or long periods of continued existence. All of these developments have been accompanied by extensive ethical debate and legal activity.

DEFINING DEATH

An early issue that spawned debate about death and dying involved the definition of death. At common law there was no all-encompassing definition of death.[1] Nobody needed one. Occasionally, however, a court had to decide when somebody had died. The typical situation involved married couples who died in a common disaster, for instance, a buggy accident. If each spouse had a will that left all their property to the other if he or she survived the will-maker's death, but left the property to different persons in the event of spousal nonsurvival, it became critical to decide which spouse died first.

In this kind of "simultaneous death" case the courts said that a person was dead when breathing stopped and the heart stopped beating.[2] That made perfect sense. Brain death was an unknown concept. People without heart beats and respiration did not come back to life. Cessation of heart beat and respiration could be easily diagnosed by a lay person. All that was necessary was to feel for a pulse, listen for a heart beat, or place a mirror under the person's nose to see if the mirror fogged.

Unfortunately, legal reference books, like *Black's Law Dictionary*,[3] picked up the cessation of heart beat and respiration language from the simultaneous death cases and purported to define death as the cessation of heart beat and respiration. Even though legal dictionaries have no legal authority, this led people to believe that cessation of heart beat and respiration was the definition of death.[4]

By the 1960s and '70s, however, technological change made many persons think that cessation of heart beat and respiration was no longer an adequate definition of death. Heart-lung machines and respirators made it possible to sustain heart beat and respiration even after the possibility that a person might return to meaningful existence, or even consciousness, had disappeared. Clinical agreement developed about when a person had reached the point at which he could not return to a cognizant state.[5] The electroencephalogram (EEG) permitted corroboration of the clinical diagnosis. Organ transplants had become possible, and there was an increasing need for fresh organs to transplant. Organs from persons who had been maintained for a long time on artificial life support were not satisfactory for transplantation purposes. Thus, persons who believed that there was a definition of death, that it was the cessation of heart beat and respiration, that this definition no longer made scientific sense, and that it impeded organ transplantation, sought a "new" definition of death.

The only way to have death defined quickly and comprehensively was through enacting state or (better still) federal legislation that defined death. Thus, scholars began proposing and legislatures began adopting death definition statutes.[6] Typical statutes followed one of two models, which were very similar in practical effect. One approach defined death as *either* the cessation of heart beat and respiration *or* the complete cessation of all brain function.[7] The other defined death as the end of life and provided that death was to be *determined by* the cessation of heart beat and respiration *unless* the patient's heart beat and respiration were being artificially maintained, in which case it was to be determined by the complete cessation of all brain function.[8]

Using either approach, the result under the new definition was clear: If a patient was being maintained on a respirator so that he or she continued to breathe and the heart continued to beat, the patient could, nonetheless, be declared dead if there was total failure of brain function. Once the patient was declared dead, the respirator could be turned off and/or the patient's organs could be removed for transplantation.

A small number of commentators, including this author, disagreed with this approach.[9] They argued that there was no cessation of heart beat and respiration standard for when death occurred except in simultaneous death cases. Therefore, no "definition" that posed an impediment to turning off respirators or obtaining transplantable organs existed. They maintained that what was really at stake was not the definition of death, but whether and when respirators could be turned off and organs transplanted; what mattered was not the definition but the consequences of the definition. Purporting to solve the problem by definition simply made it too easy to pretend there was no problem in turning off someone's respirator or removing his organs, because, by definition, he was already dead. They argued that "death" is simply a shorthand description for a situation from which many consequences, including many nonmedical consequences such as transfer of property, the possibility of remarriage, and prosecution for murder, follow. In each case it is the consequence, not the definition that matters.

Different policies govern questions about whether to remove a person's organs, convict the person who assaulted the patient of murder, or transfer the victim's property to his heirs. Moreover, for some purposes death is not even viewed as a biological phenomenon, but, for example, as a consequence of being absent without tidings for an extended period of time.[10] Finally, when death is viewed as a biological phenomenon, the law should not adopt a definition that freezes developments at a particular moment in scientific and technological development. By the mid-1970s, for example, many experts thought that brain death was already an outmoded concept that should be replaced by the idea that a person was dead when he had suffered permanent loss of function of the neocortex.[11]

For all those reasons these commentators argued that there should be no definition of death. Instead, there should be independent analyses of the social policies relevant to deciding each substantive question—remarriage, conviction, inheritance, transplantation, and removal of respirators.

Today neither side has won the debate. Most states have adopted a statutory definition of death that includes brain death as an acceptable criterion for death.[12] The Commissioners on Uniform State Laws have recommended such a statute,[13] and thirty-two jurisdictions have adopted their version or a modification of it.[14] The President's Commission has called for a federal legislative definition of death,[15] but Congress has not yet enacted one. A proposed new Simultaneous Death Act reduces the importance of determining the time of death while permitting death to be determined by either brain death or the cessation of heart beat and respiration.[16] Meanwhile, courts, acting without the benefit of statutes, have treated brain death as death for the purpose of convicting assaulters of murder.[17] States have also retained their statutes that treat persons as dead when they have been missing for a long time.[18] Thus, the reality is that even in states with definition of death statutes there are multiple definitions for multiple purposes and multiple standards (cessation of heart beat and respiration and brain death) for medical purposes.

Finally, some commentators have recently called for a change in the definition of death to define anencephalic infants as dead.[19] The purpose of that redefinition is to permit removal of organs from such newborns in order to transplant them into other persons. This suggestion demonstrates the futility and the danger of attempting to solve social problems by definition. The effort is futile because the definition cannot anticipate and keep pace with changing circumstances. Its existence is an illusion. The definition only lasts until it becomes inconvenient. Definition is dangerous because it allows us to avoid analysis and do bad things to persons without concern by defining them out of existence. Whether to transplant tissues from anencephalic infants is a difficult question. It becomes frighteningly easy if we simply define the infants as already dead. In this regard even the most influential proponent of defining death has opposed redefinition for anencephalics, arguing that the question should be what consequences to allow to follow from anencephaly, not whether to beg the question by redefining death.[20]

FACILITATING DEATH

Much more important than whether or how to define death is the question of whether, how, in what circumstances, and on whose authority to allow an undeniably living person to die, or even to expedite his death. Of course, we are not discussing here the law of capital punishment or war. Our question is posed, once again, by biomedical advance. As noted earlier, it is now possible to keep even permanently comatose persons alive almost indefinitely. Does the ability to keep them alive require us to do so? If not, does that imply that under some circumstances we are also free to expedite the deaths of persons who are not being artificially maintained but who are suffering or simply tired of life? Increasingly, persons and groups who are committed to "death with dignity" have brought those questions to public attention.

Until 1976, the date of the famous Karen Ann Quinlan case,[21] American law on the subject of facilitating death was a fascinating mix of highly restrictive formal law and highly permissive practice. Theoretically, any intentional conduct that resulted in another person's death was a serious crime. In the medical context, either killing a patient or purposely allowing a patient to die was murder in the first degree. Classically, first degree murder means the deliberate, premeditated, and malicious killing of another human being.[22] Almost any medical situation one can imagine would obviously be deliberate and premeditated. It would also be malicious, because the legal definition of malice in the homicide context is not the same as the common definition of malice. For murder, malice does not require ill will or malevolence; it requires only that the killing be done in the absence of any specifically recognized mitigating factor, such as the sudden heat of passion brought on by a legally sufficient provocation.[23] The law did not recognize the well-motivated desire to let a patient die with dignity as a factor that could make a deliberate killing nonmalicious.[24] Moreover, for legal purposes, it was theoretically clear that the physician who withheld or withdrew life support had killed the patient. Even if one characterizes the doctor's behavior as a failure to act (an omission), omissions are sufficient acts on which to predicate criminal liability in cases in which the accused person had a duty to act on behalf of the victim.[25] Doctors have such a duty toward their patients.[26] Finally, the doctor caused the patient's death as far as the law is concerned. In law one who hastens a result is said to have caused it.[27] Everybody dies some time; even conventional murderers only hasten their victim's deaths, causing them to die now rather than in the future. That, and not that one be the primary cause of death, is all that the law requires.

Under some more modern criminal codes death facilitating behavior by a physician would be a lesser offense, like second degree murder or manslaughter.[28] In some states it could also be treated as assisting suicide.[29] The important point, however, is that it was always a serious crime—in theory.

In reality, the situation was quite different. As of 1976 American law did not contain a single example of a physician or other health care professional having been convicted of any crime for any behavior that expedited or facilitated a patient's death. Hardly any had even been prosecuted. Yet both social scientific and anecdotal evidence made plain the fact that physicians practiced death facilitation frequently and routinely.[30] A larger gap between the law in practice and the law on the books could not be imagined.

One can only speculate about the reasons for this enormous gap. Surely, it had something to do with the secrecy with which medicine was practiced, behind closed office and hospital doors. Probably it had more to do with the good sense and circumspection of doctors, who did not abuse their power and only facilitated death when everybody around (patient, family, nurses) agreed with their decision. Criminal prosecution usually results from somebody who is angry complaining to the authorities; by behaving sensibly doctors gave no one cause for anger. Finally, the good sense of prosecuting attorneys probably contributed significantly to the situation. Anyone with an ounce of sense knew that the homicide laws were not designed with medical death facilitation in mind, even though they could be applied in that context. In the absence of complaints or evidence of abusive behavior by doctors, prosecutors either did not think about death facilitation or exercised their discretion by ignoring it.

Whatever the reasons for the gulf between the written and the applied law, the pre-1976 situation struck many persons as anomalous.[31] In fact, it was not as anomalous as it appears. First, prosecuting attorneys have well-recognized discretion to refrain from prosecuting conduct that is theoretically prohibited. If they did not, the criminal justice system would bankrupt the nation and collapse of its own weight. Second, in the death facilitation context one can even argue that the pre-1976 situation was as close to ideal as a system designed and run by mortals can be. It allowed physicians to practice good and humane medicine; it gave patients considerable control over the manner and timing of their deaths; its theoretical threat reduced the risk of abusive killings by doctors; and the written law took the moral high ground of formally stating the society's respect for life. What could be better than that?

Not surprisingly, many persons thought a great deal could be better. Many patients did not know that they could get the kind of end-of-life care they wanted, and surely most patients lacked the sophistication to shop for a doctor who would agree to facilitate the patient's death. Many doctors were unwilling to rely on the continued good sense of prosecutors and were afraid to practice death facilitation even if they thought it was appropriate. Undoubtedly, some doctors also refrained from practicing death facilitation because they understood it to be against the law, and, therefore, out of keeping with their view of themselves as law-abiding citizens. Finally, purists, never content to accept situations merely because they work, and not understanding the crucial role of discretion in the law, saw the situation as representing a mockery of the rule of law. Therefore, a significant movement arose to change the status quo. Reformers sought change from both the legislatures and the courts.

Judicial Reform

Regrettably, two unfortunate circumstances controlled the nature of the judicial response and distorted the developing law. First, the earliest cases that came before the courts all involved patients who were incompetent. This forced courts to deal with the hardest cases first and led them to take some positions they might have eschewed if cases about competent persons had arisen first.

Second, and ironically, judicial reform of death with dignity law started in New Jersey, the home of Karen Ann Quinlan. New Jersey was the worst possible place for reform to begin because in 1971, only five years before *Quinlan*, the New Jersey Supreme Court had ruled that "there is no constitutional right to choose to die."[32] In *John F. Kennedy Memorial Hospital v. Heston* a severely injured Jehovah's Witness refused for religious reasons to accept blood transfusions that were necessary to keep her alive. The court affirmed a trial court order that had required the appointment of a guardian to consent to the transfusions. In denying the existence of a right to choose to die, even when the choice was religiously based, the court emphasized the state's interest in preventing suicide and maintaining life and the interest of the hospital staff in practicing medicine as they think proper.

Courts can resolve disputes that come before them; they cannot control the rush of events. In 1976 the same court that had decided *Heston* encountered Karen Ann Quinlan.[33] Ms. Quinlan was a 22-year-old, unmarried woman who had slipped into a coma from which she never emerged. By the time the case reached the court, everyone agreed that Ms. Quinlan was in a persistent vegetative state from which she could not recover. She was maintained on a respirator, and the relevant experts believed that she would die quickly if removed from the respirator. Joseph Quinlan, Karen's father, sought to be appointed Karen's guardian for the purpose of ending life-supporting medical treatment, that is, to have the respirator removed. His petition was necessary because the doctors and hospital in charge of Karen's care refused to withdraw the respirator and allow Karen to die. The Quinlans were a devoted family. Mr. Quinlan was a devout Roman Catholic who had reached his decision only after consultation with his parish priest and an extended period of soul searching. No reason to question his motives existed. After the trial court refused to grant Mr. Quinlan's petititon, he appealed to the New Jersey Supreme Court.

That court assumed that before it could decide the rights of an incompetent person, like Karen, it had to decide what rights a competent person who wanted to choose to die would have.[34] Focusing on the right of privacy the court stated, "Presumably this right is broad enough to encompass a patient's decision to decline medical treatment under certain circumstances, in much the same way as it is broad enough to encompass a woman's decision to terminate pregnancy under certain conditions."[35] Thus, if Karen Ann Quinlan were competent, she could choose to be removed from her respirator.

The obvious explanation for the difference in outcome between *Quinlan* and *Heston* is that the United States Supreme Court decided *Roe v. Wade*[36] in 1973, between the two New Jersey death cases. Therefore, a perfectly sensible approach for New Jersey to have taken in *Quinlan* would have been to overrule *Heston* on the basis of *Roe v. Wade*. That would have been the obvious response to the court's view about the breadth of the right of privacy that the Supreme Court had recognized in *Roe*.

Unfortunately, however, the New Jersey Supreme Court distinguished *Heston*, rather than overruling it. *Heston* differed from *Quinlan* in that Ms. Heston, unlike Ms. Quinlan, was "salvable to long life and vibrant health."[37] While that is true, it is an unsound and dangerous basis for treating the two cases differently. The impossibility of a return to good health can hardly explain why Ms. Quinlan should have a constitutional right that Ms. Heston lacked. While the Constitution may be applied in a way that recognizes important differences among persons, there is no reason to believe that the hopelessly ill have more constitutional rights than the rest of us. Presumably, the court did not really mean to suggest that only the hopelessly ill have a right to decline medical treatment. It must have meant that the greater the patient's chance of recovering to a full, healthy life, the greater interest the state has in overriding the patient's right to reject medical care.

This suggestion, however, is very troubling. If taken seriously, it could lead to a situation in which the right to decline medical treatment provides no help to those who are most able to choose to use it and in which it might even become a tool for abuse of the disabled. That concern gains credibility from a review of several early Massachusetts cases.

The year after the *Quinlan* decision Massachusetts's highest court joined New Jersey in recognizing a right to reject life-saving medical treatment in some circumstances. In *Superintendent of Belchertown State School v. Saikewicz*[38] the court applied that right in the case of a 67-year-old mentally retarded man who had never been competent and who was suffering from acute myeloblastic monocytic leukemia. The court authorized the patient's guardian to refuse chemotherapy for the patient, even though that decision would necessarily prove fatal. After recognizing the existence of a right to refuse life-sustaining medical care, the court recognized four state interests that can be weighed against the individual's right: an interest in (1) the preservation of life, (2) the protection of innocent third parties, (3) the prevention of suicide, and (4) preservation of the ethical integrity of the medical profession.[39] Virtually every right to die case since *Saikewicz* has recognized those four state interests.[40] Taken literally those interests could always be applied to defeat an individual's choice to reject life-prolonging care. After all, that choice is always at odds with the state's interest in the preservation of life. The more likely use of the state's interests, however is to prevent patients with a good prognosis from effectuating their decision to die, thereby rendering the *Quinlan-Saikewicz* right virtually useless for those most able to exercise it. Indeed, when necessary, the Massachusetts courts have even recognized other state interests to prevent salvable patients from effectively choosing to die. For example, in one case an intermediate appellate court authorized the Commissioner of Corrections to use whatever force was necessary to compel a prison inmate to undergo dialysis treatments that were necessary to preserve his life. The court recognized that the prisoner had a right to refuse the treatments, but it held that his right was outweighed by the state's interest in maintaining prison discipline.[41]

On the other hand, the right to refuse life-saving treatment sometimes overrides state interests, including the interest in preserving life, in cases where one wonders whose interests are really being served. Consider, for example, the case of Earle N. Spring.[42] Mr. Spring, a 77-year-old man, was suffering from end-stage renal disease, which required him to be dialyzed three times a week in a town some distance from his home. He also suffered from chronic organic brain syndrome, which made him difficult to deal with. He was disoriented; he did not recognize his wife or son; and he engaged in disruptive behavior—wandering aimlessly, kicking nurses, resisting transportation for dialysis, and pulling dialysis tubing from his body.

Mr. Spring had been married to one woman for 55 years. The Springs' son lived near them and visited them daily. Mr. Spring had been an active man when he was in good health. About a year after Mr. Spring became ill, his wife suffered a stroke, which the son attributed to the strain and exhaustion of caring for Mr. Spring. After treatment, Mrs. Spring returned home and was making good progress toward recovery. Mr. Spring remained in a nursing home with no prospect for improvement in his health.

Mr. Spring's wife and son sought an order to terminate Mr. Spring's life-saving dialysis treatments. Despite the fact that Mr. Spring had never expressed any desire to die or to have the treatments discontinued, the trial court found that Mr. Spring would not want to live in his present condition and granted the order. The Appellate and Supreme Judicial Courts both affirmed.

This case is very troubling. By recognizing the existence of a "right," to which all are entitled, and by utilizing that right in the case of an incompetent person who never evinced any interest in exercising it, the court has allowed a person who was a nuisance to have his life shortened (or at least not prolonged as long as a less bothersome person's life would have been), largely on the basis of self-interested testimony from his wife and son. That is, the court has converted the right to decline medical treatment into an obligation of the annoying and troublesome to die, at least when their families are ready to be finished with them.

This result is made possible by two fundamental mistakes. First, the courts created a right, rather than simply recognizing that persons have interests in avoiding suffering and in exercising control over what is done to them. Second, since the decision in *Quinlan*, the courts have assumed that incompetent persons, who cannot make choices,[43] must have the same rights as persons who can make choices. This required that substitute decision makers be appointed to exercise incompetent persons' rights and created the risk that the substitutes and the courts would act in their own or society's interests while deluding the rest of us, and, perhaps, themselves, into believing that they are respecting the dignity, autonomy, and well-being of the incompetent person.

Fortunately, later cases have somewhat alleviated both the concern about the denial of rights to competent persons and the fear of abuse of incompetent persons. Several states have now allowed competent persons to refuse life-prolonging treatment.[44] Significantly, even though the New Jersey Supreme Court recognized that a competent person's right to refuse treatment must be balanced against the usual four state interests, the court stated that a competent person's interest in self-determination "generally outweighs" any interest of the state.[45] How secure this notion is remains unclear because, in a companion case, the court did reintroduce *Quinlan*'s focus on prognosis.[46] Nonetheless, several state courts have now allowed competent persons to choose to die.[47]

Similarly, recent cases have been more careful than *Spring* about protecting incompetent persons. In particular, a 1985 New Jersey case[48] and 1981 and 1988 New York cases[49] have been vigilant in protecting incompetent persons from premature termination of life support. Most significantly, the United States Supreme Court seems to have recognized that it does not make any sense to treat incompetent persons as if they were competent.[50]

As noted above, until the decision in the famous *Cruzan* case[51] almost all courts had said that the rights of incompetent persons must be the same as the rights of competent persons. They stated that any other position would be inconsistent with respect for all persons and recognition of the dignity of persons with handicaps.[52] While this sounds attractive, it is not clear why it should be so. The Constitution applies differentially to other groups, for example, children. Moreover, treating all persons as if they are alike actually demeans incompetent persons by denying one of the central features of their existence and insisting that their interests be accommodated to a competent person's model of humanity rather than requiring that the legal system accommodate itself to the incompetent person's reality and needs. The dangers of that approach are evident in cases like *Spring*. In *Cruzan* the Supreme Court recognized the error of treating incompetent persons as if they were competent and dealt with the question of whether to allow an incompetent person to die on its own terms.[53]

If incompetent persons have any kind of a right to have life-sustaining treatment withheld or withdrawn, the questions of (1) what standard ought to govern the decision whether to withhold or withdraw treatment, (2) who is to make the decision, and (3) what procedures they should follow in reaching their decision, all must be resolved.

Two major competing standards have been offered for deciding whether withholding or withdrawing life-sustaining treatment is appropriate, although, as a string of New Jersey cases has taught us, an infinite variety of standards is possible. The critical issue in settling upon a standard is whether to attempt to do what is objectively best for the patient or to attempt, somehow, to ascertain and do what the particular patient would subjectively have wanted done. So far, no standards that forthrightly consider the interests, needs, or desires of persons other than the patient have been applied.

An objective standard would simply ask what is in the best interests of the patient.[54] Assuming that focusing exclusively on the patient is appropriate, this seems the best standard to apply. It is both easier and more realistic to apply than a standard that purports to discover or impute a nonexistent intention to the patient, and it is broad enough to permit consideration of everything that is relevant to the patient's well-being, including social, emotional, and financial considerations as well as physical ones. However, the best interests approach is susceptible to significant criticism. It is not really very easy to decide what is best for another person, especially one who is incompetent and very ill or dying. The standard could easily be abused by a surrogate decision maker who decided to do what was best for himself (for example, terminate life support to save money for his inheritance) under the guise of doing what is best for the patient. Finally, if one thinks that incompetent persons should be treated like competent ones, the best interests approach is unsatisfactory because competent patients are entitled to have their choices honored even if the choices are in some objective sense bad for them; incompetent persons should have the same right. In *Cruzan*, the only United States Supreme Court case about a right to refuse treatment for an incompetent person, Justice Stevens was the only member of the Court to support a best interests approach.[55]

The alternative, more subjective, standard for determining whether to remove or withhold life support is the substituted judgment approach.[56] Under this standard a substitute decision maker is supposed to make the same decision for the incompetent person that the incompetent person would make for himself if he were able. Two different forms of substituted judgment analysis have been applied. *Saikewicz* involved a patient who had never been competent. Nonetheless, the court held that the substitute decision maker was to make the same decision the patient would make if he were miraculously to become competent for one moment during which he knew all the relevant facts, including that he would never be competent again.[57] This absurd formulation led one expert to say that substituted judgment was like asking, "If it snowed all summer, would it then be winter?"[58]

The alternative form of substituted judgment requires the substitute decision maker to apply whatever evidence of the patient's real desires may exist and to follow the patient's ascertained wishes.[59] Two problems exist even with this more sensible approach. First it is unclear why even the clearly expressed views of a once competent person should be controlling once the person is no longer competent. To take the extreme case, what interest does a permanently comatose person who neither thinks nor experiences anything have in the effectuation of wishes he had when he was healthy? The only apparent interest here is the interest of competent persons in being able to rest, secure in the notion that what they now think they want will be done later. This security is of some value, but, given the problems inherent in a substituted judgment approach, it hardly seems important enough to make the case for substituted judgment. Second, this form of substituted judgment applies in a very limited range of cases. Obviously, it can never be used in the case of a patient who has never been competent. In the real world it will also prove useless for many patients who were competent but who never expressed their views, or who expressed them in inconsistent ways or without sufficient detail to make them useful guides to decision making.

Whenever the substituted judgment approach does not work, the decision maker will be forced back to a best interests analysis. The preference for substituted judgment, however, will force somebody to decide whether a particular case is one in which substituted judgment will not work. Thus, in many instances substituted judgment is simply best interests complicated by an extra procedural step. This hardly represents an advance over a straightforward best interests approach, and it is certainly no less susceptible to abuse.

Often some evidence of an incompetent patient's previous wishes will exist, but it will not be very persuasive. If one is unwilling simply to fall back onto a best interests approach in such cases, one could attempt to devise a middle ground that took some account both of the patient's supposed desires and of what was best for him. This is what New Jersey has tried to do.

Claire Conroy was "an elderly nursing-home resident who is suffering from serious and permanent mental and physical impairments, who will probably die within approximately one year even with the treatment, and who, though formerly competent, is now incompetent to make decisions about her life-sustaining treatment and is unlikely to regain such competence."[60] In cases involving similarly situated patients, the New Jersey court adopted three alternative tests to be used in different circumstances to decide whether treatment should be removed. Under the (1) so-called subjective test, if there is clear evidence that the patient would have refused treatment, the surrogate decision maker may refuse it for her.[61] In the absence of such clear evidence, a (2) limited objective test is to be used if there is some trustworthy evidence that the patient would have refused the treatment. Given such evidence, the surrogate may refuse the treatment if "it is clear that the burdens of the patient's continued life with the treatment outweigh the benefits of that life for him."[62] This means that the patient is suffering and will continue to suffer unavoidable pain and that the pain and suffering of life with treatment (minus the pain and suffering he will experience if treatment is removed) will "markedly outweigh" any physical, mental, or emotional satisfactions the patient may get from life.[63] If there is no trustworthy evidence that the patient would have refused the treatment, then a (3) pure objective test applies. Under that test the treatment may be withheld or withdrawn if the net burdens of the patient's life with treatment markedly outweigh the benefits *and* "the recurring, unavoidable and severe pain of the patient's life with the treatment should be such that the effect of administering life-sustaining treatment would be inhumane."[64]

The *Conroy* approach has been criticized on several grounds, including its emphasis on pain as the exclusive burden to be considered in deciding whether to allow patients to die under the limited objective and objective tests.[65] For our purposes, however, the principal criticisms of *Conroy* are that it is unintelligible, that it fills the law with complexity, and that, as complicated as its approach may be, it still only covers a very small number of cases. In other words, *Conroy* is an example of over-legalization and the failure to advert to the limits of law.

Conroy requires a decision maker to decide whether there is clear evidence, merely trustworthy evidence, or no trustworthy evidence of an incompetent patient's wishes. In the absence of a living will or similar document, what kind of evidence is either clear or trustworthy? How clear or trustworthy is clear or trustworthy enough? Even if the patient has a living will, how are its age and its failure to anticipate the patient's precise situation to affect determinations about clarity and trustworthiness? And once one decides which of the three tests should apply, how is one to make the pain judgments (about incompetent persons whose communications cannot be trusted) and the burden-benefit analyses that the two objective tests require? Neither *Conroy*'s terms nor how to apply them is clear. The case is unintelligible. What is clear, however, is that it fills the law with complexity. It creates three tests, two of them with multiple parts, and each requiring litigation to flesh out its meaning. This complexity, however, is only the beginning. *Conroy* applies only to the very few cases that meet its factual description. That is, it does not apply to patients who are not in nursing homes, to those whose death with treatment is probably more than one year away, to patients who were never competent, or to those who cannot experience either the burdens or benefits of life because, for example, they are in a persistent vegetative state.

The court has applied different rules to each of those situations.[66] What the court's inability to craft one rule for all cases demonstrates is that the variety of death cases is simply too great to permit across-the-board decision making. This suggests that case by case, common law decision making would be better than any attempt to fashion rules if it were not for the fact that people must act on some assumption about what the law is in these cases. A major purpose of the law in entering the death and dying area is to provide conduct control—to tell doctors what to do, and to guide ordinary persons in planning their deaths. After-the-fact, common law decision making cannot effectively control the conduct of individuals. Therefore, if the law is to serve its conduct control function, it must develop a small number of clear, easily understandable rules for people to follow. If the complexity of the death and dying area is so great that this is not possible, then the law should either retreat from the area, eschewing both conduct control and the threat of sanctions while trusting other social institutions to protect against abuse, or it should develop a new procedure to produce fast, reliable, nuanced, and individualized decisions on which persons can base their conduct. Before exploring the desirability of that approach, we should examine the decision makers and decision-making machinery that are available now.

The list of potential candidates for the role of surrogate decision maker for an incompetent person includes members of the person's family, a guardian or other health care representative, one or more doctors, a court, a hospital ethics committee, or some combination of those. Legislation often authorizes patients to sign a living will or to appoint a health care representative. The problem we are discussing arises when the patient has not done so (and, perhaps, was never competent to do so). In those situations, if anybody raises the issue, a court must decide who the decision maker is to be.

The dilemma that confronts the courts is obvious. They lack the time and inclination to hear every case about whether to let a person die, but they are reluctant to remit total decision-making authority to relatives, guardians, or doctors, who may have conflicts of interest with the patient, or who may lack the ability to apply the substantive standard of decision making that the court has adopted. Courts have imposed different procedural requirements to attempt to solve this dilemma.

In *Quinlan* the New Jersey Supreme Court took the position that application to a court for authority to withhold or withdraw life support is generally inappropriate. It is both a gratuitous encroachment on the medical profession's field of competence and impossibly cumbersome.[67] Rather than requiring resort to the courts, *Quinlan* adopted a three-part procedure.[68] Under it (1) the patient's guardian must decide whether the patient would exercise her right to have life support withdrawn if she were able. If she would, then the guardian may authorize withdrawal if (2) the patient's doctors decide that there is no reasonable possibility of the patient emerging to a cognitive, sapient state and that life support should be discontinued, and if (3) a hospital ethics committee agrees. Even if all three conditions are met, the decision to terminate life support is permitted, not required.

The *Quinlan* approach is problematic in a number of ways. Substantively, it adopts a strange mix of substituted judgment, prognosis, and value judgments about what ought to be done. Procedurally, it requires, in essence, that every

New Jersey hospital create an ethics committee without adopting any requirements about the committee's membership or procedures, thus raising serious questions about the committee's legitimacy; it requires physicians and the committee, both of whose only expertise is in medicine, to make a social value judgment; and it leaves open the question of what to do if the three decision makers agree that termination of life support would be appropriate but the hospital refuses to comply. A "right" to refuse care is not worth much if one is not entitled to exercise it even after all its preconditions have been met.

The one apparent virtue of the *Quinlan* procedure was that it was clear and relatively simple. However, the apparent simplicity has turned out to be illusory. The procedures apply only in cases like *Quinlan*. In other cases other procedures are mandated. Thus, for example, in *Conroy*[69] the court adopted the following procedures that must be followed before life support may be withheld or withdrawn from elderly, once-competent, nursing home patients with about one year to live: (1) First, there must be a judicial decision (so much for keeping the courts out of the process) that the patient is incompetent to make the specific decision in question. (2) A guardian must be appointed. (3) New Jersey's Ombudsman for the Institutionalized Elderly must be notified that withdrawing life support is being considered. (4) The Ombudsman must investigate and report to the Commissioner of Human Services. (5) Evidence of the patient's condition must be presented by the patient's doctors and nurses and two unaffiliated doctors, who must be appointed by the Ombudsman or a judge. (6) The guardian and the attending physician must agree in good faith that one of the three tests (subjective, limited objective, or objective) applies. (7) The Ombudsman must agree. (8) If the limited objective or pure objective test applies, the patient's spouse, parents, children, and next-of-kin must also agree.

In 1987 New Jersey adopted still different procedures for cases involving competent patients;[70] elderly, comatose, nursing home patients who have executed a power of attorney for health care to someone close to them;[71] and incompetent, nonelderly patients who are not in a nursing home.[72] The New Jersey situation is chaotic.

In *Saikewicz*, Massachusetts, the other early entrant into the death and dying field, rejected New Jersey's view that judicial decision making is an imposition on medical discretion and required that cases be submitted to the probate court for possible authorization to withhold or withdraw life support. In that court a guardian ad litem for the patient is to make all arguments in favor of prolonging life.[73]

The decision to require judicial determination of death and dying questions produced great consternation in Massachusetts. Physicians became afraid to issue no-code (do not resuscitate) orders without obtaining judicial authorization,[74] and the specter of Massachusetts's hospitals filling up with nearly dead patients awaiting judicial determinations about whether they should be allowed to die hovered over medical practice in the state.

Although the *Spring*[75] case, which we discussed earlier, did not raise the question of what procedures had to be followed in no-code cases or other cases about terminating care for incompetent persons, the court used the case as a vehicle for "clarifying" its position. *Spring* reconfirmed the requirement to submit cases to the probate court, but, mystifyingly, noted that there is no requirement to obtain judicial approval that would not otherwise exist. It spelled out a number of factors to be considered in deciding whether a hearing is necessary; unfortunately, those factors have more to do with what the result of the hearing should be than with whether to have the hearing in the first place. If the doctor makes an incorrect determination that no hearing is required, the doctor will be exposed to liability. The guardian ad litem is still required to make all arguments in favor of prolonging life, but he has no duty to present arguments he thinks have no merit, and he has no duty to take appeals as a matter of course.

This is all, obviously, unintelligible. Clearly, what the court wants to do is to retain judicial control and physician accountability without having to decide every case. Unfortunately, it has not yet discovered a way to do that.

Increasingly, courts are recognizing the limits of their abilities to deal satisfactorily with issues surrounding the withholding or withdrawal of life-sustaining care from incompetent persons. In Wisconsin, for example, the state Supreme Court has authorized guardians of patients who have not previously expressed their wishes with regard to continuing care and who are in a persistent vegetative state, to consent to the withholding or withdrawal of care from the patient as long as (1) the patient's attending physician and two independent physicians certify that the patient is in a persistent vegetative state and has no reasonable chance of returning to a cognitive and sentient life, and (2) the guardian determines in good faith, after considering certain factors, that withholding or withdrawing treatment is in the best interests of the patient.[76] Agreeing with the Supreme Court of Washington that judicial decision making is "an unresponsive and cumbersome mechanism for decisions of this nature,"[77] the court held that the guardian need not seek judicial approval of his action.[78] However, one of the factors he is to consider is the opinion of the hospital's ethics committee, if it has one.[79] The courts remain available to resolve disputes if any interested party challenges the guardian's decision.[80] This approach, essentially withdrawing from the field and relying on complaints from interested persons to prevent abuses, is one sensible approach for courts to adopt.

A similar, even less intrusive alternative would be to remit full authority to a hospital ethics committee. Most hospitals now have such committees, and the Joint Commission on the Accreditation of Health Care Institutions requires them in all its accredited hospitals.[81]

Ethics committees are typically composed of doctors, nurses, hospital administrators, lawyers, and medical ethicists. At present, they serve widely differing functions in different hospitals. As sources of decision making about allowing incompetent patients to die, their varied membership suggests that they may be able to do as good a job as one could fairly expect of bringing together ethical, legal, and medical expertise in a setting that also assures consideration of institutional needs.

In order for ethics committees to take over the function of deciding cases about allowing incompetent persons to die, some existing legal institution has to give them that authority. In *Quinlan* the New Jersey Supreme Court simply assigned a role in the process to ethics committees at a time when such committees were in their infancy. More recently, the Wisconsin Supreme Court incorporated ethics committees into the decision-making process if the patient was in a hospital that had such a committee. In both cases, however, the committee has only a partial role to play in the decision-making process. It is almost inconceivable that ethics committees could become the ultimate decision makers unless legislatures assign them that role. It is also impossible to imagine that a legislature would make such an assignment without mandating not only the membership of the committee, but also its procedures and the substantive standard it is to follow. Once the committee empowerment bill gets through the legislature, the committee will have lost its role as an informal decision maker and will have turned into an administrative agency. Moreover, once the committee has become empowered, its decisions will almost surely be made subject to judicial review. Thus, the act of empowering the informal body will destroy its informality.

The loss of informality is essential if one believes that a significant risk of abuse exists. Careful procedures and judicial oversight are the best legal ways to avoid abuses. If, however, one believes that the best practical way to avoid abuses is through consensus decision making, then one might see legal structures aimed at abuse prevention as wasteful and unnecessary. If that is one's view, then an approach like Wisconsin's that lets those closest to a decision make it, while retaining the possibility of judicial oversight to calm the fears of those who worry about abuses, may be as close to ideal as we can come. In no event are over-legalized procedures, like those in New Jersey and Massachusetts, desirable. Those approaches consume time and money while turning an effort to achieve death with dignity into a drawn-out nightmare of litigation, all for a hypothetical and, at most, very small benefit in terms of avoiding abuses.

If a state nonetheless wishes to adopt highly legalistic procedures for deciding whether to allow an incompetent person to die, it is apparently free to do so. The only United States Supreme Court case on the subject granted states broad latitude in designing their procedures.

Cruzan v. Director, Missouri Department of Health[82] involved a patient who was in a persistent vegetative state as a result of an automobile accident and who had no realistic chance of regaining her ability to function mentally. In the face of evidence that Ms. Cruzan had once told a housemate that she would not wish to live "unless she could live at least halfway normally," the Missouri Supreme

Court had refused to authorize Ms. Cruzan's parents to have her artificial nutrition and hydration withdrawn. That court required clear and convincing evidence of an incompetent person's desire to refuse continued life support and found that the evidence in Ms. Cruzan's case was not clear and convincing.[83] The United States Supreme Court affirmed the Missouri Supreme Court's action.

Chief Justice Rehnquist's majority opinion noted that existing Supreme Court decisions supported the inference that competent persons have a constitutionally protected interest in refusing treatment and then *assumed* that the Constitution grants competent persons the right to refuse nutrition and hydration.[84] These rights, if they exist, are liberty interests rooted in the fourteenth amendment.[85] As an opponent of *Roe v. Wade*, the Chief Justice did not seek to locate a right of treatment refusal in a constitutional right of privacy.

If a treatment refusal right exists, a state may override it for sufficiently good reasons. In *Cruzan*, Missouri offered two state interests to weigh against the right, an interest in the protection and preservation of human life, and an interest in safeguarding the personal element of choice. The clear and convincing evidence requirement serves both ends. Therefore, Missouri is free to impose that requirement if it chooses to do so.[86]

Justice Brennan dissented,[87] finding that the clear and convincing evidentiary standard inappropriately stacked the deck in favor of prolonging life and against the exercise of the constitutional right to refuse treatment. Justice Stevens also dissented.[88] He thought that Missouri erred by defining death in purely physical terms and ignoring the context of the patient's life. As might be expected, Justice Scalia concurred with the majority and went farther, cautioning the Court against getting into another situation similar to the abortion morass.[89] Justice O'Connor also joined the majority, but she was careful to reserve for another day questions about whether the Constitution requires states to honor the decisions of patients' duly appointed surrogate decision makers.[90]

Despite all the publicity it attracted, *Cruzan* is not a very important case. It simply allowed Missouri to take a conservative position about the circumstances in which incompetent patients will be allowed to die. It did not require any state to take that position, and New York[91] and Maryland[92] appear to be the only states besides Missouri that would adopt such a restrictive view. The Court did not even definitively recognize a constitutional right to refuse treatment, although if one counts judicial noses, at least five Justices seemed committed to the view that such a right exists.[93]

There is no need to recognize a constitutional right to refuse treatment. Every state recognizes a common law right of refusal.[94] Given that, and given the abortion controversy as a cautionary tale, the Supreme Court would be well advised to refrain from formally recognizing any right in the treatment refusal context and to withdraw from the field.

The only remaining issue before we turn to legislative reform and then to issues of active euthanasia and medical futility, is whether the type of treatment being refused is relevant to whether a patient may refuse it. Specifically, some persons have attempted to distinguish artificial nutrition and hydration from other types of life prolongation and have suggested that it is never appropriate to withhold or withdraw nutrition and hydration.[95] Everyone concedes the symbolic significance of food and water. However, when nutrition and hydration can only be provided through surgically inserted tubes and bear no realistic resemblance to a meal, most persons agree that providing nutrition and hydration is medical care—just like providing the ability to breathe by means of a respirator—and that, like all other medical care, it may be withheld or withdrawn in appropriate circumstances.[96] This seems clearly the better view, and it is the position the Supreme Court adopted in *Cruzan*.[97]

Legislative Reform

Since 1976 judicial activity in the area of death and dying has removed a difficult and intensely personal decision from the control of doctors, patients, and families, and has formalized it and remitted decision making authority to courts, ombudsmen, ethics committees, and others. It has failed to provide workable criteria for determining whether and when to withhold or withdraw life support. It has created risks to doctors and patients alike. It has caused confusion and uncertainty. It has flirted with creating a constitutional right to die, recognition of which could only lead to a repeat of the abortion fiasco in another area. And it has created a climate in which it becomes plausible to ask whether there is a constitutional right to be killed. Still, judicial activity is only half the story of legal involvement in the area of facilitating death.

During this period of judicial activity every state has also dealt with issues of death and dying by passing legislation,[98] and Congress has attempted to assure that the residents of every state learn what their options under state law are. The federal Patient Self-Determination Act[99] requires all hospitals (and some other health care institutions) that receive medicare or medicaid funding to inform each patient at the time of admission to the facility of their state's law with regard to advance directives for health care. State legislation about such so-called advance directives is the primary legislative response to the issues we are considering here.

Generally state legislation authorizes one or both of two kinds of patient advance planning for death, living wills and the appointment of health care representatives. Naturally, statutes differ from state to state, but they have many features in common. The Commissioners on Uniform State Laws adopted a Uniform Rights of the Terminally Ill Act in 1985[100] and replaced it with another act of the same name in 1989.[101] Seven states have adopted the 1989 act;[102] six others adopted and retain the 1985 act.[103]

Typical living will statutes authorize competent adults to sign a document (a living will) directing that life-prolonging procedures be withheld or withdrawn in certain circumstances; prescribe the effect that such documents are to have; provide immunities for those who act under the documents; provide penalties for various kinds of misconduct; contain miscellaneous provisions about the effects of using the documents on other matters, like insurance, tort suits, and homicide prosecutions; and declare that the statutes do not authorize euthanasia.[104]

The statutes are generally less helpful to persons who wish to control the manner and timing of their deaths than might be assumed. First, of course, the statutes apply only to cases of persons who execute a living will while they are competent. The statutes have no application to children, never-competent adults, and persons who, for one reason or another, never made a living will. All those cases remain for judicial resolution. In addition, the statutes are usually made inoperable during pregnancy, so that the living will of a pregnant woman will not be honored.[105]

The statutes do authorize competent persons to complete living wills. Often they provide a model form that the document might take, sometimes requiring that it be in substantially the statutory form.[106] This raises questions about how close to the statutory model a living will must be and what effect a noncomplying document will have. This ambiguity creates a trap for the unwary and hinders persons who want to personalize their living wills by providing details about their treatment preferences. Some statutes require living wills to meet other technical requirements, like being witnessed by a specified number of disinterested persons.[107]

If one has a valid living will, it becomes operative when one becomes qualified.[108] Under the Uniform Act a person becomes qualified when his attending physician has determined him to be in a terminal condition.[109] A terminal condition is defined as "an incurable and irreversible condition that, without the administration of life-sustaining treatment will . . . result in death within a relatively short time."[110] Some state statutes have more complicated and confusing definitions of terminal conditions.[111] All the statutes, however, require that the patient, in fact, be terminal, that is, dying, before life-prolonging treatment may be withheld or withdrawn.[112] Living wills do not apply to patients who are suffering horribly and simply seek release from life.

All definitions of terminal, of course, require some temporal relationship between the proposed cessation of life support and the time when the patient would die anyway. This is essential because everybody will die some time; the statutes must be fairly restrictive in order to avoid becoming suicide authorization acts. However, the necessity of defining terminal conditions in terms of time presents two problems. First, it again limits the use of living wills; indeed, that is its purpose. This demonstrates yet again the modest utility of living will statutes for persons who want to exercise control over their death.

Second, there is no good way to describe the time that is required. Three possibilities exist. Some statutes require death to be imminent before a patient may be considered terminal.[113] That approach essentially destroys any utility of a living will for the patient and defeats the purpose of living will legislation by refusing to allow life support to be withheld or withdrawn until the patient is already virtually dead.

A second approach adopts a specific time within which death would occur without treatment as the criterion for determining whether a patient is in a terminal condition.[114] For example, a patient could be said not to be in a terminal condition unless he would die within six months or one year. This approach is impossible to apply. Doctors simply cannot make accurate predictions about when patients will die. Moreover, adopting a specific time period exacerbates the arbitrariness of insisting that patients be in a terminal condition before their living will becomes effective. What sound legislative policy would support allowing an incompetent person to die if he had a year of life left, but not if he had 53 weeks?

The third approach is the one adopted in the Uniform Act. It provides that a patient is in a terminal condition if, without treatment, he will die in a relatively short time.[115] This is obviously a more sensible approach than either of the others. Nonetheless, the resort to a flexible system that depends upon physicians' judgments about what a relatively short time is only masks the arbitrariness of insisting that the patient's condition be terminal; it does not avoid the arbitrariness. Moreover, the need for discretion and judgment is a good reason not to try to resolve the death with dignity question through legislation. Legislation should reduce the likelihood that decisions will depend on who the decision maker is. If sensible decisions require discretionary decision making, then legislation should be avoided. What sense does it make to adopt a statute that provides, in essence, that it will only become operative when a reasonable person, who is not accountable to anybody, thinks that it becomes operative?

If a patient has a terminal condition and meets any other criteria for being qualified, then his living will becomes operative. Often that means that the patient's physician *may* withhold or withdraw life-supporting procedures.[116] The statutes usually do not require the physician to honor the patient's wishes.[117] The Uniform Act gives the patient more control by requiring a doctor who is unwilling to comply with the living will to transfer the patient to a different physician who will honor it.[118] Other statutes contain more cumbersome and less workable transfer requirements that permit a doctor who wishes to do so to easily avoid the transfer obligation.[119]

Living wills permit the withholding or withdrawal of life-prolonging or life-sustaining procedures. Obviously, the question of what constitutes a life-prolonging or life-sustaining procedure is of critical importance. The Uniform Act defines life-sustaining treatment as any medical procedure or intervention that "will serve only to prolong the process of dying."[120] This means that medical activity that both prolongs the process of dying and does something else, like alleviate pain, need not be withheld or withdrawn. The Act makes this clear by providing that it does not affect the physician's obligation "to provide treatment, including nutrition and hydration, for a patient's comfort care or alleviation of pain."[121]

This way of dealing with the provision of nutrition and hydration is quite interesting. Under the Uniform Act comfort care and pain relief must be provided. Nutrition and hydration must be provided when they are part of comfort care or necessary to relieve pain. Otherwise, they may be withheld or withdrawn. This is quite different from the approach in a few states, which simply do not permit the withholding or withdrawal of some kinds of treatment. The Kentucky statute, for example, specifically excludes medication, procedures to alleviate pain, and nutrition and hydration from its definition of life-prolonging procedures that may be withheld or withdrawn.[122] This means that nutrition and hydration must be provided even when they are not necessary for comfort care or relief of pain.

Definitions of life-prolonging procedures like Kentucky's render living wills statutes of very little use to patients. For example, excluding the administration of medication from the definition of life-prolonging procedures means that antibiotics must be provided to a qualified patient with a living will who develops pneumonia. Pneumonia, which has often been called "the old man's friend," may be killed, but the old man will not be allowed to die. Justice Welliver of the Missouri Supreme Court called his state's living wills statute, which is very similar to Kentucky's, a fraud on the people of Missouri.[123]

Living wills statutes, then, provide very little assistance to persons who want to make binding decisions about their own deaths while they are still in a position to do so. Other types of statutes may be more helpful. Many states now authorize persons to appoint another individual to make health care decisions, including decisions about withholding and withdrawing life support, for them. Even if a state has no statute specifically designed for that purpose, a statute that authorizes the creation of a durable power of attorney can accomplish the same thing. A power of attorney simply authorizes one person (who is called an "attorney in fact," to distinguish him from a lawyer, who is an attorney at law) to act on behalf of another. A durable power of attorney retains its validity even after the person who granted the power becomes incompetent. Thus, if a person appoints an attorney in fact for all purposes, or for health care purposes, under a durable power of attorney, the attorney in fact may make the same health care decisions for the person who appointed him that the person could make for himself if he were still competent.

Durable power of attorney statutes leave several problems unresolved. First, if a person has created a general durable power of attorney without reference to health care, there may be no reason to assume that he meant to turn medical decision making over to the attorney in fact. Therefore, to be useful, a durable power of attorney must specifically refer to health care.

Second, a court may appoint a guardian for an incompetent person. If the incompetent person also has an attorney in fact, somebody will have to decide whose decisions control in the event that the guardian and the attorney in fact disagree. The Uniform Durable Power of Attorney Act,[124] which has been adopted by twenty-six states and the District of Columbia,[125] gives the guardian authority to revoke the power of attorney,[126] thereby destroying the effectiveness of the patient's appointment of an attorney in fact. However, the patient may reduce the likelihood of this outcome by using the durable power of attorney to nominate his own future guardian. In most cases the court is supposed to honor the nomination.

The biggest problem with the durable power of attorney approach, however, is that, as we have seen, the law is not clear about how to resolve cases of decision making for incompetent persons. If a competent person made clear his wishes about withholding or withdrawing treatment and then became incompetent, his views would be honored to the extent that they did not exceed what state law will allow. Under *Cruzan* the states may insist on a very high level of proof of the person's desires, and, as noted, some states would not allow a person to refuse nutrition and hydration, at least not under their living wills statutes.

If a person did not make clear any preference other than that some other named person make decisions for him, it is not clear whether a state would have to honor the decisions of the named attorney in fact. In her separate opinion in *Cruzan*, Justice O'Connor suggested that states do have to honor such decisions.[127] However, it is not yet clear whether her view will prevail. Thus, a person cannot be sure that turning decision-making authority over to an attorney in fact will be successful, especially if the attorney in fact tries to do more than a state's living wills act would allow.

Some of the problems with the durable power of attorney approach are solved by statutes that authorize the appointment of health care representatives, persons specifically authorized to make health care decisions for the person who appointed them.[128] Obviously, there can be no doubt about whether a health care representative's authority applies to health care. Conflicts between a health care representative and a guardian may still arise unless the statute resolves them in advance. The most important questions, however, involve the scope of the health care representative's authority. Like an attorney in fact, a health care representative's authority cannot exceed a patient's own authority. Thus, health care representative legislation cannot avoid ultimate judicial resolution of questions about what treatments may be withheld or withdrawn.

A special problem can arise if a state's living will statute and its health care consent law appear to be inconsistent with each other. For example, in Indiana until 1994 the Living Wills Act precluded cessation of appropriate nutrition and hydration;[129] the Health Care Consent Law did not.[130] In a case involving a never-competent person who, of course, had never executed a living will or appointed a health care representative, the state Supreme Court allowed the patient's parents, acting as her health care representatives, to decline artificial nutrition and hydration on her behalf.[131] The question that remained was what would have happened in Indiana if a competent person appointed a health care representative and then became incompetent? The patient, while competent, could not have validly refused appropriate nutrition and hydration through a living will. Could he have accomplished the same end by appointing a health care representative? Good sense suggests that the answer should be yes. Why should a once-competent person be forced to endure a treatment that a never-competent person could avoid, and why should the nature of the treatment destroy the once-competent patient's decision-making authority? On the other hand, however, reaching that result obviously would frustrate the will of the legislature in drafting the living wills statute the way it did.

This dilemma points up a pervasive difficulty with legislative solutions to problems. Often a legislature will fail to advert to existing legislation on a subject when it enacts new legislation. This creates the possibility of inconsistent or conflicting treatments of a problem. If this happens even when the relationship between two statutes is obvious, as in the case of living will and health care representative laws, imagine how often it happens when the overlap is more subtle. If a legislature, caught up in the excitement of some perceived new threat from biomedical developments, decides to enter the field, it is important that it carefully review existing legislation before it acts and that it assure the consistency of all its legislation on a topic.

To date, legislation about withholding and withdrawing care has made modest progress in extending patients' opportunities to control the manner and timing of their deaths. It has not solved all the problems in the area, and it has not created a situation in which patients can feel secure that their wishes will be followed. Judicial and legislative developments since 1976 have certainly increased conversation about allowing patients to die. Whether they have had much impact on the actual practice of medicine and on the reality of patients' control of their own destinies is not so clear.

Assisted Suicide and Euthanasia

All of the judicial and legislative reforms to date have been in the direction of authorizing patients and their representatives to reject life-prolonging medical care and authorizing medical personnel to withhold or withdraw that care. The reforms have stopped short of authorizing anyone to take affirmative steps to shorten a patient's life. Indeed, typical living will statutes specifically note that they are not to be construed as authorizing euthanasia.[132]

Nonetheless, some affirmative acts to end a person's life may be far more merciful and consistent with human dignity than allowing that person to die of dehydration or to withstand unbearable suffering. Ought the law to authorize euthanasia or assisted suicide?

At the outset, we must note a problem of terminology, which reflects a problem of conception. "Euthanasia," which comes from the Greek meaning "good death," is used in different ways by different persons. Some would include withholding or withdrawing life-prolonging care within the definition of euthanasia, while others would not. Some would call withholding or withdrawing life support "passive euthanasia," to distinguish it from affirmative acts of killing, or "active euthanasia." Some would consider furnishing a person with the wherewithal to kill himself, knowing that he intended to do so, euthanasia, while others would call it assisting suicide.

For our purposes, we shall refer to providing a person with the tools to kill himself or instructions about how to do so as assisted suicide because in such situations the person who wishes to die inflicts the mortal "blow" upon himself. We shall refer to well-motivated affirmative acts by someone other than the person who dies to purposely bring about or hasten that person's death as euthanasia. The conceptual problem is immediately apparent: Has a physician who turns off a respirator or clamps a feeding tube performed an affirmative act to shorten another person's life, or merely withdrawn life support? Obviously, one can phrase the matter either way. Indeed, almost any action can be described either affirmatively as an act of commission or negatively as an act of ommission.

The problem is not merely semantic. If a doctor removes a respirator from a person who needs it to breathe and who could live on the respirator for months, the doctor really has shortened the person's life as surely as a doctor shortens the life of a suffering cancer patient with months to live if he administers a lethal injection to the patient. The recognition of this reality is what leads many persons to argue that it is impossible to distinguish killing from letting die, euthanasia from withholding or withdrawing life support, at least in the medical setting.[133] The obvious implication of this argument is that we must choose between authorizing all forms of death facilitation, including euthanasia, and authorizing none. Since we allow the removal of life support, we must allow euthanasia (and, of course, assisted suicide).

Despite the appealing logic of this position, it has not yet prevailed;[134] Oregon has authorized physician-assisted suicide in limited circumstances, but enforcement of its enactment has been enjoined.[135] Other similar state referenda have been defeated, and opposition to euthanasia and support for letting people die seem to share widespread public support, often from the same people. Obviously, something more than logic is at work here.

One can speculate about why most members of western societies find it relatively easy to support withholding and withdrawing care and so hard to support assisted suicide and euthanasia. Perhaps the stigma that attaches to ordinary suicide (an unhappy person jumping off a bridge or blowing his brains out) infects consideration of medically assisted suicide for suffering or dying patients. Perhaps the involvement of another person to *assist* the suicide or perform euthanasia makes the inadequacy of thinking about dying as an independent act of an autonomous will too obvious to permit continued self-deception. Perhaps the legacy of Nazi misuse of the concept of euthanasia, and fear that any use will inevitably start us on the slippery slope to genocide, convince people who, for some reason, do not think the slope gets slippery at the level of withholding and withdrawing care. Perhaps there really is a difference between omission and commission, between killing and letting die, even if it is a difference that eludes logical explanation.

For purposes of evaluating the legal system's ability to respond to bioethical problems, however, the existence of the widespread view that euthanasia and assisted suicide are more problematic than withholding or withdrawing care is more important than the reasons for that view. Given the widespread opposition to assisted suicide and euthanasia, what should the legal system's response be?

Clearly, the law should not recognize a constitutional right to commit suicide, to commit or undergo euthanasia, or to die. Euthanasia and assisted suicide share most of the characteristics that made constitutional adjudication an unsatisfactory response to the abortion problem. Like abortion, euthanasia and assisted suicide are characterized by problems that are highly fact specific and not susceptible to across-the-board resolution. Many of the relevant facts will be rapidly changing, scientific facts, beyond the ability of the judges to understand or to keep up. The area is beset by widely divergent, deeply held views that cannot be contained by a pronouncement from the Supreme Court. No constitutional text plausibly supports a relevant right, which means that the legitimacy of Supreme Court action recognizing such a right would be suspect. Questions of euthanasia and assisted suicide have nothing to do with the nature and structure of American government, the area of clearest Supreme Court power and expertise.

The judicial decisions about withholding and withdrawing care, which we discussed above, hint at the difficulties that will beset the courts if they recognize a broader constitutional right. The right will not be unlimited. Rights never are. The courts will have to articulate the scope and limits of the right, its importance in the pantheon of rights, the state interests that may conflict with it, and the procedures that may or must be devised to accommodate the right with the competing state interests. They will be unable to do any of these things satisfactorily because the constitutional roots of the right will be unclear or nonexistent, and because every factual situation that arises will resonate differently with different members of the court. The fiascos of New Jersey's and Massachusetts's approaches to the relatively easy problems of withholding and withdrawing care will be replayed and extended when the question is the harder one of euthanasia or assisted suicide; and the difficulty of drawing the line between killing and letting die will bog the courts down in a hopeless quagmire of unpersuasive distinctions. The Supreme Court was wise in *Cruzan* simply to assume the existence of a right and find that even if it existed, Missouri's restriction on it was acceptable. If forced to decide, the Court would be well advised to take advantage of the opening it left itself in *Cruzan* and deny the existence of a death-related constitutional right. Better still, it should simply refrain from considering cases on the issue at all.

Certainly, the Court has not yet committed itself to recognizing a constitutional right to die. As noted, it has simply assumed for the sake of argument a constitutional liberty interest in refusing life-prolonging artificial nutrition and hydration.

One of the most telling criticisms of *Roe v. Wade* is that its language is so loose and its rationale so fuzzy that it could be taken as support for finding a great many constitutional rights in areas far removed from abortion. One could easily say, as the New Jersey Supreme Court did in *Quinlan*, that if the right of privacy is broad enough to include a woman's decision whether to terminate her pregnancy, it must also be broad enough to include a person's right to decide whether to accept medical care, and by extension whether to accept continued life. After all, the burdens of an unwanted pregnancy and childbirth are surely less onerous than the burdens of an entire unwanted life.

One could say that, but one does not have to. In other areas the Court has refused to go where the logic of *Roe* seemed to push it, and we have known for many decades that "The life of the law has not been logic, it has been experience."[136] Surely, the experience with *Roe v. Wade* would not lead an intelligent Court to undergo the same kind of experience again.

The Supreme Court has plainly stepped away from *Roe*, and in *Cruzan* the majority was careful to distance itself from the suggestion that the right of privacy was at stake in a treatment removal case. If any constitutional right was at stake, it was a vague Fourteenth Amendment liberty interest. Such an interest, if it exists, can readily be defined not to include an interest in dying however one chooses. Moreover, the Court was careful in *Cruzan* to refrain from suggesting that the right at stake, if any, was a fundamental right. If there were a fundamental right at stake, a state could only justify infringing on the right to the extent that the infringement was necessary to a compelling state interest. If a right of lesser importance is involved, then a state infringement is constitutional as long as it bears a rational relationship to a legitimate state end. In the real world of constitutional law, state infringements on fundamental rights are almost never upheld; state infringements on lesser rights almost always are.

Thus, the Supreme Court is not committed to recognizing any constitutional right in the death facilitation area. If it does recognize a right, it may well stop short of including assisted suicide and euthanasia within it, and it will probably make the right easy to override. Thus, for the moment, at least, the Court is free to do what prudence suggests—refrain from resolving the euthanasia and assisted suicide questions by constitutional adjudication.

If federal constitutional adjudication would be an unwise institutional response to euthanasia and assisted suicide, state constitutional amendments, adopted by referenda, would be only slightly less so. State constitutional referenda would eliminate two of the problems with federal constitutional adjudication. They would provide a text that would give legitimacy and some bounds to the right they created; and they would be limited to whatever states adopted them, thereby making the costs of mistakes under them less than with a constitutional right that applied nationwide. The other problems with constitutional resolution of the problem—fact dependency, rapidly changing science, widespread disagreement, and the lack of subject matter about which courts can claim to have special expertise—would all remain.

Rejection of a constitutional approach leaves legislation as the only practical way to deal with the euthanasia-assisted suicide issue. A common law response is unsatisfactory because it provides too little conduct control, and such a response is difficult to imagine anyway. No one is going to win a tort suit against somebody for failing to kill him or furnish him with the means to kill himself. If two persons entered into a contract that bound one to kill the other under certain circumstances for a fee, it is inconceivable that a court would order the contract to be performed. Receiving damages for breach of the contract to kill would be unlikely, because the contract would probably violate public policy and because the size of the proper damage award would be speculative; if damages were awarded, they would probably be low, and they obviously would not accomplish the goals of the person who wanted to be killed.

An administrative response to euthanasia and assisted suicide is possible, but first a legislature would have to empower an agency to deal with the problem. Thus, there is no avoiding the need for legislative attention if the legal system is to consider the issues outside of a constitutional context.

At present, every state prohibits homicide, and at least thirty-three states prohibit assisted suicide.[137] Criminal legislation is the legal system's present response to these issues. Therefore, the questions become whether the criminal homicide statutes should be amended to remove criminal penalties from euthanasia and whether a state without an anti-assisted suicide statute should enact one, or a state with such a statute should repeal it.

These are difficult questions to answer. If one applies Professor Packer's prudential factors, discussed in chapter 2, one reaches the conclusion that euthanasia and assisted suicide should not be crimes. There is nothing close to universal agreement that these types of behavior are immoral. They involve conduct to which people are often driven by forces stronger than the deterrent efficacy of the criminal law. Our nation's history reveals that as a people we have no desire to imprison persons who commit these activities. The benefits to be gained from criminalization are insufficient to justify the costs of enforcement and prosecution. And criminalizing euthanasia and assisted suicide has the unwanted side effects of making criminals out of usually law-abiding citizens or creating a crime tariff that will drive persons seeking relief into the arms of "back alley mercy killers." Thus, it would seem that euthanasia and assisted suicide should not be subject to criminalization.

However, the question is not that easy. Nobody proposes repealing the basic criminal prohibitions against homicide. Therefore, if euthanasia is to be decriminalized, existing homicide statutes will have to be amended. It is extremely difficult to imagine drafting a statute that will really accomplish the ends of the legislature even if one could imagine that the members were in total agreement about what they wanted to accomplish. One of the reasons not to constitutionalize a right to die also suggests that we ought not try to legislate its equivalent: Cases are simply too complex and fact specific to permit one form of words to capture the richness of the situations that will arise.

In addition, decriminalizing euthanasia is different from decriminalizing abortion. No woman will ever suffer an abortion against her will because abortion is no longer a crime. The woman herself must seek an abortion in order to get one. Euthanasia, on the other hand, is practiced on one person by another in circumstances in which the person to be killed is often secluded from public awareness and in no physical or mental condition to protect himself. Thus, the symbolic act of "allowing" euthanasia runs some risk of abuse that the decriminalization of abortion does not. In a period of intense concern about containing the costs of health care this risk of abuse may be all too real.

Finally, while questions about euthanasia are interesting and affect some real persons, euthanasia is hardly one of the central issues facing our country. Moreover, one way or another, many persons surely do receive assistance in dying in ways more circumspect than those practiced by the highly visible "suicide doctor," Jack Kevorkian. The gains of decriminalizing euthanasia are simply too slight to expend precious legislative time and stir up intense public emotion on the matter. To let sleeping dogs lie remains one of the soundest of all bits of legal/political advice.

The same points are valid with regard to assisted suicide in states where it is already illegal. The game of decriminalization is simply not worth the candle. Where assisted suicide is not a crime, the prudential considerations against the use of the criminal sanction suggest that legislators should not vote to make it one. The result of this approach is that assisted suicide will be legal (but, of course, subject to ethical restraints and social pressures) in some states and illegal in others. That is good. If we, as a nation, are not sure how we feel about a practice, using the states as laboratories to help us work out our collective point of view is a useful way to avoid excesses and reduce the costs of mistakes. After all, there is little point in having fifty states if the laws of each of them must be the same.

One remaining legal response is possible. A legislature could adopt a statute that passed decision-making authority about euthanasia and/or assisted suicide to an administrative body. This could be an existing agency, like the state's Board of Health, or a new one. Authority could be assigned to one statewide body, again, like the Board of Health, or to several more local ones, like county hospital boards, or even individual hospital ethics committees. This too would not be a useful thing to do. As with any legislative response this approach would be expensive in terms of legislative time. Any authority to authorize euthanasia or assisted suicide would require decriminalization, with the attendant costs of unnecessary polarization of views that would attend any decriminalization efforts. The result of the process would be the creation of a bureaucratic mechanism to deal with a situation that manages to get dealt with reasonably well without serious legal involvement, much like cessation of treatment was dealt with before 1976. What our experience with withholding and withdrawing treatment should teach us is that the law has no mechanism to improve significantly on the status quo. Sometimes the best legal response to an issue is to do nothing. This seems to be one of those times.

Medical Futility

One of the consequences of open discussion of death and dying and the growing consensus that sometimes it is acceptable to allow a patient to die is that an increasing number of persons have begun to suggest that under some circumstances a person has an obligation to die.[138] To put it differently, they suggest that doctors have no obligation to try to keep a person alive if in the doctors' judgment the effort would be medically futile.[139] In this argument the focus shifts from concern with the patient's autonomous choice to refuse treatment to the physician's autonomous choice to refuse to treat.

Everyone agrees that physicians have no obligation to provide whatever treatment a patient may demand. Obviously, no physician has to put a cast on a patient's leg to treat a bruise, or, to provide a more plausible example, to prescribe antibiotics for a viral infection just because the patient thinks they will work and asks for them.[140] Thus, if a treatment is so plainly futile that no competent physician would resort to it, the patient's demand for the treatment cannot bind the doctor. The patient's freedom of choice ends at the limits of medical rationality.

This principle seems to apply to end-of-life decisions as well as to all others. Nothing is to be gained beyond making a fetish out of patient autonomy by trying to force physicians to treat the untreatable.

However, stopping or refusing to start life-prolonging treatment is different in some ways from refusing to cast a bruise or provide antibiotics for viral infections. Nobody with a viral infection can receive a benefit related to his infection from being treated with antibiotics; indeed, the inappropriate treatment can be harmful. No bruised leg can benefit from being placed in a cast. Resuscitation, the use of respirators, and other similar life-prolonging treatments, however, are useful to many patients who are in some stage of the same disease process as the person for whom the treatments are now deemed futile. In asking a doctor to continue the respirator, the patient or surrogate decision maker is not asking the doctor to do something crazy. He is simply asking the doctor to do something sensible for a longer period of time than the doctor thinks is sensible. This is an important distinction for two reasons. First, it suggests that a doctor who ceases treatment because he thinks it is futile is more likely to have made a mistake than a doctor who refuses to comply with a demand to prescribe antibiotics to a patient with a viral infection. Second, because of the inherently sensible nature of what the patient or his representative is asking for, those around the patient and strangers who learn about the case are much less likely to accept the doctor's contrary conclusion.

Other reasons also suggest caution in adopting the analogy to never-indicated treatments in the dying patient context. This is death we are talking about. A decision not to treat is quite final. In the more typical case discussed above, in which the patient wants to be allowed to die, we have taken the patient's choice to be sufficient to overcome the normal preference for erring on the side of life. Here, however, the patient's preference and the presumption in favor of life both point in the same direction. It is hard to see what could justify overriding them both.

Presumably, the primary reason to override the patient's wishes and the preference for life is to avoid waste. Doctors, hospital beds, and all other parts of the medical system are limited resources. It does seem a shame to use them to no good end. Moreover, almost everyone agrees that medical care costs our country more than it should. Again, spending money on unnecessary, useless medical care is difficult to justify.

I have argued elsewhere that considering the impact of a bioethical decision on the society as a whole is inappropriate because it will always result in decisions against the poor, the powerless, and the despised.[141] We will save society's health care dollars by refusing to provide futile care for Homeless Joe, not for Donald Trump. On the other hand, significant negative impacts on real, identifiable persons should be considered.[142] If there really are too few beds to go around, it makes sense to take a bed from a person whose treatment is futile and give it to someone with a realistic chance to recover. It also makes sense to consider the real impact on a physician of having to provide futile care. If providing the care will reduce the physician from five to four hours of sleep a night and prey on his mind to the extent that it demoralizes him and reduces his effectiveness as a physician, those are real costs that should not be ignored. The best decision about whether to stop or refuse to begin futile care should be reached by balancing the real interests of all identifiable persons who will be affected in a significant way by the decision, and then following the course of conduct that will, on balance, do the least harm.

Whether one agrees with that conclusion or not, the question remains, what can and should be the legal system's response to medical futility?

Any extreme response would obviously be ill-advised. The competing values of preservation of life, patient autonomy, professional autonomy, just distribution of scarce resources, and cost containment cannot be resolved once and for all by an across-the-board pronouncement from the Supreme Court or a legislature. What is needed is nuanced, fact-sensitive decision making that rebalances the competing interests in each case based on the particular facts of the cases, evolving technology, and our developing sense of ethics. There is no point in trying seriously to control the conduct of doctors because we, as a society, do not yet know what we want doctors to do. What we need is a response that places primary reliance on the medical expertise and ethical sensitivity of physicians, while retaining enough legal oversight to minimize the risks of abuse. The common law tort system can accomplish those goals.

Medical malpractice law makes physicians responsible for the reasonableness of their behavior. It remits basic medical decision-making authority to doctors, but it holds them accountable if their decisions are unreasonable, that is, negligent. The malpractice system requires physicians to conform their behavior to that of other members of their own medical specialty.[143] If disagreement exists within a given medical community, then a doctor may act in accordance with the practices of any significant school of thought.[144]

Before a doctor may be held liable for malpractice, a patient must have been injured and must succeed in proving that the injury was caused by the doctor's negligence. Ordinarily, expert testimony from other members of the doctor's speciality is required both to establish negligence and causation.[145] Thus, if questions of futility are left to the malpractice system, the likelihood of a doctor being held liable for behavior that any respectable segment of the professional community would support is small. Even if a doctor is held liable, the doctor will not bear the resulting loss personally but will pass it on to his insurance company and, through it, ultimately to the consumers of medical care. A common law response, thus, does not pose much of a threat to physicians.

On the other hand, the common law response does provide some protection to patients. Decades of experience with what doctors like to call the "malpractice crisis" have demonstrated that even the threat of litigation does deter doctors from behaving in ways that the courts are likely to deem socially unacceptable. That is the point of the oft-repeated claim that malpractice law leads to the practice of "defensive medicine."[146] The threat alone reduces the risk of abuse. Moreover, doctors' behavior is overseen by others with incentives to minimize abuse. If a patient is in a hospital, the hospital will police the doctor's behavior to protect itself from liability. Malpractice insurers also can provide some quality control to further reduce the risks of abuse.

If, despite everything, a doctor does negligently fail to provide treatment that would not really have been futile, the patient's family will receive compensation for their loss and the doctor will be exposed to the possibility of professional discipline. Thus, a common law response backed up by existing disciplinary mechanisms provides a desirable balance in the futility cases. It remits primary decision-making authority to the experts and protects physician autonomy, while protecting patients, minimizing the risks of abuse, and remaining flexible so that different responses are possible as facts of cases, technology, and values change. No reason exists to seriously consider pursuing more extreme responses like the ones the law has made to other death and dying questions.

SERIOUSLY ILL NEWBORNS

The difficulty of resolving hard bioethical problems by intrusive legal responses is illustrated yet again by the law's efforts to deal with the poignant problems raised by the birth of children with serious birth defects. Some defects are incompatible with long life. Many are compatible with long but severely impaired life. If a child with a defect needs medical or surgical intervention to survive, questions arise about whether the intervention must be provided, and about who may make that decision.

At first blush these cases seem simply to be additional examples of issues we have discussed before. They raise the question of whether parents or guardians may reject life-prolonging treatment for patients who have never been competent. However, certain features of the defective newborn cases may require further thought about at least some of them.

Some cases involve babies who will live for many years if treatment is provided. Those cases, which involve patients with good prognoses for length, if not quality, of life, are obviously different from cases about incompetent persons with terminal conditions. In addition, children with some serious physical defects can achieve full intellectual capacity if they survive. Thus, some defective newborn cases are similar to ordinary medical-care-for-children cases; they involve patients who have never *yet* been competent, not patients who have never been and will never become competent.

Ordinarily the law requires the consent of a parent to authorize medical treatment for a child.[147] Certain exceptions exist,[148] but in the usual situation treating a child without a parent's consent would constitute a battery on the child.[149] When the result of failing to treat will certainly be death, however, the absolute dominance of the parents may be questioned.

Early cases that challenged parental control did not involve seriously ill newborns. Rather, they involved parents who rejected conventional cancer therapy for their children in favor of treatment with laetrile, vitamins, and nutritional therapy,[150] and parents who refused surgery to correct serious malformations in their children[151] or who rejected the blood transfusions that were necessary to make recommended surgery acceptably safe.[152] The cases split on the question of whether parental refusals could be overridden, some emphasizing the importance of parental rights and family autonomy,[153] and others emphasizing the importance of doing what was best for the child and not making the child a martyr to the parent's peculiar ideas.[154]

The split reveals the problem. Deciding about medical care for children in the face of parental opposition is a classic example of the need to mediate between right and right. On the one hand, following medical advice will almost always be the wisest course in terms of the physical well-being of the child. It is difficult to justify exposing a child to suffering and death because he had the bad luck to be born to parents with bizarre ideas. And it is hard to see why simply being a parent should give one person the power to ruin or terminate the life of another. On the other hand, however, our country is based upon a plurality of ideas and the rejection of mandatory orthodoxy. What seems bizarre to the majority may in fact turn out to be better than the conventional view. Parents almost always have their children's best interests at heart, and in a world full of uncertainty, why shouldn't their loving preferences be honored?

Moreover, the child must live somewhere, and almost always that means with the parents and in their community. Therefore, overriding the parents' wishes for the child's physical well-being may not be best for the child if psychological and social well-being are added to the equation. Conversely, a child may well be better off alive in a less than optimal social and psychological situation than dead. The parents' interests and the complexity of considering the full range of the child's interests suggest that accommodation, not choosing one set of values that always must prevail, is the prudent approach to issues of medical care for children.

In the case of seriously impaired newborns, these themes are played out in the starkest terms. Here, if the parents refuse to agree to treatment, the child will die. One would have to envision a pretty hideous life to conclude comfortably that living would be a fate worse than death. On the other hand, nobody is better situated than the child's parents to think about those alternatives from the vantage point of loving concern for the child. But, the parents will have to bear the brunt of the burdens of caring for the child if it lives; therefore, they have a conflict of interest, and we are uneasy about accepting their choices. Again, however, the parents are persons too. Is it so clear that their interests in living a decent life are not entitled to some consideration? And who is better situated than the parents to consider the interests of other persons, like the sick child's siblings, whose needs are also arguably relevant? One wants to throw up one's hands in dismay.

When problems are this hard and involve so much that seems right on both sides, the one response that cannot possibly be sound is to choose an across-the-board solution that always prefers one set of interests to the other—a choice that always opts for treatment, or one that always opts for parental choice.

During the 1980s the national administration tried to impose a view that always resolved questions in favor of treatment. Its efforts were not successful in either legal or practical terms.

A highly publicized case that arose in Bloomington, Indiana, piqued federal interest.[155] A baby, who became known as Baby Doe, was born with Down's syndrome and esophogeal atresia, a condition that prevents food from reaching the infant's stomach. Without surgical repair, an easy procedure, the baby would never be able to eat, and he would starve to death. With surgery, the baby could expect a long (although probably shorter than average) life. He would be mentally retarded, but the degree of retardation could not be predicted. He would have the characteristic appearance of a person with Down's syndrome, and he would have a greater than normal risk of heart disease and leukemia. The parents, who had no advance warning that their child would be other than normal, received information about the child's prognosis in an emotionally charged atmosphere immediately after the child's birth. The obstetrician, who provided them with their first information, presented a very bleak prognosis, in accordance with his social philosophy. The pediatrician, who entered the scene a bit later, attempted to impose his strongly interventionist views. The parents decided not to authorize surgery. After extensive, if rushed litigation, the Indiana Supreme Court upheld the parents' decision,[156] and the baby died before a hearing in the United States Supreme Court could be sought.

The Reagan administration, which generally opposed federal intervention and extensive government regulation, decided that the result in the Baby Doe case was intolerable and should not recur. Not surprisingly, no federal statute specifically governed withholding medical care from seriously ill newborns. However, the administration took the position that an existing statute that had been drafted for entirely different purposes was applicable. Section 504 of the Rehabilitation Act of 1973[157] was designed to prevent discrimination against handicapped persons. It provided, "No otherwise qualified handicapped individual . . . shall, solely by reason of his handicap, . . . be subjected to discrimination under any program or activity receiving Federal financial assistance." The administration asserted that if a hospital that received federal financial aid (as almost all hospitals do), allowed a baby to die without the performance of lifesaving measures, that hospital had discriminated against an "otherwise qualified handicapped individual," even if the baby's parents refused to consent to the intervention. Acting on that interpretation, the Department of Health and Human Services issued regulations designed to require hospitals to assure that all future affected newborns receive treatment.[158]

The so-called Baby Doe regulations required hospitals to post notices stating that section 504 prohibits discrimination on the basis of handicap and that "nourishment and medically beneficial treatment . . . should not be withheld from handicapped infants solely on the basis of their present or anticipated mental or physical impairments."[159] The notices had to inform people of a 24-hour toll free number at DHHS for reporting perceived violations and promise confidentiality for those who made reports.[160] Once a report was made, a team from DHHS could appear at the hospital and demand expedited access to the hospital's records about the baby and obtain an expedited restraining order that required that the baby be treated.[161] The regulations also required state agencies to develop procedures to assure the treatment of handicapped infants.[162]

The regulations were absurdly one-sided and intrusive. They created the specter and the reality of "Baby Doe Squads" arriving at hospitals and launching emergency investigations on the basis of anonymous tips while the hospital's efforts to treat its patients were disrupted. They also attempted to require state agencies with limited resources to use those resources in one way, without regard for the impact of doing so on the agencies' ability to carry out their other, also health related, functions.

The Supreme Court struck the regulations down on the ground that they exceeded the authority that section 504 gave to the Secretary of DHHS.[163] The Court of Appeals had held that section 504 does not apply to treatment decisions about handicapped newborns.[164] The Supreme Court did not go that far.

Instead, the plurality opinion took two main positions: First, section 504 only prohibits discrimination by recipients of federal assistance against "otherwise qualified handicapped individuals." If there is any discrimination in Baby Doe cases, no evidence suggests that it is discrimination by recipients of federal funds. Any discrimination that exists is discrimination by the babies' parents in withholding their consent to treatment, not by hospitals. Moreover, without parental consent or a substitute for it, the babies are not "otherwise qualified."[165] Second, the reporting and enforcement regulations have nothing to do with discrimination. Rather, they are a federal mandate to the states to use their resources in a particular way. Requirements of federalism preclude that in the absence of clear Congressional intent.[166]

Both the Court of Appeals' and the Supreme Court's approaches teach an important lesson about legislation. While it is sometimes possible to twist an existing statute to serve a novel and legislatively unintended end, doing so is seldom a very good idea. A statute designed for one purpose may not be readily adaptable to another. Judicial nullification of the attempted extension seems both likely and appropriate. When the executive branch attempts to use a statute designed for one purpose for an entirely different purpose, it is attempting to avoid the exercise of the democratic process in resolving the new problem. Therefore, judicial restraint in the face of the popular will is neither called for, nor likely to be exercised. When new problems arise, new legislation that addresses the novel questions should be enacted, if legislation is an appropriate response to the problems at all.

In fact, Congress did eventually enact legislation specifically designed to deal with the Baby Doe issue. In 1984 Congress amended the Child Abuse Prevention and Treatment Act in an effort to assure the treatment of seriously handicapped newborns.[167] The Act imposes requirements that states must meet in order to obtain federal funding for child abuse prevention and treatment programs under the Social Security Act. The 1984 amendments added requirements related to treatment of handicapped newborns.

The amendments define withholding medically indicated treatment as the failure to respond to an infant's life-threatening conditions by providing treatment (including appropriate nutrition, hydration, and medication) which, in the treating physician's reasonable medical judgment, will be most likely to be effective in ameliorating or correcting all such conditions, *except* that the term does not include failure to provide treatment (other than appropriate nutrition, hydration, and medication) to an infant when in the physician's reasonable medical judgment (1) the infant is chronically and irreversibly comatose; (2) the provision of treatment would (a) merely prolong dying, (b) not be effective in ameliorating or correcting all the infant's life-threatening conditions, or (c) otherwise be futile in terms of the survival of the infant; or (3) the provision of treatment would be "virtually futile" in terms of survival, and treatment under the circumstances would be inhumane.[168]

The amendments then required states, as a condition of getting funding for child abuse prevention and treatment, to set up a program to respond to reports of medical neglect, including withholding of medically indicated treatment. The program must provide for coordination, prompt notice of suspected cases, and authority under state law to pursue legal remedies.[169] The Secretary of DHHS was required to publish regulations to implement the requirements and model guidelines for the state programs.[170]

This approach makes no sense. It proceeds from two premises—that non-treatment of handicapped newborns is a form of child abuse, and that there is a problem of inappropriate nontreatment that is so big that it warrants federal intervention. The first premise is highly debatable. Letting a seriously ill newborn die bears little resemblance to the kind of child beating and sexual imposition that one normally thinks of as child abuse. No reason exists to preclude a state from obtaining resources to combat conventional child abuse unless that state is also willing to tackle a different problem in the way the federal government suggests.

The second premise is simply wrong. As the Supreme Court plurality noted in striking down the original Baby Doe regulations, there is no evidence that hospitals are letting babies die in any significant number.[171] An occasional parent may refuse to consent to care. When that happens, hospitals usually seek judicial clarification of their obligations. In any event, occasional lapses by parents is hardly a reason to impose onerous burdens on states, and through them, on hospitals. Not only are the amendments shooting a cannon at a gnat, but also they attempt to hide their highly controversial intrusion into parental decision making by directing their requirements at hospitals and states.

The amendments are unsound in other ways as well. They are either overly intrusive or totally insignificant. Their definition of medically indicated treatment depends upon reasonable medical judgment, which is defined in the regulations the Secretary adopted, as the judgment a reasonably prudent physician would make.[172] They also modify their requirements about nutrition, hydration, and medication by use of the word, "appropriate."[173] Focus on reasonable medical judgment and appropriateness may provide a gigantic loophole for hospitals and states to use if they want to justify nontreatment in a particular case, or may simply be a trap for unwary hospitals if a federal bureaucrat interprets the terms in light of the apparent intent of the legislation to require aggressive treatment in every case. The intrusive possibilities appear likely, since the amendments seem to require that nutrition, hydration, and medication be provided even to chronically and irreversibly comatose infants, a reading that is specifically reinforced in the appendix to the Secretary's regulations.[174] Finally, the use of meaningless terms such as "virtually futile" again either invites gross overregulation or offers the promise of nullification of the legislature's intention.

Efforts to date reveal that federal legislation, even legislation specifically addressed to the issue of treatment for handicapped newborns, fails. Several reasons for the failure exist. First, there is no public consensus around which to build a statute. That is why the statute that finally emerged is vague and self-contradictory. Second, legislation is too blunt an instrument to deal with the issues involved, given their factual variability. Third, the statute that finally emerged is too indirect to be effective in achieving its goals—trying to get at a problem of family and medical decision making by attaching strings to state child abuse funding. The reason for the indirect nature of the response is that handicapped newborn issues are so private and local in their nature that Congress had no other basis to get at them. Perhaps more direct state legislation could be more effective. Fourth, there was no need for legislation in the first place. One dramatic case that some people think was wrongly decided is not sufficient warrant to crank up the vast legislative machine. Handicapped newborn cases can best be dealt with at the lowest and most fact-sensitive legal level, through case by case adjudication without resort to the Constitution, without resort to the criminal law, without resort to legislation, and without any legal consideration at all except when the consensus of those involved in a case breaks down so that somebody insists on legal involvement.

When courts must decide, reasonable persons will disagree about what the best decision in any particular case will be. One possibly attractive approach would be to follow the path that does as good a job as possible of serving the law's normal medical law policies while taking account of the special reality of the child's condition. That approach would note the law's emphasis on patient autonomy and would maximize the child's opportunity to achieve autonomy, in cases where that is factually possible. Under this approach a court should always order treatment for a child with a reasonable chance of achieving autonomy (unless, perhaps, the treatment is so hideous that it shocks the conscience). For example, courts should always require treatment for children with spina bifida.

If a child does not have a reasonable chance of achieving autonomy, then a court should fall back onto medical law's secondary goal—the provision of good medical care. If doctors agree on a course of treatment as medically indicated, the court should require it. Parents have no independent right to injure or kill their children.

If a child has no reasonable chance to achieve autonomy, and if there is a legitimate split among physicians about what good medical care requires, then no reason to intervene exists. A court should follow the parents' preference.

Regardless of whether one adopts this substantive model for decision making, the important point is that all decisions should be based on the facts of the particular case. The limits of the law's ability and the lack of a pressing social problem counsel the avoidance of any more intrusive approach.

CONCLUSION

Since at least 1976 issues of death and dying have captured the imagination of the public and the attention of ethicists and legal institutions. Public and scholarly ethical attention may have contributed to increasing the humanity of treatment for persons at the end of life. But twenty years of statutes, cases, and claims about rights seem to have been a tempest in a teapot that have contributed little, if anything, to improving persons' lives or deaths. This is because these are the kinds of issues for which the law, especially in its more intrusive modes, is unsuited—issues of intense moral controversy, involving almost infinite factual variability and rapidly and constantly changing scientific facts.

SEVEN

Controlling Research

Administrative Law, Human Subjects, and the Power of the Purse

Medical advances do not just happen. Despite occasional examples of serendipity most developments, like the ones we have been exploring in this book, are the results of painstaking and very deliberate research. Biomedical research presents the legal system with two major problems: It is expensive, and it may be dangerous. In a world of limited resources somebody has to decide both which kinds of research and which specific research projects to pursue. In addition, somebody must decide which research is too dangerous in the abstract, or as compared to its potential benefits, to go forward, and what safeguards to impose on permitted research.

While the role of administrative agencies in responding to the issues we have discussed so far has been relatively slight, administrative agencies have been the dominant legal institutions involved in the funding and regulation of research. As discussed in chapter 1, administrative law is law made by relatively unaccountable appointed officials who have expertise in the area under their control. In theory these officials may proceed relatively informally, and they may both make rules and adjudicate.

SETTING THE RESEARCH AGENDA

Research is expensive. Private foundations and corporations can fund and carry out research, but the United States has decided, as a political matter, that we need more research than the private sector will produce. Therefore, most biomedical research is funded by the federal government.

The questions of how much money to spend on research and what kinds of research to support are, quite properly, political questions. We elect representatives to decide questions that have no inherently right answers, like how much money to spend on research as opposed to highways or defense; how much to spend on biomedical research as opposed to research in physics or sociology; how much to spend on basic and how much on applied research; and how much to spend on each of an almost infinite number of worthy ends—cure versus prevention, AIDS versus birth defects, and so forth.

After Congress has established general levels of research funding and made very general assignments of support to various kinds of research, administrative agencies decide which specific research projects to fund. Biomedical research is supported by many different agencies, including the Department of Energy and the Department of Defense, but most support for research of this type comes from the Department of Health and Human Services and its subsidiaries, such as the National Institutes of Health.

Typically, an individual or an institution that wants to do federally funded research prepares an extensive and detailed research grant application, which it then submits to a potential funding source within the government. An officer of the granting agency assigns the application to a so-called study section for evaluation. Study sections are comprised of distinguished scientists with expertise in the general area of the grant application. Members of the study section prepare a written evaluation of the proposal, assign it a priority score, and make a recommendation about its proposed budget. The agency then considers all pending applications in terms of the study section evaluations, the needs of the agency, and available resources, and makes a recommendation to the Secretary of DHHS about whether and at what rate to fund the proposal. The Secretary normally follows these recommendations.[1]

This system of so-called peer review is occasionally criticized on several grounds. One obvious objection is that the experts who review grant applications are in some sense competitors of the persons whose applications they are reviewing; thus, conflict of interest is a problem. Another potential criticism is that decision making by established experts inevitably discriminates against young investigators, whose reputations are not yet established; against new or small institutions that lack the most advanced equipment and research support; and against proponents of maverick projects which might challenge well-entrenched ideas but which might also hold out the most exciting prospects for major breakthroughs.

These criticisms, while valid, do not seem very telling. The conflict of interest objection is a special example of the well-known phenomenon of "capture." The only persons with enough expertise to make informed decisions are the persons the administrative scheme is supposed to regulate. This problem pervades administrative law. For example, only doctors know enough about medicine to regulate it, but allowing them to do so means that the medical profession is regulating itself, which is probably not a very good idea.

Nonetheless, in the peer review setting the problem does not seem very serious. First, research grants are primarily designed to promote research, not to regulate researchers. Second, the study sections are not adopting rules that favor their group (researchers) over the rest of us. They are choosing among applicants from within their group. Third, any conflicts of interest between study section members and applicants are attenuated; study section members may not participate in decisions in which they have a direct conflict of interest.[2] And fourth, study section members, who are usually persons of distinction, often have enough grants to satisfy their needs, so that conflicts with applicants are even more attenuated than they would otherwise be.

Objections to the peer review system on the ground that it is inherently conservative are really objections to government funding of science. One can hardly imagine a system in which the proper thing for the government to do would be to spend taxpayers' money on wild-eyed proposals from unheard of investigators at ill-equipped institutions. The present system does include special funding opportunities for investigators who are members of minority groups.[3] In addition, Congress requires the inclusion of women and minority group members as subjects in clinical research,[4] and it sometimes makes funds available to study special health problems of politically underrepresented groups, like programs directed against sickle cell anemia, a genetic disease that mostly affects black persons.[5] Moreover, the scientists who sit on study sections are in the business of seeking breakthroughs and are probably more receptive to far-reaching ideas than a group of disinterested bureaucrats would be. One may well quarrel with a political judgment that one thinks allocates too little money to a perceived need, but a general criticism of the granting process as too conservative must be dismissed as a plea for fiscal imprudence.

Disappointed grant applicants seldom seek judicial review of decisions not to fund their proposals. If an applicant does sue, the time and effort devoted to preparing the grant and other intangible losses that accompany the denial will be enough to obtain a hearing for the applicant.[6] However, the agency's decision to deny funding will be upheld unless the agency acted in violation of the Constitution, its statutory mandate, or its own procedures.[7] An applicant's victory in the courts is extremely unlikely. This makes sense, because if litigation to overturn negative grant decisions were easy to win, such litigation would be frequent and would involve the courts in deciding issues they lack the ability to understand, thus undermining the entire purpose of the peer review system of judgment by experts.

ASSURING THE SAFETY OF RESEARCH

Some biomedical research is dangerous. It may create risks to human or animal research subjects or to the environment, or it may produce knowledge that is dangerous or that can lead to dangerous applications or misapplications. The legal system could respond to the potential dangers of research simply by allowing persons who suffer research-caused injuries to seek compensation through lawsuits, but that is an inadequate response. Research that poses dangers to the environment or to society at large cannot be adequately regulated by private damage awards. Some injuries to private individuals are too serious to tolerate even if compensation is available, and some dignitary injuries cannot be adequately redressed by after-the-fact compensation. Some broader response is required.

The trick in crafting broad responses to social problems, of course, is to avoid making them too broad and draconian. In the area of biomedical research, the law has attempted to provide a measured response through administrative controls. This approach, which has largely been successful, can be illustrated by discussing the law's response to the use of human subjects in research.

Research with Human Subjects

Protection of human research subjects did not attract much systematic attention until the world was shocked by experiments carried out under the auspices of the Nazi regime in Germany. Shortly after the revelation of those atrocities, reports of grossly inappropriate uses of human subjects in the United States dispelled any notion that it couldn't happen here. For example, in what are probably the two most widely reported examples of the abuse of human subjects in the United States, patients at the Jewish Chronic Disease Hospital in Brooklyn, New York, were injected with live cancer cells without even being told what they were receiving,[8] and black residents of Tuskegee, Alabama, were denied antibiotic treatment for syphilis they thought was being treated so that investigators could monitor the natural history of the disease.[9] As these examples illustrate, research with human subjects may expose the subjects to danger, may threaten their dignity and autonomy by dealing with them without their voluntary and informed consent, or both.

Abuses of human subjects led to the formulation of several highly influential declarations of ethical principles governing research with human subjects,[10] and eventually, in the United States, to the adoption of regulations to govern the activity. The major regulations are those of the Department of Health and Human Services, which govern research at institutions that receive federal research support,[11] and those of the Food and Drug Administration, which govern the development of new drugs.[12] For our purposes it will be sufficient to consider the DHHS regulations.

With certain exceptions the regulations apply to all research involving human subjects that is conducted, supported, or regulated by DHHS or by any other agency of the United States government that makes them applicable to research it conducts, supports, or regulates.[13] The exceptions are for research in which serious risks to human beings are not present, such as research that maintains confidentiality and uses previously collected information or specimens,[14] and research about the relative merits of different instructional techniques.[15] "Research" means "systematic investigation . . . designed to develop or contribute to generalizable knowledge."[16] "Human subject" means a living person about whom an investigator, conducting research, obtains data through interacting or intervening with the person, or obtains identifiable private information.[17]

The regulations protect human subjects of research through an ingenious system that creates and passes authority to local decision-making bodies that are subject to federal oversight and that gives those bodies minimal substantive guidance about the limits of acceptable research. The regulations require each institution to appoint an Institutional Review Board (IRB) that must approve any proposed use of human subjects before the research can be funded.[18] Each IRB must have at least five members; at least one must be a scientist, and at least one must be a nonscientist; at least one member must come from outside the institution; membership must be diverse with regard to expertise and to race, gender, cultural background, and sensitivity to community attitudes; it must include persons with competence to evaluate research in terms of institutional commitments, regulations, and law;[19] and if the IRB regularly considers research that involves vulnerable populations such as children or prisoners, consideration is to be given to appointing someone with knowledge and experience in working with those subjects.[20] The IRB is allowed to consult with outside experts when a proposal exceeds the expertise of the IRB's members.[21]

All research proposals to DHHS and other cooperating agencies must be submitted to the sponsoring institution's IRB.[22] In deciding whether to approve the research, the IRB is to consider eight criteria, six involving the proposed research itself, and two having to do with informed consent. For research to be approved, (1) risks to subjects must be minimized; (2) risks to subjects must be reasonable in relation to anticipated benefits to them, if any, and in relation to the importance of the knowledge that the research may reasonably be expected to produce; (3) selection of subjects must be equitable; (4) when appropriate, data must be monitored to assure the subjects' safety; (5) when appropriate, privacy and confidentiality must be protected; (6) additional safeguards must be taken to protect especially vulnerable subjects; (7) informed consent must be sought; and (8) informed consent must be documented.[23]

Of these requirements, only those about seeking and documenting informed consent are substantially fleshed out in the regulations. IRB approval of a research proposal requires that informed consent be *sought* from each subject or the subject's legally authorized representative.[24] No investigator may use a subject, however, unless the investigator actually *obtains* that informed consent.[25] The investigator must seek consent in circumstances that provide adequate opportunity for the subject to decide whether to consent and that minimize the risk of coercion or undue influence.[26] The information must be given in language understandable to the subject or representative.[27] It may not include any exculpatory language.[28] In order for a consent to be adequately informed, the information presented to the subject or representative must include the following elements:

(1) A statement that the study involves research; explanations of its pur-

poses, the expected duration of the subject's participation, and the procedures to be followed; and identification of any experimental procedures.

(2) A description of any reasonably foreseeable risks or discomforts to the subject.

(3) A description of any reasonably expected benefits of the research to the subject or others.

(4) Disclosure of any appropriate alternative treatments or procedures that might be advantageous to the subject.

(5) A description of the amount of confidentiality about the subject that will be maintained.

(6) An explanation of compensation and treatment plans available for injury from research that involves more than minimal risk.

(7) Information about whom to contact about questions or treatment.

(8) A statement that participation is voluntary, that refusal to participate will not involve any penalty or loss of benefits the subject is entitled to, and that the subject may discontinue participation at any time without penalty or loss of such benefits.[29]

In addition, when appropriate, one or more of the following items must also be provided:

(1) A statement that the procedure may involve unforeseeable risks.

(2) A statement of anticipated circumstances under which the investigator may terminate the subject's participation without regard to the subject's consent.

(3) Information about any additional costs to the subject that may result from participating in the research.

(4) Explanation of the consequences of the subject's decision to withdraw from the research and procedures for orderly termination of the subject's participation.

(5) A statement that significant new findings that may affect the subject's willingness to continue to participate will be provided to the subject.

(6) The approximate number of subjects involved in the study.[30]

In most circumstances a signed consent form is required to document the fact that the necessary information has been provided and that the subject or the subject's legal representative has consented to participate.[31]

In comparison to the detailed and specific requirements for informed consent, the criteria for evaluating the acceptability of research, assuming that the subjects consent, are quite vague and open-ended. The mere existence of the criteria, however, makes the crucial point: some research is simply unacceptable, even if individuals agree to act as subjects. There are limits to what persons may agree to have done to themselves and limits to the kind of activities society will tolerate, even if all the participants are willing ones. This central feature of the regulations reflects multiple interests—the interest of the nation in not having uncivilized things done in its name or under it auspices; the interest in avoiding injuries, even when doing so requires that people be protected from themselves; and the interest in the equitable selection of research subjects, avoiding the overuse of poor persons and others with reduced ability to make unconstrained choices. It is, thus, a manifestation of an interesting complex of paternalistic, egalitarian, and virtue-based views that makes plain the inadequacy of a simple ethic of individual autonomy for the resolution of bioethical issues.

The criteria themselves are not very enlightening. Basically, they require the risks of research to be reasonable and to be no greater than necessary to accomplish the purpose of the research; confidentiality; and equitable selection of subjects.[32] In assessing the reasonableness of risks, the IRB is not to consider possible long-range consequences of applying knowledge gained from the research.[33] Thus, the regulations make it clear that they are regulations about protecting the *human subjects* of research, not about passing judgment on the social desirability of pursuing certain lines of inquiry. This is quite appropriate. IRBs have no expertise in general matters of social policy and no accountability or legitimacy that would justify their taking positions on such issues.

The regulations, by addressing only issues of subject safety, also make plain that the job of IRBs is not to evaluate the scientific merit of research proposals. The distinction between assessment of risks and evaluation of scientific merit is, however, easier to state than to apply. The regulations themselves require the reasonableness of risks to be determined in comparison to anticipated benefits of the research.[34] Indeed, it is difficult to see how else it could be evaluated. The potential benefits of the research, however, are partly determined by the scientific merit of the proposal. Thus, some consideration of scientific merit is inevitable. Nonetheless, the basic point remains: If research is not dangerous, or if risks are adequately protected against, an IRB is not to withhold its approval on the ground that the members of the IRB are not favorably impressed by the research proposal or do not think it should be funded.

The approach adopted by the DHHS regulations is generally sensible, and it works remarkably well. Nevertheless, the regulations do have several faults. First, by assigning decision-making authority to committees appointed by each institution that seeks federal funding, the regulations create a level of decentralization that could lead to uneven decision making from one IRB to another. This turns out not to be a big problem, however, because IRB approval is not binding on the funding agency. IRB decisions are centrally overseen, which adds another level of protection for subjects and minimizes the risk of inconsistent decision making by different IRBs. The only real risk is that a local IRB will require more protection for human subjects than DHHS would think necessary.

A more serious potential problem arises from the contrast between the specificity of the informed consent requirements and the generality of the requirements for approval of the research itself. Confronted with one set of vague guidelines and one list of specific requirements, a decision maker may focus on the more specific requirements. That would mean that IRBs would devote excessive attention to informed consent, in the comforting belief that if they could get the consent procedures just right, everything would be okay. That, in turn, would lead to too little attention being paid to the fundamental question of whether the research is acceptable and create the risk that inappropriately dangerous research would be approved.

In my experience IRBs do tend to focus on informed consent more than on the general question of acceptability. However, there is no evidence that they are ignoring acceptability entirely. Nonetheless, the regulations should probably be amended to assure that IRBs pay serious attention to the question of whether research projects are too dangerous or ill conceived to allow people to agree to participate in them. In order to maintain the utility of the IRB system, however, any amendments should retain the ability of IRBs to make subtle, fact-sensitive decisions on a case by case basis.

Investigators sometimes object to the regulations because they require paperwork, consume time in the grant application process, and involve someone looking over the investigator's shoulder to assure that the investigator is not acting improperly. While all of these objections are understandable, none is very important. Paperwork and bureaucracy for their own sake are objectionable, but when their purpose is to protect human beings from the kinds of abuses that led to the adoption of the regulations, they seem quite worthwhile. Some expenditure of time and effort is part of the price we pay for being able to live in a civilized community. All researchers who use human subjects must comply with the regulations, so nobody is disadvantaged vis-à-vis anyone else by the time and effort that compliance requires. Moreover, the regulations provide for expedited review of certain kinds of research projects that pose only minimal risk,[35] so that in many cases the delay is slight. Finally, although each researcher will believe that regulations are unnecessary as to him because he would never mistreat human subjects, all sensible persons will recognize that some investigators would misuse human subjects if no constraints were in place. No way exists in the abstract to identify possible wrongdoers and regulate only them. Therefore, everybody must be subject to the regulations. There is nothing surprising or special about this; it is the way all regulatory law works.

The most serious criticism of the regulations is that they do not provide an effective method for monitoring research after it has been initially approved. The regulations require IRBs to conduct at least annual reviews of ongoing research and authorize them "to suspend or terminate approval of research that is not being conducted in accordance with the IRB's requirements or that has been associated with unexpected serious harm to subjects."[36] However, as a practical matter, it is hard to expect an IRB to do more by way of monitoring than to require and review annual reports from investigators. IRB members are uncompensated for their service; most of them have full-time jobs. None of them is likely to have training or expertise in policing research, and collectively they could not possibly have expertise in more than a few possible research areas. Therefore, using IRB members to police research in a serious way is not feasible. Moreover, serious policing would be very intrusive and deleterious to the research process.

DHHS does have an Office of Research Risks that investigates complaints about research on human subjects. Its director reported in 1994 that his office had investigated 115 complaints in the last four years.[37] That seems a small enough number to suggest that further expenditures for policing activities are probably unwarranted. Most recent shocking revelations about human subjects abuses in the United States are reports of incidents that occurred before the present regulations and their accompanying mechanisms were in place.

The DHHS regulations seem a sensible response to the issues of experimentation with human subjects. They pass primary decision making authority to a small, easily convened, local group at the site of the proposed research. The group contains representatives from a variety of backgrounds, some but not all of whom have scientific expertise. Centralized review of the local group's decisions is built into the process. Review is designed to protect subjects' autonomy, well-being, privacy, and confidentiality, while refraining from taking across-the-board positions that would prohibit or significantly slow down research or certain types of research simply because they depended upon the use of human subjects. The process is flexible and case oriented. Except in the area of informed consent, decision making criteria are broad and flexible and leave plenty of room for IRBs to make subtle, fact-based distinctions. By placing primary reliance on the granting or withholding of funds as the instrument of conduct control, the regulations and the statutes that authorize them refrain from extreme responses, like prohibiting conduct or stigmatizing persons, that are so prevalent elsewhere in the law. Finally, the regulations work. Their adoption has not impeded research in the United States, and abuses of human subjects in research subject to the regulations occur infrequently.

The human subjects regulations are an example of a way in which the legal system can make small, measured responses to issues posed by biomedical advance in areas where the common law is inadequate because of the need for conduct control and scientific expertise. Such small, measured responses never satisfy everybody. On the one hand, they do represent some legal involvement, which annoys those who would rather be left alone. On the other hand, they do not provide perfect protection, and it is easy to imagine scenarios in which something bad could occur. Nonetheless, they represent the best *practical* response, a response that provides all the protection one can reasonably expect without sacrificing all the gains that an important activity such as research offers.

The success of the regulations in their attempts to deal with research involving especially vulnerable groups of subjects—fetuses and pregnant women, prisoners, and children—is more mixed. The regulations concerning fetuses and pregnant women reflect some of the political fallout of the abortion debate. Those about prisoners and children are more straightforward.

Prisoners are a singularly powerless group. Not only are they under the domination of others, but the bleak nature of their circumstances may lead them to agree to participate in activities they would not engage in outside of an institution. This is especially true if early release from the institution is offered as an inducement to obtain their participation. Some would argue that the likelihood that research that uses prisoners as subjects will be abusive is so high, and the likelihood that a prisoner's consent will be truly voluntary and informed is so low, that we should not allow researchers to use prisoners as subjects.

On the other hand, a strong case can be made that the use of prisoners is acceptable. Prisoners may be especially useful subjects because of the relative ease of controlling their environment to avoid confounding variables. This, of course, would not justify the use of prisoners as subjects if that use were otherwise abusive. However, two considerations suggest that using prisoners may be more respectful of the prisoners as human beings than refusing to allow them to be subjects. First, persons in prison have almost no opportunity to contribute to the well-being of society or their fellow human beings. Some prisoners may see participating in research as an opportunity to make a contribution and to make up for the harm they have caused. It seems singularly vindictive to deny a person the chance to reestablish his self-worth by refusing to allow him to participate in an activity he sees as expiating some of his guilt. Second, as we argued earlier in our discussion of surrogate motherhood, all persons do things because of inducements. To argue that a prisoner should not be allowed to participate in research because he would not choose to do so if he were not a prisoner is like arguing that a poor person should be denied a menial job because he would not choose to take it if he were rich. This argument denies the prisoner what may be his best or only realistic chance to improve his position. All human choices are constrained by circumstances; that does not mean that all human choices should be denied.

The regulations resolve this argument by taking a restrictive position, allowing quite limited use of prisoners as research subjects. Prisoners may only serve as subjects if the research involves only

(1) study of possible causes, effects, and processes of incarceration and criminal behavior, as long as the research "presents no more than minimal risk and no more than inconvenience to the subjects"; " 'Minimal risk' is the probability and magnitude of physical or psychological harm that is normally encountered in the normal lives, or in the routine medical, dental, or psychological examination of healthy persons";

(2) "Studies of prisons as institutional structures or of prisoners as incarcerated persons," again subject to the minimal risk and inconvenience proviso;

(3) research on conditions that particularly affect prisoners if the Secretary of DHHS has first consulted with experts and published in the Federal Register notice of intent to approve such research;

(4) research on practices that are intended to, and have a reasonable probability of improving the health or well-being of the subject.[38]

In addition to its other responsibilities, the IRB, which now must include a prisoner or prisoner representative,[39] must make several additional findings before it may approve a research proposal. It must find

(1) that the research falls into one of the four permitted categories;

(2) that any possible advantages to the prisoner of participating in the research are not great enough to impair the prisoner's ability to weigh the risks and benefits of participation "in the limited choice environment of the prison";

(3) that the risks are "commensurate with risks" that nonimprisoned volunteers would accept;

(4) that procedures for selection of the subjects within the prison are fair;

(5) that information is presented in language understandable to the subject population;

(6) that parole boards will not take participation in research into account in deciding whether to grant parole, and that prisoners will be told that before they participate;

(7) that adequate provision exists for any necessary postparticipation examination or care of the subjects.[40]

These regulations effectively eliminate prisoners as potential subjects of most kinds of biomedical research and remove one of the two main motivations for prisoners to choose to participate—early release or other benefits. This reflects a very different attitude than is reflected in the basic human subjects regulations. It is unfortunate for two reasons. First, arguably, the decision to curtail most research with prisoner subjects is not the best decision on the merits. It further dehumanizes prisoners by removing one more aspect of control over their lives from them, and it denies them both tangible and psychic benefits. An unfortunate side effect of this denial is to remove a very useful population of potential research subjects from participating in research. Allowing prisoners to participate, under regulations that protect them from abuse, might have been a better way to serve the interests of the prisoners, the research community, and the public. Second, the detailed nature of the prisoner regulations prevents the kind of careful case-by-case decision making that the basic human subjects regulations foster, thereby preventing IRBs from being able to paint with a fine brush.

The regulations governing research with children are more permissive and more flexible than the prisoner-subject regulations, and they demonstrate that vulnerable groups can be protected without handicapping research or removing those subjects from the research pool. Children, of course, differ from prisoners in many ways besides their age. Most obviously, they are usually under the legal authority of a private person (parent or guardian) rather than the state; their parent or guardian is presumed to have their best interests at heart; they lack capacity to consent and, therefore, to strike deals on their own behalf;

and they lack the incentive to try to strike deals to gain expiation or some major benefit, like early parole. In addition, unlike prisoners, children strike a responsive and sympathetic chord in almost everybody.

Interestingly, this sympathetic, protective response has not led to restrictions on children participating in research that are nearly as strict as those that apply to prisoners. One can only speculate about why this is so. Perhaps the explanation lies in the fact that it is more important to use children than prisoners as subjects; child subjects are essential to research on childhood disease. Alternatively, the discrepancy may simply reflect the fact that dehumanization and denial of benefits to prisoners, especially the benefit of early release, is not a major concern of DHHS. A third, quite different hypothesis would suggest that society's feelings about children are more ambivalent and hypocritical than we care to admit, and that easier use of children than prisoners as research subjects is consistent with allowing many things—beating, imposition of a religion—to be done to children that we would never tolerate if they were done to prisoners.[41]

The regulations divide research using children as subjects into four categories: (1) research that does not involve greater than minimal risk; (2) research that does involve greater than minimal risk, but that presents the prospect of direct benefit to the individual child subjects; (3) research that involves greater than minimal risk and no prospect of direct benefit to individual subjects, but which is likely to produce generalizable knowledge about the subject's disorder or condition; and (4) research that is not otherwise approvable that presents an opportunity to understand, prevent, or alleviate a serious problem that affects the health or welfare of children.[42] They adopt different requirements for approving each of the four types of research. "Minimal risk" is not defined specifically in these regulations as it is in the regulations about prisoners, but the term is defined in the basic human subjects regulations. "Minimal risk" means that the risks are not greater than risks encountered in daily life or during the performance of routine physical or psychological exams.[43]

The child-subject regulations do define and give importance to the terms "assent" and "permission" which, between them, are used instead of "consent." "Assent" is a *child's* affirmative agreement to participate in research.[44] "Permission" is the *parent's or guardian's* agreement to allow the child to participate.[45]

If the IRB finds that research involves no more than minimal risk to children, the research may be approved as long as the IRB also finds that adequate provisions exist for soliciting the assent of the children and the permission of their parents or guardians.[46]

If the research involves more than minimal risk but presents the prospect of direct benefit to individual subjects, then it may be approved if the IRB finds (1) that the risk is justified by the anticipated benefit to the subjects; (2) the relation of anticipated benefit to risk is at least as favorable to subjects as that presented by available alternative approaches; and (3) adequate provisions for soliciting assent and permission have been made.[47]

If the research involves more than minimal risk and does not offer the prospect of direct benefit to the individual subjects, then it may only be approved if the IRB finds that (1) "The risk represents a minor increase over minimal risk"; (2) the research presents the child with experiences that are "reasonably commensurate" with experiences inherent in the child's "actual or expected medical, dental, psychological, social, or educational situations"; (3) the research is likely to provide generalizable knowledge about the subject's condition that is of "vital importance" to understanding or ameliorating the condition; and (4) adequate provisions for soliciting assent and permission exist.[48]

Finally, DHHS will fund research that does not appear to fall into any of the first three categories if (1) the IRB finds that the research presents a reasonable opportunity to further the understanding, prevention, or alleviation of a serious child health or child welfare problem; (2) the Secretary, after consultation with experts and a chance for public review and comment, finds that the research really does fall into one of the first three categories, or finds (1) that the research presents a reasonable opportunity to further the understanding, prevention or alleviation of a serious child health or child welfare problem (the same finding required of the IRB); (2) "The research will be conducted in accordance with sound ethical principles"; and (3) adequate provisions for soliciting assent and permission have been made.[49]

IRBs are given authority to waive the assent requirement if they find either that consulting the young subjects is not reasonable because of the children's lack of capacity, or that the research activity holds out a prospect of a direct benefit that is important to the subjects and that cannot be obtained without the research.[50] They may waive the permission requirement in order to protect the children in cases in which the requirement is unreasonable (for example, cases involving abused children) as long as an appropriate protective mechanism is substituted for parental permission.[51] In the normal case, in which parental permission is required, the IRB may accept permission from one parent for minimal risk and direct benefit research, but must insist on permission from both parents for the other two categories of research unless one parent is dead, unknown, incompetent, or unavailable, or only one parent has legal custody of the child.[52]

It would be easy to criticize the child-subject regulations. Aside from simply disagreeing with them about whether and when children should be allowed to serve as research subjects, one could point to a number of internal problems with the regulations. Such criticisms would view the regulations as the equivalent of legislation that is supposed to constitute rules of conduct. Looked at in that way, the regulations leave a lot to be desired.

For example, in the direct benefit provision, the requirement that the relation of anticipated benefit to risk be at least as favorable to subjects as that presented by available alternative approaches seems to require the IRB to make an impossible calculation. One cannot compare the known risks and benefits of existing treatments, for example, with the hypothetical risks and benefits of research.

The provision governing research that does not offer the prospect of direct benefit is unclear. What constitutes a "minor increase over minimal risk" is difficult to say, given that what is minor lies in the eye of the beholder. What the regulation means when it limits the research to that which presents the child with experiences that are "reasonably commensurate" with experiences inherent in the child's "actual or expected medical, dental, psychological, social, or educational situations," is anybody's guess. And how important knowledge has to be before it qualifies as being of "vital importance" is no more clear.

The provision governing research that appears not to fall into one of the first three categories takes the cake for meaningless gibberish, however, when it requires the Secretary of DHHS to determine that "research will be conducted in accordance with sound ethical principles." Not only is there no agreement about what constitutes sound ethical principles, but the whole purpose of the regulations is to flesh out what constitute sound ethical principles in the context of research on children. This provision is the equivalent of a regulation that required people to act properly and defined acting properly as engaging in proper behavior.

Each of these criticisms is valid if one thinks of the regulations as rules. However, that is not a realistic way to think of them. Regulations that are clear and meaningful could be written, but they would inevitably be destructive. Clarity divorced from factual situations requires the drafter to adopt one position and stay with it wherever it leads. Clear rules would either restrict the use of children so tightly that important, nonabusive research could not be done, or provide so little protection for children that the rules would provide inadequate safeguards against abuse. The DHHS regulations attempt to avoid both pitfalls.

The regulations are not rules of conduct. Rather, they are an assignment of authority to a decision-making body that is in a position to make decisions based on the facts of the particular cases that are presented to them. DHHS could simply have given full authority to IRBs and trusted them to make sound decisions. Rather than adopt that risky and maximally decentralized position, however, the Department adopted a middle course—it gave authority to the IRBs, but it constrained them in the exercise of their authority by adopting a few specific rules and general language that points the IRBs in the direction they are to go.

Viewed in this way, the provisions criticized above do not look so foolish. Nobody can really compare risks and benefits of research to risks and benefits of existing treatments; but the idea that the IRB is not to allow the use of a child in research if a safe and effective alternative approach to the child's needs exists is plain enough. A "minor increase over minimal risk" conveys the general idea that research may not be performed on children if it will expose them to serious or highly probable harm. The "reasonably commensurate" language means that the research is not supposed to upset the child's life. "[V]ital importance" is not quantifiable, but it clearly conveys the notion that the knowledge to be gained may not be just any old knowledge or pretty important knowledge; it has to be darned important. Even the reference to sound ethical principles at least makes the point that the importance of the knowledge sought is not enough to justify the use of a child as a research subject; another set of considerations must always be weighed.

When the regulations governing research with children are seen as expressions of general instructions to decentralized decision making bodies rather than as rules of conduct, they are more consonant with the approach of the basic human subjects regulations than the regulations about research with prisoners are, and they strike a much better balance. They allow really important research to proceed without exposing children to inappropriate risks, and they leave the primary decisions about what research is really important and what risks are inappropriate to those who are in the best position to judge.

The regulations governing research involving fetuses and pregnant women[53] (which are coupled with regulations governing research that involves human in vitro fertilization)[54] constitute one small corner of the legal response to the abortion debate. Basically, the regulations seem to proceed on the assumption that, left to their own devices, a significant number of women would obtain abortions so that their fetuses could become subjects of research, and a significant number of scientists would attempt to persuade them to do so. The regulations seek to make that unlikely by making it virtually impossible to do research that uses pregnant women or fetuses as subjects.

First, the regulations prohibit any use of pregnant women as research subjects unless (1) the purpose of the research is to meet health needs of the mother, and the fetus will be placed at risk only to the minimum extent necessary to meet those needs; or (2) the risk to the fetus is minimal.[55] Even then the research will not be permitted unless the mother and father of the fetus are both competent and both consent, unless the research is to meet health needs of the mother, or the father is unknown or not reasonably available, or the pregnancy resulted from rape.[56] This provision is outrageous. One can easily imagine a competent, known, available father whose relationship with the mother is abusive, hostile, or nonexistent, and who desires no involvement with any baby the mother might bear, but who, nonetheless, wishes to object to research on the mother to play out his feelings of hostility. Why such a man should have anything to say about the mother's use as a research subject is unclear. And prohibiting a woman from serving as a research subject if the fetus's father is incompetent truly makes no sense. Given the requirement that risk to the fetus be minimal, the provision is even hard to understand as reflecting an excess of caution about fetal well-being.

States may not condition abortion on paternal consent or even on notification to the father of the mother's intent to obtain an abortion.[57] Thus, it would seem to follow that restricting experimentation on pregnant women by a paternal consent requirement would also be unconstitutional were it not for the decision in *Rust v. Sullivan*,[58] discussed in chapter 2. *Rust* permitted even the restriction of speech when the restriction came in the form of a limitation on the government's willingness to provide funding for family planning programs. Presumably, the same rule would apply in the case of funding research. That is, *Rust* seems to suggest that the government can impose rules that restrict constitutional rights when it does so by imposing conditions on the grant of federal funds. Nonetheless, the restriction seems unwise, even if it is not unconstitutional, and it plainly represents opposition to abortion rather than concern about research.

Fetuses in utero may not be subjects of research unless (1) the purpose of the research is to meet the particular fetus's health needs, and the research will place the fetus at the minimum risk necessary to meet those needs; or (2) the risk to the fetus is minimal, and the research is to develop important biomedical knowledge that cannot be obtained any other way.[59]

A fetus that is outside the mother's uterus may not be used as a research subject until someone has determined whether the fetus is viable unless there will be *no* added risk to the fetus from the research *and* the research is to develop important biomedical knowledge that cannot be obtained any other way; or the purpose of the research activity is to increase the particular fetus's chance of achieving viability.[60] If a fetus is not viable it may only be used as a research subject if (1) its vital functions will not be artificially maintained; (2) experimental activities that would terminate the fetus's heartbeat or respiration will not be used; and (3) the research is to obtain important biomedical knowledge that cannot be obtained another way.[61] If a fetus is viable, research with it is governed by the regulations on children as research subjects.[62]

In addition to the restrictions mentioned, research may not be performed on fetuses in utero or on nonviable fetuses or fetuses of undetermined viability without the consent of the mother and father, except that the consent of the father is unnecessary if he is unknown or unavailable or the pregnancy resulted from rape.[63]

Further, no research may be performed on pregnant women or fetuses unless any risk to the fetus is the least possible risk for achieving the objectives of the research and, unless the research is to meet the health needs of the mother or the fetus, the risk to the fetus is minimal.[64] No one involved in the research may participate in determining the timing, method, or procedures used to terminate the pregnancy or in determining viability.[65] No inducements to terminate a pregnancy may be offered.[66] IRBs must determine not only that all these requirements are met, but also that adequate consideration has been given to how subjects will be selected and to monitoring the actual informed consent process.[67]

Finally, the regulations require the appointment of one or more Ethical Advisory Boards (EABs) to advise the Secretary about ethical issues in research with fetuses or pregnant women.[68] An EAB may establish classes of proposals that cannot be funded without being submitted to an EAB as well as an IRB.[69]

Obviously, the regulations make it virtually impossible to do research with fetuses or pregnant women. On the merits this is probably an unwise position for the government to have adopted, and its unarticulated premise, that severe restrictions are necessary to prevent abortion from becoming especially attractive to women who would like to contribute to science, seems particularly absurd. As a legal process matter, the regulations governing research with fetuses and pregnant women demonstrate that the administrative process is no panacea for those who are interested in controlling science through law. These regulations show that an administrative agency can draft requirements that are just as inflexible as any that a legislature might devise, and that agencies, like legislatures, are likely to be governed by political considerations. Clearly, politics, rather than any kind of administrative expertise, underlies these regulations.

Nonetheless, the administrative process, when it regulates in flexible, general terms rather than in detailed, specific ones, and when it regulates in positive ways by making funding available to those who comply rather than punishing those who do not, can be a helpful, if limited tool in the law's response to rapidly changing science.

EIGHT

Conclusion

Living with Limits—The Value of Half a Loaf

The law's ability to regulate developments in biology and medicine is severely limited. As our exploration of the law's responses to abortion, sterilization, assisted reproduction, genetics, death and dying, and regulating research has shown, the law fails most miserably when it tries to regulate most fully or to take principled positions. It comes closest to succeeding when it hardly regulates at all. The questions that remain are why this is so, whether anything can be done about it, and whether the limited ability of law to control biomedical science and technology is to be decried or celebrated.

Some of the reasons for the limited utility of law apply to all legal responses, while others differ from one legal institution to another. The most pervasive reason for the law's limitations is the limits of human ability. All legal institutions are devised and operated by human beings. No human being or collection of human beings, developing or working within a legal institution, can know enough about existing science and technology or be prescient enough to avoid making mistakes. More significantly, no human being or group of human beings can attain the wisdom to resolve the social issues posed by biology and medicine with confidence that their resolution is correct even if their understanding of the underlying scientific facts is right.

Time and again we have seen the consequences of lawmakers' inability to understand or keep pace with science. Thus, one reason the Supreme Court has dealt so unsatisfactorily with abortion is that while the Court rightly recognizes that abortion cases differ depending on their facts, it has been unable to come to grips with the facts that seem relevant. The Court thinks the viability of the fetus is relevant, but it cannot make sound constitutional law that is dependent on viability because viability must be determined medically one case at a time, because viability differs depending on whether it is determined before or after an abortion has been performed, because medical advances are continually changing the time of viability, and because viability differs from community to community depending on available medical resources. Similarly, the Court thinks maternal health is relevant, but developing medical technology continually changes the medical requisites of maternal well-being.

If one believed that eugenic sterilization legislation would be socially desirable, one would be prevented from drafting scientifically sound legislation by the limitations of our understanding of genetics and of the interplay of genetics and environment in the etiology of many handicapping conditions. Fortunately, similar factors would restrict efforts to regulate assisted reproduction to make it a eugenic tool. Advances in genetics are occurring so fast that the legal system's efforts to keep pace are futile. Technologies that allow us to maintain life for ever longer periods and changing techniques for affecting the quality of life develop outside the awareness of legal decision makers. And research, which, by definition, is on the cutting edge of knowledge, defies the ability of all but the members of an elite research community to understand and keep up.

Even if lawmakers were able to understand and keep pace with scientific change, however, human legal institutions would be unable to effect wise, principled, or across-the-board responses to the social issues posed by biomedical advance. As noted at the outset, the law "mediates most significantly between right and right."[1] Every serious social question posed by biomedical advance involves conflict between right and right. Principled or across-the-board responses will always be wrong because they will always represent the sacrifice of one right to another rather than mediation or accommodation between them.

Thus, for example, the abortion controversy cannot be resolved in favor of either pro-life or pro-choice forces without sacrificing a good that is too valuable to lose—a woman's reproductive liberty or a fetus's opportunity to live. Sterilization cannot be prohibited without sacrificing the vital needs of those persons whose liberty and physical and mental well-being require them to be sterilized, but it cannot simply be permitted because of the discrimination and abuse of the helpless that easy access to sterilization would guarantee. Assisted reproduction pits the desires of infertile couples to achieve parenthood and of individuals to capitalize on their physical resources against concerns about demeaning and imposing on women and irresponsible treatment of children. When utilized to permit single parent, gay, or lesbian parenthood, assisted reproduction raises still more conflicts between right and right—avoiding discrimination versus avoiding affront, protecting the expectations of gamete providers, and (some would say) protecting children. The conflicts between goods in the area of genetics are almost too numerous to count—autonomy versus the group good, confidentiality versus public safety, maximizing information versus blissful ignorance, rational differentiation versus avoiding discrimination, and many more. In the area of death and dying one confronts the sanctity of life versus the quality of life, autonomy versus the good of the group, protection of the weak versus preserving limited resources for those who will benefit from them the most, and so forth. Research poses issues of competing uses for scarce resources, safety for research subjects versus medical advance, respecting the autonomy of potential participants in research versus protecting them from harm, and more.

While human beings are capable of thinking about these issues, and while sophisticated ethical analysis may improve the quality of that thought, only the most extreme hubris would support confidence in the issues' proper resolutions, and surely no legal institutions devised by mortals could be counted on to get them right.

Moreover, the closer the legal institution comes to making a choice between competing goods, the less satisfactory the legal response will be. Constitutional adjudication and criminal legislation are blunt instruments, incapable of dealing with the sophisticated questions posed by biomedical advance. When those blunt responses try to become fine-pointed and flexible, they demonstrate their inability to do so and sacrifice the supposed advantages that caused people to turn to them in the first place. Common law adjudication, on the other hand, has the enormous advantage of developing in such a way that its mistakes are likely to be small, inexpensive, and easily correctable, but those who seek conduct control, certainty, or scientific sophistication from their law will not find them in the common law. Legislation that addresses small problems in moderate ways can, on occasion, be helpful and can provide more conduct control than the common law, but, as we have seen, the vagaries of language and politics and the limitations of human wisdom often render legislation worthless or even counterproductive. Administrative agencies can be helpful when they restrict their lawmaking to their spheres of expertise and try to regulate as nondisruptively as possible, but they too can go off the political deep end, can exceed their competence, and can become largely nonaccountable adjuncts to the political process.

If our present legal institutions offer as little as I have suggested to the resolution of social issues posed by biomedical advance, the question of whether we should create new institutions obviously arises. In fact, one new legal institution, a so-called "science court," has been seriously proposed, and several developments that could be called new institutions have been tried.

The science court proposal was an effort to overcome the lack of scientific expertise that characterizes most lawmakers and existing legal institutions. Under the proposal, whenever an issue of public policy involved a scientific question, a "court" staffed by persons with expertise in the relevant scientific area would be appointed to resolve the relevant scientific questions. The court's resolution would be definitive. Lawmakers addressing the public policy issue would assume the scientific correctness of the science court's resolution and make law based on that court's decisions about what the "facts" are.[2]

This well-intended proposal is seriously flawed. First, as we have seen, lawmakers' scientific ignorance is only one factor in the law's inability to deal well with issues posed by biomedical developments. Even if the science court could overcome the scientific ignorance problem, all the others would remain.

Second, unfortunately, the proposal cannot even overcome the scientific ignorance problem for several reasons. The proposal proceeds on the assumption that it is possible to separate issues of fact from issues of value. Regrettably, however, that is not so. What questions one asks (and fails to ask), how one goes about finding the answers, and how certain one must be before one accepts an answer as correct are all matters of value, not fact. Who is appointed to the science court and by what process are political or value questions that must affect the answers the court provides. The "fact" that a majority of the members of the science court agree about what the evidence shows provides no assurance that the majority is right. Determining supposedly objective scientific "truth" is hardly a matter of majority vote.

Moreover, the nature of evolving science will not permit honest experts to decide what the truth is. Often evidence will be developing and changing quickly and constantly. The honest expert will be unable to do more than assess the balance of probabilities at a given moment. Of course, the moment itself may be inopportune. By the time somebody recognizes a problem, convenes a science court, and obtains a resolution, the social problem may have resolved itself or developed beyond resolution. The science court would slow down, not speed up the legal process.

Finally, the extent to which we should even want objective, scientific resolution of so-called factual questions is unclear. Every opportunity to make social policy presents a new opportunity to decide what the proper role of scientific accuracy in lawmaking is. Sometimes the best law may not be the most scientifically accurate law.

For example, insanity has long been a defense to a charge of crime. For many years a great deal of effort was devoted to determining what "insanity" really means. Especially in the District of Columbia courts made a real effort to make the law scientifically accurate.[3] However, efforts at scientific accuracy were abandoned because scientific accuracy was not consistent with the law's goals.[4] The law needs to know whether the ends of justice, public safety, and crime prevention require that a particular person be convicted of a crime, not what the best current psychiatric views of mental illness are. Therefore, even if a science court could decide what the true meaning of "insanity" is, that would not tell us very much. The view that best serves social ends may not be the most scientifically accurate view.

For all of these reasons the science court was doomed to fail, and the idea never really got off the ground.

Other additions to the conventional legal armamentarium have appeared in recent years, but none of them is as formal a suggestion for a new institution as the science court was. One increasingly popular adjunct to existing legal mechanisms is the expert commission. For example, The President's Commission for the Study of Ethical Problems in Medicine and Biomedical and Behavioral Research studied and made policy recommendations about many bioethical issues during the late 1970s and early '80s.[5] Similar state commissions have performed similar functions for their jurisdictions.[6] Typically, expert commissions are created under a legislative directive. They often have highly qualified members who represent diverse constituencies, and typically they are also able to hire first rate staffs.

These commissions can make significant contributions. Their expertise, diverse membership, partial insulation from the political process, substantial research budgets, and relative lack of time pressures can produce very helpful analyses and recommendations. However, expert commissions cannot overcome the basic failings of the legal system.

Commissions are most useful when they recommend legislation. However, as we have seen, legislation is often an unsound response to social issues posed by rapid change. Commissions provide relatively little assistance to courts functioning in either their common law or their constitutional capacities. Moreover, by proposing across-the-board solutions to difficult problems, largely on the basis of abstract analysis, commissions do not tend to promote the kind of experimentation with real problems that is likely to lead in the long run to the soundest results. Commissions are undemocratic. They are peopled by virtually unaccountable experts. Therefore, they have some of the vices of the largely unaccountable courts, but, in a strange way, they transfer that unrepresentative outlook to the legislature, where it will not be balanced by the constraints that bind the judiciary. Finally, commissions are not effective legal institutions no matter how well they do their jobs. The most a commission can do is make recommendations. Legislatures are to be applauded for using commissions to increase their knowledge and to take advantage of the expertise of persons who have it. However, the bottom line remains—what legislatures do with commission recommendations is subject to all the vagaries of the legislative process.

Perhaps the most promising new approach to dealing with issues posed by rapid developments in biology and medicine is the increasing use of local committees to decide a variety of specific questions. We have seen ethics committees at work when we considered issues of death and dying in chapter 6, and IRBs functioning as the first-line decision makers for questions about the use of human subjects in research, which we discussed in chapter 7. Local committees for deciding specific questions have a great deal to recommend them. They decide one case at a time, and they work locally. Both of those features mean that the costs of their mistakes are likely to be relatively small. When well constituted, local committees are a very attractive decision-making group; they combine a high level of all relevant kinds of expertise with an element of popular representation. Their decisions, which will often be consensus decisions, are as likely to be sound as the decisions of any institution one can imagine. They are able to work quickly, informally, and inexpensively, and they lack the power to stigmatize persons or expose them to inappropriately severe legal sanctions. These are very appealing new institutions.

Of course, local committees are no panacea. Real questions exist about their legitimacy and accountability. To the extent, for example, that hospital ethics committees are appointed by the officers or board of the hospital, they lack the normal vetting by the political process that we have come to expect. To the extent that they meet informally and secretly, they lack the level of accountability that we normally rely on as protection against abuse. Often committee procedures are informal, and the opportunity for the committee to miss something important is real. Committees do not have the essential legal attribute of decisiveness; if somebody does not like a committee's resolution of a dispute, the unhappy person may bring the issue to court. Therefore, it is possible that local committees will simply become an additional layer of bureaucracy on the road to closure of disputes. Finally, some persons would see the decentralized feature of committees as a vice rather than a virtue. Certainly, if one wants to impose a "right" answer to a bioethical question on the entire United States, local committee decisions are not the way to achieve that goal.

Nonetheless, the ease, informality, cheapness, expertise, decentralization, and case-by-case decision making of local committees make them a useful, if limited tool in the law's approach to bioethics.

CONCLUSION

The lesson of our brief survey of American legal tools for responding to rapid change in biology and medicine is clear: Less is more, slow and steady wins the race, half-a-loaf is better than a whole one. Given our present legal institutions and any that seem likely to emerge, the soundest response to a social issue posed by biomedical advance is to begin by assuming that no legal response is necessary. Lawyers and fearful persons can always conjure up catastrophes. Given the costs and perils of legal involvement, lawmakers should refrain from acting until it is plain that a *real* problem, not a hypothetical one, exists *and* that the certain costs of legal involvement will not be greater than the costs of the problem to be solved.

Thus, wise jurisdictions have refrained from enacting legislation to solve the easily imagined, but rare problems posed by artificial insemination. When, occasionally, real issues have arisen, the common law courts have dealt with them perfectly satisfactorily. The states that adopted statutes to solve problems that did not exist and the Commissioners for Uniform State Laws, on the other hand, *created* problems by succumbing to the normal human desire to *do something*, ignoring the first mandate of sound remediation: If it ain't broke, don't fix it.

Similarly, it is hard to see that two decades of legal involvement in the area of death and dying have significantly improved the situation for patients, their loved ones, or their physicians. What used to be a simple and dignified encounter among patient, family, and doctor, has now been formalized to require legal documents and often judicial hearings and other procedural steps. The law, in the name of death with dignity, has created traps for the unwary without foreclosing the possibility that occasional abuses may occur. Indeed, in cases like that of Earl Spring, which we discussed in chapter 6, well-motivated law may actually have fostered abuses. The law of death facilitation before *Quinlan* was not the problem. If there was a problem, it was with physician attitudes, insufficient attention to medical ethics, and reformers' Quixotic search for guarantees. The law should have left well enough alone.

Sometimes, of course, a problem really does exist. Then, perhaps, something should be done about it. The least intrusive way for the law to approach a real problem is through common law adjudication. One feature of the common law is that it cannot be galvanized into action unless a problem does exist: Before there can be a lawsuit, something must have happened that made somebody angry enough to sue. To the extent that law should be forward-looking and preventative, this is a drawback; to the extent that it protects against unnecessary meddling with hypothetical problems, it is a virtue.

If a legal response to a problem is necessary, the common law should be the presumptive first-line response. For all its drawbacks, the common law has one enormous advantage over other types of legal responses: its mistakes are cheap and easy to correct. Common law differs from state to state, and what the law requires differs from one factual situation to the next. Mistaken decisions can be ignored in other jurisdictions, distinguished out of existence, or even overruled, without causing major upheavals or injustices. And because the common law is sensitive to subtle factual differences, it can paint with a finer brush than any other legal response and is likely to decide more cases correctly than any other approach. The common law's satisfactory response to issues of artificial insemination and wrongful birth and life illustrates these points.

Only if a *real* problem exists that the common law is demonstrably incapable of dealing with should one consider escalating the legal response. One should ask why the common law is inadequate and adopt the legal approach that cures the common law's deficiencies most cheaply and least intrusively. For example, if the common law is inadequate because scientific expertise is necessary to deal with an issue, then the issue should be remitted to an administrative agency that has the necessary expertise. That agency should operate in the least intrusive way—deciding disputes, authorizing experiments, etc.—being careful not to exceed either its expertise or its mandate. If the common law is inadequate because sound social policy requires more or better conduct control than the common law can provide, then the legislature should either empower an agency to engage in the minimal necessary amount of regulation or should adopt minimally restrictive conduct control requirements (rules) itself. The rules should be enforced by providing private causes of action to persons injured by others' noncompliance, by license restrictions, by funding denials, or by any of a number of other noncriminal sanctions.

If neither common law, nor noncriminal legislation, nor administrative lawmaking, nor any combination of them can solve a problem, then a would-be lawmaker should reconsider the extent of the social problem. The only remaining legal responses, criminal legislation and constitutional adjudication, are so extreme that one must be convinced that one is confronting a problem of the greatest severity to seriously contemplate using them. Before resorting to either criminal law or the constitution, one should be sure (1) that a very serious problem exists; (2) that no other legal response can deal with it adequately; (3) that one's proposed solution is sound; (4) that institutional features of the criminal law or constitutional adjudication do not disable them from resolving the problem; and (5) that the negative consequences of using the criminal law or the constitution do not outweigh the benefits to be obtained. These five criteria will almost never be met, at least in the area of biomedical advance. This means that in this area we should almost never resort to criminalization or constitutionalization. The sorry history of the abortion controversy should make that abundantly clear. The history of sterilization, the constitutionalization of death and dying, and premature efforts to criminalize certain reproductive techniques reinforce the point.

Given the nature of legal institutions, we should always start from the assumption of no legal involvement with biomedical advance. When necessary, we should escalate slowly, cautiously, one step at a time, and only to the extent that we have both the need and the ability to do so.

NOTES

I. INTRODUCTION

1. James Watson & Francis Crick, *Molecular Structure of Nucleic Acids: A Structure for Deoxyribose Nucleic Acid*, 171 NATURE 737 (1953); JAMES WATSON, DOUBLE HELIX: A PERSONAL ACCOUNT OF THE DISCOVERY OF DNA (1968).

2. *See* H.L.A. HART, THE CONCEPT OF LAW 125-26 (1961).

3. O.W. HOLMES, THE COMMON LAW 108 (1881).

4. For an introduction to the so-called Critical Legal Studies movement, *see* Critical Legal Studies Symposium, 36 STAN. L. REV. 1 (1984).

5. *See* Peter Gabel & Duncan Kennedy, *Roll Over Beethoven*, 36 STAN. L. REV. 1, 7 (1984); Louis B. Schwartz, *With Gun and Camera through Darkest CLS-Land*, 36 STAN. L. REV. 413 (1984).

6. The intellectual foundations of this understanding of law were most fully developed by Professors Henry M. Hart, Jr., and Albert M. Sacks of the Harvard Law School. For many years their monumental work, THE LEGAL PROCESS, circulated as duplicated teaching materials in a 1958 tentative edition. Now, finally, Professors William N. Eskridge, Jr., and Philip P. Frickey have edited, and Foundation Press has published, a permanent edition: Henry M. Hart, Jr., & Albert M. Sacks, THE LEGAL PROCESS (William N. Eskridge, Jr., & Philip P. Frickey, eds., 1994).

7. *In re* Gault, 387 U.S. 1, 21 (1967).

8. Malinski v. New York, 324 U.S. 401, 414 (1945) (separate opinion).

9. Paul Freund, *Legal Frameworks for Human Experimentation*, in EXPERIMENTATION WITH HUMAN SUBJECTS 105 (Paul Freund, ed., 1969).

10. For a thorough and very thoughtful analysis of the common law, *see generally* MELVIN ARON EISENBERG, THE NATURE OF THE COMMON LAW (1988).

11. This theory was first articulated by Justice Brandeis. New State Ice Co. v. Liebmann, 285 U.S. 262, 280, 311 (Brandeis, J., dissenting).

12. Uniform Anatomical Gift Act (1987), 8A U.L.A. 19 (1993); Uniform Anatomical Gift Act (1968), 8A U.L.A. 63 (1993).

13. Haft v. Lone Palm Hotel, 91 Cal. Rptr. 745 (1970).

14. Helling v. Carey, 519 P.2d 981 (1974).

15. Wash. Rev. Code § 4.24.290 (West Supp. 1978).

16. Gates v. Jensen, 595 P.2d 919 (1979).

17. The history of these regulations is discussed and their fate is resolved in Bowen v. American Hospital Association, 476 U.S. 610 (1986).

18. 5 U.S.C.A. §§ 551 et seq., 701 et seq., 3105, 3344 (Supp. 1995).

19. ALFRED C. AMAN, JR. & WILLIAM T. MAYTON, ADMINISTRATIVE LAW § 13.4.1 at 447-49 (1993).

20. 410 U.S. 113 (1973).

21. Those who thought so turned out to be wrong. Bowers v. Hardwick, 478 U.S. 186 (1986).

22. For a lengthy, if flawed, analysis of the role of *stare decisis* in constitutional de-

cision making, *see* Planned Parenthood v. Casey, 112 S. Ct. 2791, 2808–2816 (1992) (O'Connor, Kennedy, and Souter, JJ.); *contrast id.*, 2855, 2860–2867 (Rehnquist, C. J., concurring in the judgment in part and dissenting in part).

23. Mapp v. Ohio, 367 U.S. 643 (1961).

2. ABORTION

1. CONN. STAT. tit. 22 §§ 14, 16 (1821), *reprinted in* Eugene Quay, *Justifiable Abortion—Medical & Legal Foundations*, 49 GEO. L.J. 395, 435 & n.54, 453 app. I (1961) (punishing the attempt to abort a fetus by poison after quickening); *see also* Roe v. Wade, 410 U.S. 113, 138 (1973).

2. *See* C. HAAGENSEN & W. LLOYD, A HUNDRED YEARS OF MEDICINE 19 (1943), *cited in Roe*, 410 U.S. at 148–49.

3. *See* Quay, *supra* note 1, at 437.

4. ALA. CODE tit. 14 § 9 (1958); D.C. CODE ANN. § 22–201 (1967), *cited in Roe*, 410 U.S. at 139.

5. *See* D. M. Potts, *Postconceptive Control of Fertility*, 8 INT'L J. GYNAECOLOGY & OBSTETRICS 957, 967 (1970), *cited in Roe*, 410 U.S. at 149.

6. HERBERT PACKER, THE LIMITS OF CRIMINAL SANCTION (1968).

7. *Id.* at 277–82.

8. MODEL PENAL CODE § 230.3 (Proposed Official Draft 1962); *see also* LAURENCE H. TRIBE, ABORTION: THE CLASH OF ABSOLUTES 36 (1990); Edward P. Steegman, Note, *Of History & Due Process*, 63 IND. L.J. 369, 381 (1987).

9. Despite the abortion law developments described in the rest of this chapter, general legislative reform of the criminal law continued after 1973. For a list of thirty-six states that had completed recodifications by 1986 and of other states where reform efforts were pending, *see* WAYNE R. LaFAVE & AUSTIN W. SCOTT, JR., CRIMINAL LAW § 1.1 (b) at 4–5 nn.15–16 (2d ed. 1986).

10. *Roe*, 410 U.S. at 140 n.37 (collecting statutes).

11. *Id.*; *see also* TRIBE, *supra* note 8, at 46–49.

12. *See* United States v. Vuitch, 402 U.S. 62 (1971).

13. Kolender v. Lawson, 461 U.S. 352 (1983); United States v. Harriss, 347 U.S. 612 (1954); *see generally*, Note, *The Void-For-Vagueness Doctrine in the Supreme Court*, 109 U. PA. L. REV. 67 (1960).

14. LAURENCE TRIBE, AMERICAN CONSTITUTIONAL LAW 578 (1988).

15. *See, e.g.*, Coppage v. Kansas, 236 U.S. 1 (1915) (protecting the right to organize unions); Adair v. United States, 208 U.S. 161 (1908) (same); Lochner v. New York, 198 U.S. 45 (1905) (protecting freedom of contract); Allgeyer v. Louisiana, 165 U.S. 578 (1897) (same). The first 30 years of the twentieth century are known as the *"Lochner* Era," during which the Court used substantive due process as a protection of economic and property rights; see TRIBE, *supra* note 14, at 567.

16. West Coast Hotel v. Parrish, 300 U.S. 379 (1937) (upholding a minimum wage law and rejecting a claim that deprivation of freedom of contract violated Due Process since the Constitution does not speak of such freedom).

17. American Federation of Labor v. American Sash & Door Co., 335 U.S. 538 (1949); Lincoln Fed. Labor Union No. 19129 v. Northwestern Iron & Metal Co., 335 U.S. 525 (1949) (sustaining state laws requiring that employment decision not be based on union membership); Whitaker v. South Carolina, 335 U.S. 525 (1949).

18. Ferguson v. Skrupa, 372 U.S. 726, 730 (1963) (stating that the doctrine prevailing in *Lochner, Coppage*, and *Adkins* had "long since been discarded," and returning to the "original constitutional proposition that courts do not substitute their social and economic beliefs for the judgment of legislative bodies").

19. The statute stated:

> Any person who uses any drug, medicinal article or instrument for the purpose of preventing conception shall be fined, not less than fifty dollars or imprisoned not less than sixty days nor more than one year or be both fined and imprisoned.

CONN. GEN. STAT. § 53-32 (1958), *reprinted in* Griswold v. Connecticut, 381 U.S. 479, 480 (1965).

20. 318 U.S. 44 (1943).

21. 367 U.S. 497 (1961).

22. 381 U.S. 479 (1965).

23. *Id.* at 484.

24. "The enumeration in the Constitution, of certain rights, shall not be construed to deny or disparage others retained by the people." U.S. CONST. amend. IX.

25. *Griswold*, 381 U.S. at 486.

26. *Id.* at 485.

27. *Id.* at 502 (White, J., concurring).

28. *Id.* at 499 (Harlan, J., concurring).

29. *Id.* at 486 (Goldberg, J., concurring).

30. *Id.* at 507 (Black, J., dissenting).

31. *Id.* at 527 (Stewart, J., dissenting).

32. *Id.*

33. Roe v. Wade, 410 U.S. 113, 168 (1973) (Stewart, J., concurring).

34. *Id.* at 209, 212 n.4 (Douglas, J., concurring).

35. United Sates v. Vuitch, 402 U.S. 62 (1971).

36. 405 U.S. 438 (1972).

37. TRIBE, *supra* note 14, at 1439–40 & n.4, 1454, 1465–66.

38. *Eisenstadt*, 405 U.S. at 453.

39. TRIBE, *supra* note 14, at 1601–02 (discussing "intermediate scrutiny" or the "middle-tier approach").

40. 410 U.S. 113 (1973).

41. 410 U.S. 179 (1973).

42. *Roe*, 410 U.S. at 153.

43. *Id.*

44. *Id.* at 152.

45. *Id.* at 163.

46. *Id.*

47. *Id.* at 165.

48. *Id.* at 163.

49. *Id.* at 163–64.

50. John Hart Ely, *The Wages of Crying Wolf: A Comment on* Roe v. Wade, 82 YALE L.J. 920 (1973).

51. *Compare, e.g., id.* (criticizing the opinion) *with* Laurence Tribe, *Forward: Toward a Model of Roles in the Due Process of Life & Law*, 87 HARV. L. REV. 1 (1973) (offering

support of the decision on the ground of choices among alternative allocations of decision-making authority).

52. Ely, *supra* note 49, at 924.

53. *Roe*, 410 U.S. at 153.

54. *Id.* at 159.

55. *Id.* at 157.

56. *Id.* at 162.

57. 428 U.S. 52 (1976).

58. *See* Maher v. Roe, 432 U.S. 464, 469 (1977).

59. Nyberg v. City of Virginia, 495 F.2d 1342 (8th Cir. 1974), *appeal dismissed*, 419 U.S. 891 (1974); Doe v. Hale Hosp., 500 F.2d 144 (1st Cir. 1974); Wolfe v. Schroering, 541 F.2d 523 (6th Cir. 1976).

60. Doe v. Poelker, 515 F.2d 544, 546 (1975), *rev'd*, 432 U.S. 519 (1976).

61. *Poelker*, 432 U.S. 519 (1976), *rev'g* 515 F.2d 544 (1975).

62. Maher v. Roe, 432 U.S. 464 (1977).

63. Harris v. McRae, 448 U.S. 297 (1980).

64. *See, e.g.*, Bellotti v. Baird (*Bellotti I*), 428 U.S. 132, 147 (1976) (holding constitutional a requirement of written parental consent unless it unduly burdens the right to seek an abortion).

65. Roe v. Wade, 410 U.S. 113, 153 (1973).

66. *Maher*, 432 U.S. at 474 (upholding the Connecticut requirement because it "imposed no restriction on access to abortions that was not already there").

67. *See id.* at 475–76.

68. Planned Parenthood Ass'n v. Ashcroft, 462 U.S. 416, 442 (1983); H.L. v. Matheson, 450 U.S. 398, 440 n.24 (1981) (Marshall, J., dissenting).

69. Bellotti v. Baird (*Bellotti II*), 443 U.S. 622, 639 (1979) (plurality).

70. *H.L.*, 450 U.S. at 418 (Powell, J., concurring); *Bellotti II*, 443 U.S. at 651.

71. Akron v. Akron Ctr. for Reproductive Health, 462 U.S. 416, 439–42 (1983); *Bellotti II*, 443 U.S. at 643.

72. *Bellotti II*, 443 U.S. at 643.

73. *Id.* at 649 n.29.

74. *H.L.*, 450 U.S. 398.

75. Hodgson v. Minnesota, 497 U.S. 417 (1990).

76. Ohio v. Akron Ctr. for Reproductive Health, 497 U.S. 512 (1990).

77. *H.L.*, 450 U.S. at 412.

78. *Id.* at 411.

79. 443 U.S. 622 (1979) (plurality).

80. *Id.* at 640 (footnotes omitted).

81. *Id.* at 642.

82. *Id.* at 642–43.

83. *Id.* at 647–48.

84. 462 U.S. 416 (1983).

85. *Id.* at 419–20.

86. *Id.* at 427.

87. *Id.* at 429–30.

88. *Id.* at 439.

89. *Id.* at 429 n.11.

90. *Id.* at 431 n.15.

91. 410 U.S. 179 (1973).

92. *Akron*, 462 U.S. at 434–39.

93. *Id*. at 431.

94. *Id*. at 452 (O'Connor, J., dissenting).

95. *Id*. at 461–62.

96. Planned Parenthood v. Casey, 112 S. Ct. 2791, 2820–21 (1992) (plurality) (stating that "an undue burden is an unconstitutional burden").

97. *Id*. at 464.

98. *Id*.

99. *Id*. at 442–49.

100. 492 U.S. 490 (1989).

101. 111 S. Ct. 1759 (1991).

102. *Webster*, 492 U.S. at 507. Section 188.210 stated that it "shall be unlawful for any public employee within the scope of his employment to perform or assist an abortion, not necessary to save the life of the mother." *Id*.

103. *Id*. Section 188.215 made it "unlawful for any public facility to be used for the purpose of performing or assisting an abortion not necessary to save the life of the mother."

104. *Id*. at 504–507.

105. *Id*. at 513 (footnote omitted).

106. *Id*. at 532. (Scalia, J., concurring).

107. *Id*. at 514.

108. *Id*.

109. *Id*. at 525 (O'Connor, J., concurring).

110. *See, e.g.*, Planned Parenthood v. Danforth, 428 U.S. 52, 64 (1976).

111. *Webster*, 492 U.S. at 527 (O'Connor, J., concurring).

112. *Id*. at 515–16 (Rehnquist, J., joined by JJ. White & Kennedy); *id*. at 525–28 (O'Connor, J., concurring); *id*. at 542–44 (Blackmun, J., concurring in part and dissenting in part, joined by JJ. Brennan & Marshall); *id*. at 560–61 (Stevens, J., concurring in part and dissenting in part); *id*. at 537 (Scalia, J., concurring in part and concurring in judgment).

113. *Id*. at 530 (O'Connor, J., concurring).

114. *Id*. at 517–20.

115. *Id*. at 549–52 (Blackmun, J., concurring in part and dissenting in part).

116. *Id*. at 547–49 (Blackmun, J., concurring in part and dissenting in part).

117. *See* TRIBE, *supra* note 14, at 861–86.

118. Roger B. Dworkin, *Fact Style Adjudication and the Fourth Amendment: The Limits of Lawyering*, 48 IND. L.J. 329 (1973).

119. The Fourth Amendment provides:

> The right of the people to be secure in their person, houses, papers, and effects, against unreasonable searches and seizures, shall not be violated, and no Warrants shall issue, but upon probable cause, supported by Oath or affirmation, and particularly describing the place to be searched, and the persons or things to be seized.

U.S. CONST. amend. IV; *see also* Mapp v. Ohio, 367 U.S. 643 (1961).

120. *Webster*, 492 U.S. at 549 (Blackmun, J., concurring in part and dissenting in part) (quoting Thornburgh v. American College of Obstetricians & Gynecologists, 476 U.S. 747, 777 n.5 (Stevens, J., concurring) (quoting Charles Fried, *Correspondence*, 6 PHIL. & PUB. AFF. 288–89 (1977)).

121. *See* Roe v. Wade, 410 U.S. 113, 153–54 (1973).

122. *Webster*, 492 U.S. at 549 (Blackmun, J., concurring in part and dissenting in part).

123. *Id.* at 519; *see also id.* at 552 (Blackmun, J., concurring in part and dissenting in part).

124. *Id.* at 552–54 (Blackmun, J., concurring in part and dissenting in part).

125. *Id.* at 555 (Blackmun, J., concurring in part and dissenting in part) (characterizing the plurality's "permissibly furthers" standard "to be nothing more than a dressed-up version of rational-basis review").

126. Planned Parenthood v. Casey, 112 S. Ct. 2791, 2803 (1992) (plurality).

127. *Id.* at 2832. Justices O'Connor, Kennedy, and Souter jointly wrote the opinion that announced the judgment of the Court. Justice Rehnquist authored a separate opinion in which Justices White, Scalia, and Thomas joined. *Id.* at 2855 (Rehnquist, J., concurring in judgment in part and dissenting in part).

128. *Id.* at 2826–31; *id.* at 2843 (Stevens, J., concurring in part and dissenting in part); *id.* (Blackmun, J., concurring in part, concurring in judgment and dissenting in part).

129. *Id.* at 2823–25; *id.* at 2867–68 (Rehnquist, J., concurring in judgment in part and dissenting in part).

130. *Id.* at 2825–26; *id.* at 2868 (Rehnquist, J., concurring in judgment in part and dissenting in part).

131. *Id.* at 2838 (Stevens, J., concurring in part and dissenting in part); *id.* at 2844 (Blackmun, J., concurring in part, concurring in judgment and dissenting in part).

132. *Id.* at 2855 (Rehnquist, J., concurring in judgment in part and dissenting in part).

133. *Id.* at 2860, 2867 (Rehnquist, J., concurring in judgment in part and dissenting in part).

134. *Id.* at 2804.

135. *Id.*

136. *See supra*, text accompanying note 44.

137. *See* Mapp v. Ohio, 367 U.S. 643 (1961) (establishing the exclusionary rule).

138. Miranda v. Arizona, 384 U.S. 436 (1966).

139. A public official can recover damages for defamation only upon proof that "the statement was made with 'actual malice'—that is, with knowledge that it was false or with reckless disregard of whether it was false or not." New York Times Co. v. Sullivan, 376 U.S. 254, 279–80 (1964).

140. *Casey*, 112 S. Ct. at 2808.

141. *Id.* (discussing the rule of *stare decisis*).

142. *Id.* at 2814.

143. *Id.* at 2815.

144. *Id.*

145. *Id.*

146. *Casey*, 112 S. Ct. at 2882 (Scalia, J., concurring in judgment in part and dissenting in part).

147. *Id.* at 2862–63 (Rehnquist, C. J., concurring in judgment in part and dissenting in part).

148. *Id.* at 2865–66.

149. *Id.* at 2865.

150. *Id.* at 2808 (opinion of O'Connor, Kennedy, and Souter, JJ.)

151. *Id.*

152. *See id.* (referring to situations where related principles of law have so far developed as to have left the old rule no more than a remnant of abandoned doctrine).

153. *Id.* at 2809.

154. *Id.*

155. *Id.*

156. *Id.*

157. *Id.* at 2810.

158. *See id.* at 2884 (Scalia, J., concurring in judgment in part and dissenting in part).

159. *Id.* at 2811–12 (opinion of O'Connor, Kennedy, and Souter, JJ.)

160. *Id.* at 2807.

161. *Id.*

162. *Id.* at 2807–08.

163. *Id.* at 2806 (collecting cases).

164. *Id.* (collecting cases).

165. *Id.* at 2840 (Stevens, J., concurring in part and dissenting in part).

166. *Id.* at 2846 (Blackmun, J., concurring in part, concurring in judgment and dissenting in part).

167. *Id.* at 2875 (Scalia, J., concurring in judgment in part and dissenting in part).

168. *See infra* chapter 3 notes 23–34 and accompanying text.

169. *Casey,* 112 S. Ct. at 2817.

170. *Id.*

171. *Id.*

172. *Id.*

173. *Id.* at 2816.

174. *Id.* at 2812.

175. *See infra* chapter 6.

176. *In re* Quinlan, 355 A.2d 647, 663 (N.J.), *cert den. sub nom.* Garger v. New Jersey, 429 U.S. 922 (1976).

177. Cruzan v. Director, Mo. Dep't of Health, 497 U.S. 261 (1990) (balancing liberty interest in refusing life-sustaining medical treatment against the state interest in protecting and preserving human life).

178. Bowers v. Hardwick, 478 U.S. 186 (1986).

179. 111 S. Ct. 1759 (1991).

180. 84 Stat. 1506, as amended, 42 U.S.C. §§ 300–330a-6 (1970).

181. Section 1008, 42 U.S.C. § 300a-6 (1988).

182. 53 Fed. Reg. 2923–24 (1988).

183. 42 C.F.R. 59.8(a)(1) (1994).

184. 42 C.F.R. 59.10(a).

185. 42 C.F.R. 59.9.

186. Rust v. Sullivan, 111 S. Ct. 1759, 1767–69 (1991).

187. *Id.* at 1773.

188. *Id.* at 1774.

189. *Id.* at 1776.

190. *Id.*

191. Carl E. Schneider, *Rights Discourse & Neonatal Euthanasia*, 76 CAL. L. REV. 151, 172 (1988).

192. Brown v. Board of Educ., 347 U.S. 483 (1954).

3. STERILIZATION

1. Alabama, Arizona, California, Connecticut, Delaware, Georgia, Idaho, Indiana, Iowa, Kansas, Maine, Michigan, Minnesota, Mississippi, Montana, Nebraska, Nevada, New Hampshire, New Jersey, New York, North Carolina, North Dakota, Oklahoma, Oregon, South Carolina, South Dakota, Utah, Vermont, Virginia, Washington, West Virginia, Wisconsin; *see* Elyce Z. Ferster, *Eliminating the Unfit—Is Sterilization the Answer?* 27 OHIO ST. L.J. 591, 596–97 (1966).

2. *E.g.*, CAL. PEN. CODE § 645 (Deering 1994); WASH. REV. CODE ANN. § 9.92.100 (West 1994); OKLA. STAT. ANN. tit. 57 § 171 (West 1935) (found unconstitutional in Skinner v. Oklahoma *ex rel.* Williamson, 316 U.S. 535 (1942)).

3. 274 U.S. 200 (1927).

4. *Id.* at 207.

5. *Id.* at 208.

6. Skinner v. Oklahoma *ex rel.* Williamson, 316 U.S. 535 (1942).

7. *Id.* at 541.

8. *Id.*

9. *See, e.g.*, *In re* Moe, 432 N.E.2d 712 (Mass. 1982); *In re* Terwilliger, 450 A.2d 1376 (Pa. Super. Ct. 1982).

10. *See, e.g.*, Hudson v. Hudson, 373 So.2d 310 (Ala. 1979); Frazier v. Levi, 440 S.W.2d 393 (Tex. Civ. App. 1969); *In re* Tulley, 146 Cal. Rptr. 266 (Ct. App. 1978), *cert. denied*, 440 U.S. 967 (1979).

11. Ruby v. Massey, 452 F.Supp. 361 (D. Conn. 1978).

12. Relf v. Weinberger, 372 F.Supp. 1196 (D. D.C. 1974), *vacated on other grounds* 565 F.2d 722 (D.C. Cir. 1977).

13. 410 U.S. 113 (1973).

14. *Relf*, 372 F.Supp. at 1196.

15. *Id.* at 1202.

16. *Id.* at 1203.

17. 410 U.S. at 154.

18. 428 U.S. 52 (1976).

19. *See generally* MARY ANN GLENDON, RIGHTS TALK (1991).

20. ARK. CODE ANN. § 20–49–302 (Michie 1993); CONN. GEN. STAT. ANN. § 45a-699 (1992); GA. CODE ANN. § 31-20-3 (1994); MISS. CODE ANN. § 41-45-1 (1993); N.C. GEN. STAT. § 35-36 (1993); VT. STAT. ANN. tit. 18 § 8708 (1993); VA. CODE ANN. § 54.1-2976 (1994); W. VA. CODE § 27-16-1 (1994).

21. *In re* Hayes, 608 P.2d 635 (Wash. 1980) (*en banc*).

22. *In re* C.D.M., 627 P.2d 607 (Alaska 1981); *In re* Valerie N., 707 P.2d 760 (Cal. 1985); *In re* Romero, 790 P.2d 819 (Colo. 1990); *In re* A.W., 637 P.2d 366 (Colo. 1981); P. S. by Harbin v. W. S. & P. S., 452 N. E.2d 969 (Ind. 1983); Guardianship of Matejski, 419 N.W.2d 576 (Iowa 1988); Wentzel v. Montgomery Gen. Hosp., Inc., 447 A.2d 1244 (Md. 1982); *In re* Moe, 432 N.E.2d 712 (Mass. 1982); *In re* Grady, 426 A.2d 467 (N.J. 1981); *In re* Terwilliger, 450 A.2d 1376 (Pa. Super. 1982).

23. *In re* Valerie N., 707 P.2d 760 (Cal. 1985).

24. *Id.* at 771–73.

25. *Id.* at 771–72.

26. *Id.* at 771.

27. *Id.* at 773.

28. *Id.* at 775–77.

29. *Id.* at 781 (Bird, C. J., dissenting).

30. *Id.* at 784–85.

31. *Id.* at 781.

32. *Id.* at 785.

33. *Id.*

34. *Id.* at 786–87.

4. ALTERNATIVE REPRODUCTIVE TECHNIQUES

1. United States Congress, Office of Technology Assessment, *Artificial Insemination: Practice in The United States Summary of a 1987 Survey—Background Paper* 8 (1988).

2. *In re* Adoption of Anonymous, 345 N.Y.S.2d 430 (Sur. Ct. 1973); L. v. L., 1 ALL. ENG. 141 (1949).

3. Laurene Mascola & Mary E. Guinan, *Screening to Reduce Transmission of Sexually Transmitted Diseases in Semen Used for Artificial Insemination,* 314 NEW ENG. J. MED. 1254 (1986).

4. Orford v. Orford, 49 Ont. L.R. 15, 58 D.L.R. 251 (1921).

5. 1958 Sess. Cas. 105.

6. *Id.* at 114.

7. *Id.* at 107.

8. *Id.* at 108.

9. *Id.* at 113–14.

10. *Id.* at 115.

11. *E.g.,* People v. Sorensen, 437 P.2d 495 (Cal. 1968); Strnad v. Strnad, 78 N.Y.S.2d 390 (Sup. Ct. 1948).

12. Gursky v. Gursky, 242 N.Y.S.2d 406 (Sup. Ct. 1963).

13. *See* cases summarized in *In re* Adoption of Anonymous, 345 N.Y.S.2d 430 (Sur. Ct. 1973).

14. W. J. Broad, *A Bank for Nobel Sperm,* 207 Science 1326 (1980).

15. 377 A.2d 821 (N.J. Super. Ct. 1977).

16. GA. CODE ANN. § 19-7-21 (1994).

17. R.S. v. R.S., 670 P.2d 923 (Kan. App. 1983), *rev. denied,* 234 Kan. 1077 (1983).

18. GA. CODE ANN. § 43-34-42 (1994).

19. McIntyre v. Crouch, 780 P.2d 239 (Ore. 1989), *rev. denied,* 784 P.2d 1100 (Ore. 1989), *cert. denied,* 495 U.S. 905 (1990).

20. GA. CODE ANN. § 43-34-42 (1994).

21. Unif. Parentage Act § 5, 9B U.L.A. 301 (1988).

22. Unif. Status of Children of Assisted Conception Act, 9B U.L.A. 152 (Supp. 1994).

23. VA. CODE ANN. § 20-158 (1994); N.D. CENT. CODE § 14-18-01 (1993).

24. ALA. CODE § 26-17-1 (1993); CAL. FAM. CODE § 7600 (West 1994); COLO. REV. STAT. § 19-4-101 (1993); DEL. CODE ANN. tit. 13, § 801 (1993); HAW. REV. STAT. § 584-1 (1993); ILL. ANN. STAT. ch. 40 para. 2501 (Smith-Hurd 1993); KAN. STAT. ANN. § 38-110

(1993); MINN. STAT. ANN. § 257.51 (West 1993); MO. ANN. STAT. § 210.817 (Vernon 1993); MONT. CODE ANN. § 40–6–101 to 40–6–135 (1993); NEV. REV. STAT. § 126.011 (1993); N.J. STAT. ANN. § 9:17–38 (West 1993); N.M. STAT. ANN. § 40–11–1 (Michie 1994); N.D. CENT. CODE § 14–17–01 (1993); OHIO REV. CODE ANN. § 3111.01 (Baldwin 1994); R.I. GEN. LAWS § 15–8–1 (1993); WASH. REV. CODE ANN. § 26.26.010 (West 1994); WYO. STAT. § 14-2-101 (1994).

25. 179 Cal. App. 3d 386 (1986).

26. OR. REV. STAT. § 109.239 (1993).

27. McIntyre v. Crouch, 780 P.2d 239 (Ore. 1989), *rev. denied*, 784 P.2d 1100 (Ore. 1989), *cert. denied*, 495 U.S. 905 (1990).

28. MARTHA A. FIELD, SURROGATE MOTHERHOOD (1988).

29. *See, e.g.,* THOMAS A. SHANNON, SURROGATE MOTHERHOOD: THE ETHICS OF USING HUMAN BEINGS (1988); Shari O'Brien, *Commercial Conceptions: A Breeding Ground for Surrogacy*, 65 N.C.L. REV. 127, 148–49 (1986); Andrew Kimbrell, *The Case Against the Commercialization of Childbearing*, 24 WILLAMETTE L. REV. 1035, 1045–47 (1988); *Babyselling and It's Wrong*, N.Y. Times, June 4, 1988, at 26.

30. *See, e.g.,* Matter of Baby M., 537 A.2d 1227, 1248–50 (N.J. 1988); Margaret J. Radin, *Market Inalienability*, 100 HARV. L. REV. 1849, 1928–36 (1987); Lorraine Stone, Neoslavery—"Surrogate" Motherhood Contracts v. The Thirteenth Amendment, 6 LAW AND INEQUALITY 63 (1988).

31. See the balanced discussion in Lori B. Andrews, *Alternative Modes of Reproduction*, in REPRODUCTIVE LAWS FOR THE 1990s (Sherrill Cohen & Nadine Taub, eds.), 361, 366–374 (1989); see also Herbert T. Krimmel, *The Case Against Surrogate Parenting*, 13 HASTINGS CTR. REP. 35 (1983); Stone, *supra* note 30.

32. Judith T. Younger, *What the Baby M Case Is Really All About*, 6 LAW & INEQUALITY 75, 81 (1988).

33. *See, e.g.,* Emily Buss, *Getting Beyond Discrimination: A Regulatory Solution to the Problem of Fetal Hazards in the Workplace*, 95 YALE L.J. 577 (1986); Dawn E. Johnsen, *The Creation of Fetal Rights: Conflicts with Women's Constitutional Rights to Liberty, Privacy and Equal Protection*, 95 YALE L.J. 599 (1986); Deborah Mathieu, *Respecting Liberty and Preventing Harm: Limits of State Intervention in Prenatal Choice*, 8 HARV. J.L. & PUB. POL'Y 19 (1985); Lawrence J. Nelson & Nancy Milliken, *Compelled Medical Treatment of Pregnant Women: Life, Liberty, and Law in Conflict*, 259 J.A.M.A. 1060 (Feb. 19, 1988).

34. 537 A.2d 1227 (N.J. 1988)

35. *Id.* at 1234.

36. *Id.* at 1248.

37. *Id.* at 1250.

38. *Id.* at 1246, 1248.

39. HOMER H. CLARK, JR., THE LAW OF DOMESTIC RELATIONS IN THE UNITED STATES § 19.4, at 797–98 (2nd ed. 1988).

40. Leckie v. Voorhies, 875 P.2d 521 (Ore. 1994).

41. *E.g.,* Surrogate Parenting Associates v. Commonwealth, 704 S.W.2d 209 (Ky. 1986); *In re* Baby Girl L.J., 132 Misc. 2d 972, 505 N.Y.S.2d 813 (1986); *contra, In re* Paul, 146 Misc. 2d 379, 550 N.Y.S.2d 815 (1990).

42. CLARK, *supra* note 39, § 20.6, at 903.

43. *Id.* § 19.4, at 797–98.

44. 537 A.2d at 1256.

45. *Id.* at 1258–59.

46. *Id.*

47. *See, e.g.,* Steven M. Recht, Note, *"M" Is for Money: Baby M and the Surrogate Motherhood Controversy,* 37 AM. U.L. REV. 1013 (1988).

48. *See, e.g.,* LORI B. ANDREWS, Between Strangers 187 (1989); Stone, *supra* note 30.

49. 537 A.2d at 1258–59.

50. *Id.* at 1261.

51. CLARK, *supra* note 39, § 19.4, at 811–14.

52. *Id.*

53. Stiver v. Parker, 975 F.2d 261 (6th Cir. 1992), *reh'g denied,* 1992 U.S. App. LEXIS 34150.

54. CLARK, *supra* note 39, §§ 19.6–19.7, at 820–33.

55. Hoy v. Willis, 398 A.2d 109 (N.J. Super. Ct. App. Div. 1978); Carter v. Brodrick, 644 P.2d 850 (Alaska 1982); Ross v. Hoffman, 364 A.2d 596 (Md. Ct. Spec. App. 1976). *See* Kimberly P. Carr, Comment, *Alison D. v. Virginia M.: Neglecting the Best Interests of the Children in a Nontraditional Family,* 58 BROOK. L. REV. 1021 (1991); Suzette M. Haynie, Note, *Biological Parents v. Third Parties: Whose Right to Child Custody Is Constitutionally Protected?* 20 GA. L. REV. 705 (1986).

56. Johnson v. Calvert, 851 P.2d 776 (Cal. 1993), *cert. denied,* 114 S. Ct. 206 (1993), *and cert. dismissed,* 114 S. Ct. 374 (1993).

57. Simpson v. Simpson, 586 S.W.2d 33, 36 (Ky. 1979) (Stephenson, J., dissenting) (discussing visitation rights).

58. Unif. Status of Children of Assisted Conception Act, Prefatory Note, 9B U.L.A. 152 (Supp. 1994)

59. *Id.*

60. Davis v. Davis, 1989 Tenn. App. LEXIS 641.

61. Davis v. Davis, 1990 Tenn. App. LEXIS 642.

62. Davis v. Davis, 842 S.W.2d 588, 594–96 (Tenn. 1992), *reh'g granted in part,* 1992 Tenn. LEXIS 622, *cert. denied,* 113 S. Ct. 1259 (1993).

63. *Id.* at 598–99.

64. *Id.* at 603–604.

65. *Id.* at 604.

66. *Id.*

67. Del Zio v. Columbia Presbyterian Med. Cntr., No. 74-3558 (S.D.N.Y. Apr. 12, 1978), cited in Davis v. Davis, 842 S.W.2d 588 at 602 n.25 (1992).

68. York v. Jones, 717 F. Supp. 421 (E.D. Va. 1989).

69. See George P. Smith II, *Australia's Frozen 'Orphan' Embryos: A Medical, Legal and Ethical Dilemma,* 24 J. FAM. L. 27 (1985–86).

70. Hecht v. Superior Court of Los Angeles, 16 Cal. App. 4th 836 (1993), *rev. denied,* 1993 Cal. LEXIS 4768.

71. David Mangolick, *15 Vials of Sperm: The Unusual Bequest of an Even More Unusual Man,* N.Y. Times, Apr. 29, 1994, at B18.

72. LA. REV. STAT. ANN. § 9:131 (1993).

5. THE NEW GENETICS

1. James Watson & Francis Crick, *Molecular Structure of Nucleic Acids: A Structure for Deoxyribose Nucleic Acid,* 171 NATURE 737 (1953); JAMES WATSON, DOUBLE HELIX: A PERSONAL ACCOUNT OF THE DISCOVERY OF DNA (1968).

2. WALTER WADLINGTON ET AL., CASES AND MATERIALS ON LAW AND MEDICINE 803–804 (1980) (relying on U.S. DEPARTMENT OF HEW, PUBLIC HEALTH SERVICE, NATIONAL INSTITUTES OF HEALTH, DRAFT, CONSENSUS DEVELOPMENT CONFERENCE ON ANTENATAL DIAGNOSIS, TASK FORCE REPORT: PREDICTORS OF HEREDITARY DISEASE OR CONGENITAL DEFECTS (1979)).

3. *See* Lori A. Whittaker, *The Implications of the Human Genome Project for Family Practice*, 35 J. FAM. PRAC. 294 (1992).

4. *E.g.*, MINN. STAT. ANN. § 145.424 (West 1993); S.D. CODIFIED LAWS § 21-55-2 (1994); UTAH CODE ANN. §§ 78-11-24, 78-11-25 (1994).

5. *E.g.*, Viccaro v. Milunsky, 551 N.E.2d 8 (Mass. 1990); Schroeder v. Perkel, 432 A.2d 834 (N.J. 1981); Becker v. Schwartz, 386 N.E.2d 807 (N.Y. 1978); Speck v. Finegold, 408 A.2d 496 (Pa. Super. 1979); *see generally* Roger B. Dworkin, *The New Genetics*, 1 BIOLAW 89, 95–97 (1986).

6. *Id.*

7. For examples of this approach applied in cases involving the unwanted birth of healthy children, *see, e.g.*, Sherlock v. Stillwater Clinic, 260 N.W.2d 169 (Minn. 1977); Marciniak v. Lundborg, 450 N.W.2d 243 (Wis. 1990).

8. *See, e.g.*, Dumer v. St. Michael's Hosp., 233 N.W.2d 372 (Wis. 1975); Schroeder v. Perkel, 432 A.2d 834 (N.J. 1981).

9. *See, e.g.*, Rodrigues v. State, 472 P.2d 509 (Haw. 1970); Gammon v. Osteopathic Hosp., 534 A.2d 1282 (Me. 1987).

10. *E.g.*, CAL. CIV. CODE § 3333.2 (West Supp. 1994).

11. Viccaro v. Milunsky, 551 N.E.2d 8 (Mass. 1990); Berman v. Allan, 404 A.2d 8 (N.J. 1979).

12. Smith v. Cote, 513 A.2d 341 (N.H. 1986); Howard v. Lecher, 366 N.E.2d 64 (N.Y. 1977).

13. W. PAGE KEETON ET AL., PROSSER & KEETON ON THE LAW OF TORTS § 54, at 365–66 (5th ed. 1984).

14. Howard v. Lecher, 366 N.E.2d 64 (N.Y. 1977).

15. Becker v. Schwartz, 386 N.E.2d 807 (N.Y. 1978); Dumer v. St. Michael's Hosp., 233 N.W.2d 372 (Wis. 1975); Elliott v. Brown, 361 So. 2d 546 (Ala. 1978); Gildiner v. Thomas Jefferson Univ. Hosp., 451 F. Supp. 692 (E.D. Pa. 1978).

16. Gleitman v. Cosgrove, 227 A.2d 689, 692 (N.J. 1967).

17. *In re* Quinlan, 355 A.2d 647 (N.J. 1976), *cert. denied sub nom.* Garger v. New Jersey, 429 U.S. 922 (1976).

18. *E.g.*, Turpin v. Sortini, 643 P.2d 954 (Cal. 1982); Procanik v. Cillo, 478 A.2d 755 (N.J. 1984); Harbeson v. Parke-Davis, Inc., 656 P.2d 483 (Wash. 1983).

19. *E.g.*, Hook v. Rothstein, 316 S.E.2d 690 (S.C. Ct. App. 1984), *cert. denied*, 320 S.E.2d 35 (S.C 1984).

20. *E.g.*, Arato v. Avedon, 858 P.2d 598 (Cal. 1993); Cobbs v. Grant, 502 P.2d 1 (Cal. 1972); Canterbury v. Spence, 464 F.2d 772 (D.C. Cir. 1972), *cert. denied*, 409 U.S. 1064 (1972).

21. 414 N.W.2d 399 (Minn. 1987).

22. Pratt v. University of Minnesota Affiliated Hosp. and Clinics, 403 N.W.2d 865, 869–70 (Minn. Ct. App. 1987).

23. 414 N.W.2d 399, 402.

24. McPherson v. Ellis, 287 S.E.2d 892 (N.C. 1982); Scott v. Bradford, 606 P.2d 554 (Okla. 1979).

25. Reyes v. Wyeth Lab., 498 F.2d 1264 (5th Cir. 1974), *cert. denied*, 419 U.S. 1096 (1974).

26. *E.g.*, Woolley v. Henderson, 418 A.2d 1123 (Me. 1980); Cobbs v. Grant, 502 P.2d 1 (Cal. 1972).

27. *See, e.g.*, Hammonds v. Aetna Casualty & Surety Co., 243 F. Supp. 793 (N.D. Ohio 1965); Horne v. Patton, 287 So.2d 824 (Ala. 1974); Hague v. Williams, 181 A.2d 345 (N.J. 1962).

28. *See* KEETON ET AL., *supra* note 13, § 56, at 375–77.

29. *See, e.g.*, Horne v. Patton, 287 So. 2d 824 (Ala. 1973); Hague v. Williams, 181 A.2d 345 (N.J. 1962).

30. *See* KEETON ET AL., *supra* note 13, § 56, at 375–77, and authorities collected there.

31. *Id.* § 56, at 378–84.

32. Tarasoff v. Regents of Univ. of Calif., 551 P.2d 334 (Cal. 1976).

33. *See, e.g.*, Canterbury v. Spence, 464 F.2d 772 (D.C. Cir. 1972); Cobbs v. Grant, 502 P.2d 1 (Cal. 1972).

34. *See* KEETON ET AL., *supra* note 13, § 117, at 856–57.

35. Horne v. Patton, 287 So. 2d 824 (Ala. 1974); Humphers v. First Interstate Bank, 696 P.2d 527 (Ore. 1985).

36. *E.g.*, N.J. STAT. ANN. § 26: 4–38 (West 1993); IOWA CODE § 140.4 (1993); IDAHO CODE § 39–602 (1994); GA. CODE ANN. § 31–17–2 (1994).

37. *E.g.*, N.D. CENT. CODE § 50–25.1–03 (1993); N.M. STAT ANN. § 32A-4-3 (Michie 1994); NEW HAMP. REV. STAT. ANN. 169-C:29 (1993); MONT. CODE ANN. § 41-3-201 (1993).

38. *E.g.*, HAWAII REV. STAT. § 453–14 (1993); FLA. STAT. ANN. § 790.24 (West 1993); ARK. CODE ANN. § 12–12–602 (1993); OHIO REV. CODE ANN. § 2921.22 (Baldwin 1994).

39. *E.g.*, OHIO REV. CODE ANN. § 5101.61 (Baldwin 1994) (abuse of adult); MISS. CODE ANN. § 41–35–3 (1993) (inflamation of a newborn's eyes); IND. CODE ANN. § 35–47–7–1 (Burns 1994) (ice pick wounds).

40. *See, e.g.*, Horne v. Patton, 287 So.2d 824 (Ala. 1973); Tarasoff v. Regents of Univ. of Calif., 551 P.2d 334 (Cal. 1976).

41. See the discussion in chapter 2, at 33, 38–39.

42. Hurley v. Eddingfeld, 59 N.E. 1058 (Ind. 1901).

43. See Marcia Angell, *The Case of Helga Wanglie*, 325 NEW ENG. J. MED. 511 (1991); Steven H. Miles, *Informed Demand for "Non-Beneficial" Medical Treatment*, 325 NEW ENG. J. MED. 512 (1991).

44. Compare Gotkin v. Miller, 514 F.2d 125 (2d Cir. 1975) (denying access when sought for writing a book) with MINN. STAT. ANN. § 144.335 (West Supp. 1994).

45. DAVID HENDIN & JOAN MARKS, THE GENETIC CONNECTION 40 (1978); JAMES S. THOMPSON & MARGARET W. THOMPSON, GENETICS IN MEDICINE 170–71 (2d ed. 1973).

46. Kenneth J. Burke, *The "XYY Syndrome": Genetics, Behavior and the Law*, 46 DENV. L.J. 261 (1969).

47. *See, e.g.*, Robert L. Bonn & Alexander B. Smith, *The Case Against Using Biological Indicators in Judicial Decision Making*, 7 no. 1 CRIM. JUST. ETHICS 3 (1988).

48. *See, e.g.*, DOROTHY NELKIN & LAURENCE TANCREDI, DANGEROUS DIAGNOSTICS (1989); Lawrence B. Kessler, Note, *The XYY Chromosomal Abnormalty: Use and Misuse in the Legal Process*, 9 HARV. J. ON LEGIS. 469 (1972).

49. For a discussion of this proposition in the context of maternal-fetal conflict, *see* Roger B. Dworkin, *Common Sense and Common Decency: Some Thoughts about Maternal-Fetal Conflict* in BIOETHICS AND THE FETUS, 9 BIOMEDICAL ETHICS REVS. 27–28 (James M. Humber & Robert F. Almeder, eds. (1991)).

50. *See* David R. Cox, *Medical Genetics*, 268 J.A.M.A. 368 (1992); Linda W. Engel, *The Human Genome Project; History, Goals, and Progress to Date*, 117 ARCH. PATHOL. LAB. MED. 459 (1993).

51. *See* Shirley Rainier & Andrew P. Feinberg, *Genomic Imprinting, DNA Methylation, and Cancer*, 86 J. NAT´L CANCER INST. 753 (1994).

52. *See* Boris Tabakoff, *Genetics and Biological Markers of Risk for Alcoholism*, 103 PUBLIC HEALTH REP. 690 (1988).

53. *See* WAYNE R. LaFAVE & AUSTIN W. SCOTT, JR., CRIMINAL LAW § 4.1, at 304–10 (2d ed. 1986).

54. 42 U.S.C. §§ 12101–12213 (Supp. III 1991).

55. Mark A. Rothstein, *Genetic Discrimination in Employment and the Americans with Disabilities Act*, 29 HOUSTON L. REV. 23 (1992).

6. DEATH AND DYING

1. *See* Roger B. Dworkin, *Death in Context*, 48 IND. L.J. 623, 623–24 (1973); Susan L. Brennan & Richard Delgado, *Death: Multiple Definitions or a Single Standard?* 54 S. CAL. L. REV. 1323, 1328 (1981).

2. Sauers v. Stolz, 218 P.2d 741 (Colo. 1950) (*en banc*) (testimony that witness saw man's heart beating was evidence that husband outlived his wife for a few moments when no heartbeat could be detected in her body).

3. BLACK'S LAW DICTIONARY 488 (4th ed. 1960) (cited in PRESIDENT'S COMMISSION FOR THE STUDY OF ETHICAL PROBLEMS IN MEDICINE AND BIOMEDICAL AND BEHAVIORAL RESEARCH, DEFINING DEATH: MEDICAL, LEGAL AND ETHICAL ISSUES IN THE DETERMINATION OF DEATH (1981) [hereinafter DEFINING DEATH]).

4. DEFINING DEATH, *supra* note 3, at 109.

5. Ad Hoc Committee of the Harvard Medical School to Examine the Definition of Brain Death, *A Definition of Irreversible Coma*, 205 J.A.M.A. 337 (1968) [hereinafter *Irreversible Coma*].

6. Alexander M. Capron & Leon R. Kass, *A Statutory Definition of the Standards for Determining Human Death: An Appraisal and a Proposal*, 121 U. PA. L. REV. 87 (1972) [hereinafter Capron and Kass].

7. *Id.* at 108–109 (citing the Kansas statute, "An Act relating to and defining death" codified at KAN. STAT. ANN. § 77–202 (Supp. 1971); *see generally* DEFINING DEATH, *supra* note 3, at 109–34.

8. Capron and Kass, *supra* note 6, at 111 (describing the authors' statutory proposal).

9. Dworkin, *supra* note 1.

10. Unif. Absence as Evidence of Death & Absentees' Property Act § 1, 8A U.L.A. 5 (1983) (providing a seven-year period). For discussions of the presumptions of death at different times for different purposes, *see* Dworkin, *supra* note 1, and Brennan & Delgado, *supra* note 1.

11. David R. Smith, *Legal Recognition of Neocortical Death*, 71 CORNELL L. REV. 850 (1986).

12. *Id.* at 853 (compiling thirty-three state statutes).

13. Unif. Determination of Death Act, 12 U.L.A. 414 (Supp. 1994).

14. *Id.*

15. Defining Death, *supra* note 3.

16. Unif. Simultaneous Death Act, 8A U.L.A. 322 (Supp. 1993).

17. Commonwealth v. Golston, 366 N.E.2d 744 (Mass. 1977); DEFINING DEATH, *supra* note 3, at 136–39.

18. Dworkin, *supra* note 1, at 633 n.75 (1973) (compiling state statutes).

19. David T. McDowell, *Death of an Idea: The Anencephalic as an Organ Donor*, 72 TEX. L. REV. 893 (1993).

20. Alexander M. Capron, *Anencephalic Donors: Separate the Dead From the Dying*, 17 HASTINGS CTR. REP. 5 (February 1987).

21. *In re* Quinlan, 355 A.2d 647 (N.J. 1976), *cert. denied sub nom.* Garger v. New Jersey, 429 U.S. 922 (1976).

22. WAYNE R. LAFAVE & AUSTIN W. SCOTT, JR., HANDBOOK ON CRIMINAL LAW § 7.7, at 642–43 (2d ed. 1986); Donald G. Collester, Jr., *Death, Dying & the Law: A Prosecutorial View of the Quinlan Case*, 30 RUTGERS L.J. 304, 309 (1977).

23. Collester, *supra* note 22, at 309. *See also* Leonard H. Glantz, *Withholding and Withdrawing Treatment: The Role of the Criminal Law*, 15 L. MED. HEALTH CARE 231, 232 (1987/88).

24. Collester, *supra* note 22, at 309; Donald L. Beschle, *Autonomous Decisionmaking and Social Choice: Examining the "Right to Die,"* 77 KY. L.J. 319, 323 (1988/89); *see also* Blackburn v. State, 23 Ohio St. 146, 163 (1873) ("[Assisted suicide] is declared by the law to be murder, irrespective of the wishes or the condition of the party to whom the poison is administered . . . "); People v. Roberts, 178 N.W. 690, 693 (1920) (man who prepared poison for his terminally ill wife was convicted of murder).

25. La Fave & Scott, *supra* note 22, § 3.3 at 202–203.

26. *See* Cruzan v. Director, Mo. Dep't of Health, 110 S. Ct. 2841, 2861 (1990) (Scalia, J., concurring) (citing Barrow v. State, 188 P. 351 (Okla. Crim. App. 1920); People v. Phillips, 414 P.2d 353 (Cal. 1966)); *see also* Hall v. Nagel, 39 N.E.2d 612 (Ohio 1942); Spendlove v. Georges, 295 P.2d 336 (Utah 1956); Lyons v. Grether, 239 S.E. 2d 103 (Va. 1977).

27. La Fave & Scott, *supra* note 22, § 3.12 at 280.

28. George P. Smith II, *All's Well That Ends Well: Toward a Policy of Assisted Rational Suicide or Merely Enlightened Self-Determination?* 22 U.C. DAVIS L. REV. 275, 310 n.260 (1989).

29. *Id.* at 290–91 n.106 (compiling statutes).

30. Glantz, *supra* note 23.

31. *See id.* at 234.

32. John F. Kennedy Memorial Hosp. v. Heston, 279 A.2d 670, 672 (N.J. 1971).

33. *In re* Quinlan, 355 A.2d 647 (N.J. 1976), *cert. denied sub nom.* Garger v. New Jersey, 429 U.S. 922 (1976).

34. *Id.* at 660–61.

35. *Id.* at 663.

36. 410 U.S. 113 (1973).

37. *Quinlan*, 355 A.2d at 663.

38. Superintendent of Belchertown State School v. Saikewicz, 370 N.E.2d 417 (Mass. 1977).

39. *Id.* at 425.

40. For a collection of cases, *see* John A. Alesandro, Comment, *Physician-Assisted Suicide and New York Law*, 57 ALB. L. REV. 819, 913 n.534 (1994).

41. Commissioner of Correction v. Myers, 399 N.E.2d 452 (Mass. App. 1979).

42. *In re* Spring, 405 N.E.2d 115 (Mass. 1980).

43. For a collection of cases, *see* Smith, *supra* note 11, at 861 n.49.

44. *E.g.*, Bouvia v. Superior Court, 225 Cal. Rptr. 297 (Cal. App. 1986); *In re* Farrell, 529 A.2d 404 (N.J. 1987); Beschle, *supra* note 24, at 329–30.

45. *In re* Farrell, *supra* note 44, at 415.

46. *In re* Peter, 529 A.2d 419, 424 (N.J. 1987).

47. ROBERT M. VEATCH, DEATH, DYING AND THE BIOLOGICAL REVOLUTION: OUR LAST QUEST FOR RESPONSIBILITY 91 n.1 (1989) (collecting cases).

48. *In re* Conroy, 486 A.2d 1209 (1985).

49. *In re* Storar, 420 N.E.2d 64, *cert. denied*, 454 U.S. 858 (1981); *In re* Westchester County Medical Center *ex rel.* O'Connor, 531 N.E.2d 607 (1988).

50. Cruzan v. Director, Mo. Dep't of Health, 110 S. Ct. 2841, 2852 (1990) (stating that to assert that an incompetent person *should* possess the same right to refuse life-saving treatment as a competent person "begs the question: An incompetent person is not able to make an informed and voluntary choice to *exercise* a hypothetical right to refuse treatment or any other right. Such a 'right' must be exercised for her, if at all, by some sort of surrogate").

51. *Id.*

52. *See, e.g.*, John F. Kennedy Memorial Hosp. v. Heston, 279 A.2d 670, 672 (N.J. 1971); *In re* Guardianship of Browning, 568 So.2d 4 (Fla. 1990); Rasmussen v. Fleming, 741 P.2d 674, 686 (Ariz. 1987).

53. *Cruzan*, 110 S. Ct. at 2852.

54. PRESIDENT'S COMMISSION FOR THE STUDY OF ETHICAL PROBLEMS IN MEDICINE AND BIOMEDICAL AND BEHAVIORAL RESEARCH, DECIDING TO FOREGO LIFE-SUSTAINING TREATMENT: ETHICAL, MEDICAL, AND LEGAL ISSUES IN TREATMENT DECISIONS 134–36 (1983) [hereinafter DECIDING TO FOREGO].

55. *Cruzan*, 110 S. Ct. at 2879 (Stevens, J., dissenting).

56. DECIDING TO FOREGO, *supra* note 54, at 132–34; Nancy K. Rhoden, *Litigating Life and Death*, 102 HARV. L. REV. 375, 384 (1988).

57. *Saikewicz*, 370 N.E.2d at 431.

58. *In re* Storar, 420 N.E.2d 64, 72–73 (N.Y. 1981), *cert. denied*, 454 U.S. 858 (1981).

59. *In re* Conroy, 486 A.2d 1209, 1229–32 (N.J. 1985).

60. *Id.* at 1219–20.

61. *Id.* at 1229.

62. *Id.* at 1232.

63. *Id.*

64. *Id.*

65. Rhoden, *supra* note 56, at 397.

66. Nancy J. Moore, *'Two Steps Forward, One Step Back': An Analysis of New Jersey's Latest 'Right to Die' Decisions*, 19 RUTGERS L.J. 955 (1988).

67. *In re* Quinlan, 355 A.2d 647, 669 (N.J. 1976), *cert. denied sub nom.* Garger v. New Jersey, 429 U.S. 922 (1976).

68. *Id.* at 664, 671.

69. *Conroy*, 486 A.2d 1209 (1985).

70. *In re* Farrell, 529 A.2d 404 (1987); Moore, *supra* note 66.

71. *In re* Peter, 529 A.2d 419 (1987); Moore, *supra* note 66.

72. *In re* Jobes, 529 A.2d 434 (1987); Moore, *supra* note 66.

73. Superintendent of Belchertown State School v. Saikewicz, 370 N.E.2d 417, 433 (Mass. 1977).

74. George A. Annas, *Trying to Live Forever*, 15 L. MED. & HEALTH CARE 242 (1987/88). *See also, e.g.*, Brophy v. New England Sinai Hosp., Inc., 497 N.E.2d 626, 632 (Mass. 1986); *In re* Dinnerstein, 380 N.E.2d 134 (Mass. App. 1978). Both cases are distinguished from *Saikewicz*, which required judicial resolution of whether life-prolonging treatment should be withheld from incompetent patients.

75. *In re* Spring, 405 N.E.2d 115 (Mass. 1980).

76. *In re* Guardianship of L.W., 482 N.W.2d 60 (Wis. 1992).

77. *Id.* at 75 (quoting *In re* Colyer, 660 P.2d 738, 746 (Wash. 1983)).

78. *Id.*

79. *Id.* at 73–74.

80. *Id.* at 75.

81. Susan M. Wolf, Trying Not to Talk Forever: A Tool for Change, 15 L. MED. & HEATH CARE 248 & n.5 (1987/88) (citing Joint Commission on the Accreditation of Hospitals, *New and Revised Standards Approved: Withholding Resuscitative Services*, 5 JCAH PERSPECTIVES 7 (1987)).

82. 110 S. Ct. 2841 (1990).

83. Cruzan v. Harmon, *760 S.W.2d 408 (Mo. 1988)*.

84. *110 S. Ct.* at 2851–52.

85. *Id.* at 2851 ("The Fourteenth Amendment provides that no state shall 'deprive any person of life, liberty, or property without due process of law' ").

86. *Id.* at 2852–54.

87. *Id.* at 2863–78.

88. *Id.* at 2878–92.

89. *Id.* at 2859 (Scalia, J., concurring).

90. *Id.* at 2857 (O'Connor, J., concurring).

91. *In re* Westchester County Medical Ctr. ex rel. O'Connor, 534 N.Y.S.2d 886 (N.Y. 1988) (authorizing hospital to insert nasogastric feeding tube into elderly, mentally incompetent patient since her previously expressed wishes did not constitute clear and convincing proof that she would have refused treatment under the particular circumstances); *see* Grace Plaza of Great Neck, Inc. v. Elbaum, 588 N.Y.S.2d 853 (N.Y. App. Div. 1992), *aff'd*, 623 N.E.2d 513 (N.Y. 1993) (continuing to provide life-saving medical treatment to comatose patient despite objections of patient's conservator incurs no liability by doctor or nursing home).

92. Mack v. Mack, 618 A.2d 744 (Md. 1993) (withholding nutrition and hydration from patient in persistent vegetative state not permitted absent conclusive evidence of patient's intent under such circumstances).

93. Chief Justice Rehnquist's majority opinion, assuming the "constitutionally protected right to refuse lifesaving hydration and nutrition" (*Cruzan*, 110 S. Ct. at 2852),

190

was joined by Justices White, O'Connor, and Kennedy. Justice O'Connor specifically agreed that a "protected liberty interest in refusing unwanted medical treatment may be inferred. . . . " *Id.* at 2856 (O'Connor, J., concurring). The fifth justice, Stevens, recognized "[a]n innocent person's constitutional right to be free from unwanted medical treatment" but maintained that Cruzan failed to preserve her right. *Id.* at 2882–83 (Stevens, J., dissenting). Although Justice Scalia joined the majority opinion, he asserted that the Constitution neither grants nor denies a right of refusal; *id.* at 2863 (Scalia, J., concurring).

94. Daniel Callahan, *On Feeding the Dying*, 13 HASTINGS CTR. REP. 22 (October 1983).

95. *Id.*

96. Kathleen M. Anderson, Note, *A Medical-Legal Dilemma: When Can "Inappropriate" Nutrition and Hydration Be Removed in Indiana?* 67 IND. L.J. 479, 492 n.76 (1992) (collecting cases in which courts treat artificial nutrition and hydration like any other medical treatment).

97. *Cruzan*, 110 S. Ct. at 2847–54.

98. SOCIETY FOR THE RIGHT TO DIE, REFUSAL OF TREATMENT LEGISLATION: A STATE BY STATE COMPILATION OF ENACTED AND MODEL STATUTES (1991) [hereinafter REFUSAL OF TREATMENT LEGISLATION].

99. Patient Self-Determination Act 42 U.S.C.A. §§ 1395cc, 1396a (West Supp. 1994) (effective December 1, 1992, as part of the 1990 Omnibus Budget and Reconciliation Act).

100. Unif. Rights of the Terminally Ill Act of 1985, 9B U.L.A. 609 (1987 & Supp. 1994).

101. Unif. Rights of the Terminally Ill Act of 1989, 9B U.L.A. 127 (Supp. 1994).

102. *Id.* (California, Maine, Montana, Nevada, Ohio, Oklahoma, and Rhode Island).

103. Unif. Rights of the Terminally Ill Act of 1985, 9B U.L.A. 145 (Supp. 1994) (Alaska, Arkansas, Iowa, Missouri, Nebraska, and North Dakota).

104. For a collection of state statutes, *see* REFUSAL OF TREATMENT LEGISLATION, *supra* note 98.

105. Unif. Rights of the Terminally Ill Act of 1989 § 6(c), 9B U.L.A. 138 (Supp. 1994).

106. *Id.* § 2(b).

107. *Id.* § 2(a).

108. *Id.* § 3.

109. *Id.* ((i) declaration must be communicated to attending physician and (ii) declarant is determined by doctor to be in terminal condition and unable to make decisions regarding life-sustaining treatment).

110. *Id.* § 1(9).

111. For a collection of state statutes, *see* REFUSAL OF TREATMENT LEGISLATION, *supra* note 98.

112. *Id.*

113. *E.g.*, ALA. CODE § 22–8A-3(6) (1990); OR. REV. STAT. § 127.605 (3) (1990).

114. OKLA. STAT. ANN. TIT. 63, § 3102 (8) (Supp. 1991); *see also* N.J. S.B. 1211 § 3 (1991).

115. Unif. Rights of the Terminally Ill Act of 1989 § 9, 9B U.L.A. 130 (Supp. 1994).

116. *See, e.g.*, IND. CODE ANN. § 16–36–4-8 (f) (Burns 1993).

117. *Id.*

118. Unif. Rights of the Terminally Ill Act of 1989 § 8, 9B U.L.A. 163 (Supp. 1994).

119. *E.g.*, IND. CODE ANN. § 16-36-4-13 (Burns 1993).

120. Unif. Rights of the Terminally Ill Act of 1989 § 1(4), 9B U.L.A. 129 (Supp. 1994).

121. *Id.* § 6(b).

122. KY. REV. STAT. § 311.624(5)(b) (Michie Supp. 1992).

123. Cruzan v. Harmon, 760 S.W.2d 408, 441 (Mo. 1988) (*en banc*) (Welliver, J., dissenting), *aff'd sub nom.*, Cruzan v. Director, Mo. Dep't of Health, 497 U.S. 261 (1990).

124. 8A U.L.A. 317 (1993 & Supp. 1994).

125. *Id.*

126. *Id.* § 3 (1993).

127. Cruzan v. Director, Mo. Dep't of Health, 110 S. Ct. 2841, 2858 (1990) (O'Connor, J., concurring).

128. For a collection of state statutes, *see* REFUSAL OF TREATMENT LEGISLATION, *supra* note 98.

129. IND. CODE ANN. §§ 16-36-4-1 to -22 (Burns Supp. 1994). The 1994 amendment to § 16-36-4-1 deleted subsection (b)(1) which stated that the term "life-prolonging procedure" does not include the "provision of appropriate nutrition and hydration."

130. *Id.* §§ 16-8-12-1 to -13 (Burns 1990 & Supp. 1991); *see generally* Anderson, *supra* note 96.

131. *In re* Lawrance, 579 N.E.2d 32 (Ind. 1991).

132. For a collection of state statutes, *see* REFUSAL OF TREATMENT LEGISLATION, *supra* note 98.

133. Dan W. Brock, *Taking Human Life*, 95 ETHICS 851, 854–55 (1985) (discussing the philosophy of Alan Donagan); Jeff McMahan, *Killing, Letting Die and Withdrawing Aid*, 103 ETHICS 250–79 (January 1993).

134. CARLOS F. GOMEZ, REGULATING DEATH 7, 13 (1991); Susan M. Wolf, *Holding the Line on Euthanasia*, 19 HASTINGS CTR. REP. 13 (Special Supp. January/February 1989).

135. Lee v. Oregon, 1995 U.S. Dist. LEXIS 12011 (D. Ore. Aug. 3, 1995).

136. O. HOLMES, THE COMMON LAW 1 (1881).

137. Alesandro, *supra* note 40, at 858 (citing CHOICE IN DYING, STATE LAWS REGARDING ASSISTED SUICIDE (1993), *reprinted in* RIGHT TO DIE LAW DIGEST (Dec. 1993)).

138. *See* Daniel Callahan, *Medical Futility, Medical Necessity: The Problem-Without-a-Name*, 21 HASTINGS CTR. REP. 30, 31 (July/August 1991) (citing Lawrence J. Schneiderman et al., *Medical Futility: Its Meaning and Ethical Implications*, ANNALS OF INTERNAL MED. 112, no. 12 (June 15, 1990): 949–54).

139. *Id.*

140. Marcia Angell, *The Case of Helga Wanglie: A New Kind of "Right to Die" Case*, 325 NEW ENG J. MED. 511, 512 (1991); *see also* Steven H. Miles, *Informed Demand for "Non-Beneficial" Medical Treatment*, 325 NEW ENG. J. MED. 512 (1991).

141. Roger B. Dworkin, *Medical Law and Ethics in the Post-Autonomy Age*, 68 IND. L.J. 727, 739–40 (1993).

142. *Id.* at 741.

143. W. PAGE KEETON ET AL., PROSSER & KEETON ON TORTS § 32 at 185–87 (5th ed., 1984) [hereinafter PROSSER & KEETON].

144. *Id.* § 32 at 187.

145. *Id.* § 32 at 188 and § 41 at 270.

146. Project, *The Medical Malpractice Threat: A Study of Defensive Medicine*, 1971 DUKE L.J. 939, 942–44; Cynthia J. Dollar, Note, *Promoting Better Health Care: Policy Arguments for Concurrent Quality Assurance and Attorney-Client Hospital Incident Report Privileges*, 3 HEALTH MATRIX 259, 261–62 (1993).

147. PROSSER & KEETON § 18, *supra* note 143, at 115.

148. Alexander M. Capron, *The Competence of Children as Self-Deciders in Biomedical Interventions*, *in* WHO SPEAKS FOR THE CHILD: THE PROBLEMS OF PROXY CONSENT 57, 61–65 (W. Gaylin & R. Macklin eds., 1982) (recognizing the "emergency exception," "physician judgment" statutes and "best-interests" exception).

149. PROSSER & KEETON § 18, *supra* note 143, at 116.

150. Custody of a Minor, 379 N.E.2d 1053 (Mass. 1978), *reviewed and aff'd*, 393 N.E.2d 836 (Mass. 1979); *In re* Hofbauer, 393 N.E.2d 1009 (N.Y. 1979).

151. *In re* Seiferth, 127 N.E.2d 820 (N.Y. 1955) (cleft palate); *In re* Sampson, 317 N.Y.S.2d 641 (N.Y. Fam. Ct. 1970), *aff'd*, 323 N.Y.S.2d 253 (N.Y. App. Div. 1971), *aff'd*, 278 N.E.2d 918 (N.Y. 1972) (neurofibromatosis).

152. *In re* Green, 292 A.2d 387 (Pa. 1972); *In re* Sampson, 317 N.Y.S.2d 641 (Fam. Ct. 1970), *aff'd per curiam*, 328 N.Y.S.2d 686 (Ct. App. 1972).

153. *Hofbauer*, 393 N.E.2d 1009 (N.Y. 1979).

154. *Custody of a Minor*, 393 N.E.2d 836 (Mass. 1979).

155. *In re* Infant Doe, No. GU 8204-004A (Monroe, Ind., Cir. Ct. April 12, 1982) *mandamus denied sub nom.*, State *ex rel.* Infant Doe v. Baker, No. 482 S 140 (Ind. May 27, 1982), *and cert. denied sub nom.*, Infant Doe v. Bloomington Hosp., 464 U.S. 961 (1983); *see generally* HELGA KUHSE AND PETER SINGER, SHOULD THE BABY LIVE? 11–17 (1985).

156. State *ex rel.* Infant Doe v. Baker, No. 482 S 140 (Ind. 1982).

157. As amended, 29 U.S.C.A. § 794 (Supp. 1985).

158. Bowen v. American Hosp. Ass'n, 476 U.S. 610, 612–13 (1986) (citing 45 C.F.R. § 84.55 (1985)).

159. *Id.* at 615 (citing 45 C.F.R. §§ 84.55(b)(3), (4) (1985)).

160. *Id.*

161. *Id.* at 616–17 (citing 45 C.F.R. §§ 84.55(d), (e) (1985) and 49 Fed. Reg. 1628 (1984), respectively).

162. *Id.* at 615–16 (citing 45 C.F.R. § 84.55(c)(1) (1985)).

163. *Id.* at 647.

164. United States v. University Hosp., 729 F.2d 144 (2d Cir. 1984).

165. *Bowen*, 476 U.S. at 630.

166. *Id.* at 644–45.

167. 42 U.S.C.A. §§ 5101–5116 (1983 & Supp. 1994); *see generally* Thomas H. Murray, *The Final, Anticlimactic Rule on Baby Doe*, 15 HASTINGS CTR. REP. 5 (June 1985).

168. 42 U.S.C.A. § 5106g(10) (Supp. 1994).

169. 42 U.S.C.A. § 5106a(10) (Supp. 1994).

170. 45 C.F.R. Part 1340—Child Abuse and Neglect Prevention and Treatment.

171. Bowen v. American Hosp. Ass'n, 476 U.S. 610, 642 (1986).

172. 45 C.F.R. § 1340.15(b)(3)(ii) (1993).

173. 45 C.F.R. § 1340.15(b)(2) (1993).

174. 45 C.F.R. Appendix to Part 1340—Interpretative Guidelines Regarding 45 C.F.R. § 1340.15—Services and Treatment for Disabled Infants.

7. CONTROLLING RESEARCH

1. 42 C.F.R. § 52.5 (1993).
2. 42 C.F.R. § 52h.5 (1993).
3. Minority Biomedical Research Support Program, 42 C.F.R. 52c, *as amended*, 58 Fed. Reg. 61,029 (1993).
4. 42 U.S.C.A. § 289a-2 (Supp. 1994).
5. 38 U.S.C.A. §§ 1751–52 (1991).
6. Apter v. Richardson, 510 F.2d 351 (7th Cir. 1975).
7. *Id.*; *see also* Kletschka v. Driver, 411 F.2d 436 (2d Cir. 1969).
8. Hymen v. Jewish Chronic Disease Hosp., 248 N.Y.S. 245 (N.Y. Sup. Ct. 1964).
9. JAMES H. JONES, BAD BLOOD: THE TUSKEGEE SYPHILIS EXPERIMENT (1981); UNITED STATES DEPARTMENT OF HEALTH, EDUCATION AND WELFARE, PUBLIC HEALTH SERVICE, FINAL REPORT OF THE TUSKEGEE SYPHILIS STUDY AD HOC ADVISORY PANEL (1973); Allan M. Brandt, *Racism and Research: The Case of the Tuskegee Syphilis Study*, 8 HASTINGS CTR. REP. 21 (Dec. 1978).
10. Jesse A. Goldner, *An Overview of Legal Controls on Human Experimentation and the Regulatory Implications of Taking Professor Katz Seriously*, 38 ST. LOUIS U.L.J. 63 n.175 (1993) (principles known as the "Nuremberg Code" are set forth in Office of the Judge Advocate General, Department of the Army, Trials of War Criminals Before the Nuremberg Military Tribunals, vols. 1 & 2 at 181–82 (1946–1949)); 21 C.F.R. § 312.120(b)(4) (1993) ("Declaration of Helsinki"); Henry K. Beecher, *Ethics and Clinical Research*, 274 NEW ENG. J. MED. 1354 (1966) (cited in Jay Katz, *Human Experimentation and Human Rights*, 38 ST. LOUIS U.L.J. 7, 9 (1993); ROBERT J. LEVINE, ETHICS AND REGULATION OF CLINICAL RESEARCH (2d ed. 1986).
11. 45 C.F.R. pt. 46 (1993).
12. 21 C.F.R. pt. 50 (1993).
13. 45 C.F.R. § 46.101(a) (1993).
14. 45 C.F.R. § 46.101(b)(1)(i) (1993).
15. 45 C.F.R. § 46.101(b)(1)(ii) (1993).
16. 45 C.F.R. § 46.102(d) (1993).
17. 45 C.F.R. § 46.102(f) (1993).
18. 45 C.F.R. § 46.103 (1993).
19. 45 C.F.R. § 46.107(a) (1993).
20. *Id.*
21. 45 C.F.R. § 46.107(f) (1993).
22. 45 C.F.R. § 46.109(a) (1993).
23. 45 C.F.R. § 46.111 (1993).
24. 45 C.F.R. § 46.116 (1993).
25. *Id.*
26. *Id.*
27. *Id.*
28. *Id.*
29. 45 C.F.R. § 46.116(a) (1993).
30. 45 C.F.R. § 46.116(b) (1993).
31. 45 C.F.R. § 46.117 (1993).
32. 45 C.F.R. § 46.111 (1993).

33. 45 C.F.R. § 46.111(a)(2) (1993).
34. *Id.*
35. 45 C.F.R. § 46.110 (1993).
36. 45 C.F.R. §§ 46.109(e) (reviews not less than one per year), 46.113.
37. Martin Finucane, *Better Safeguards Sought for Research Subjects,* Los Angeles Times, at A8, col. 1 (Apr. 10, 1994).
38. 45 C.F.R. §§ 46.306(a)(2), .303(d) (1993) ("defining minimal risk").
39. 45 C.F.R. § 46.304(b) (1993).
40. 45 C.F.R. § 46. 305(a) (1993).
41. I am indebted to my colleague, Professor Aviva Orenstein, for this idea.
42. 45 C.F.R. §§ 46.404–.407 (1993).
43. 45 C.F.R. § 46.406(b) (1993).
44. 45 C.F.R. § 46.402(b) (1993).
45. 45 C.F.R. § 46.402(c) (1993).
46. 45 C.F.R. § 46.408 (1993).
47. 45 C.F.R. § 46.405 (1993).
48. 45 C.F.R. § 46.406 (1993).
49. 45 C.F.R. § 46.407 (1993).
50. 45 C.F.R. § 46.408(a) (1993).
51. 45 C.F.R. § 46.408(c) (1993).
52. 45 C.F.R. § 46.408(b) (1993).
53. 45 C.F.R. §§ 46.201–.211 (1993).
54. *Id.*
55. 45 C.F.R. § 46.207(a) (1993).
56. 45 C.F.R. § 46.207(b) (1993).
57. Planned Parenthood of Southeastern Pa. v. Casey, 112 S. Ct. 2791, 2826–29 (1992).
58. 500 U.S. 173 (1991).
59. 45 C.F.R. § 46.208(a) (1993).
60. 45 C.F.R. § 46.209(a)(1), (2) (1993).
61. 45 C.F.R. § 46.209(b) (1993).
62. 45 C.F.R. § 46.209(c) (1993).
63. 45 C.F.R. § 46.209(d) (1993).
64. 45 C.F.R. § 46.206(a)(2) (1993).
65. 45 C.F.R. § 46.206(3) (1993).
66. 45 C.F.R. § 46.206(4)(b) (1993).
67. 45 C.F.R. § 46.205(a)(1), (2) (1993).
68. 45 C.F.R. § 46.204(a) (1993).
69. 45 C.F.R. § 46.204(c) (1993).

8. CONCLUSION

1. PAUL FREUND, *Legal Frameworks for Human Experimentation,* in Paul Freund, EXPERIMENTATION WITH HUMAN SUBJECTS 105 (1969).
2. *See generally,* Arthur Kantrowitz, *The Science Court Experiment,* 13 no. 3 TRIAL 48 (1977); James A. Martin, *The Proposed "Science Court,"* 75 MICH. L. REV. 1058 (1977).
3. *See* Durham v. United States, 214 F.2d 862 (D.C. Cir. 1954).
4. *See* United States v. Brawner, 471 F.2d 969 *(en banc)* (D.C. Cir. 1972).

5. The Commission's reports are available from the Superintendent of Documents, U.S. Government Printing Office, Washington, D.C. 20402.

6. *See, e.g.,* THE NEW YORK STATE TASK FORCE ON LIFE AND THE LAW, THE DE-TERMINATION OF DEATH (1986); LIFE SUSTAINING TREATMENT: MAKING DECISIONS AND APPOINTING A HEALTH CARE REPRESENTATIVE (1987); DO NOT RESUSCITATE ORDERS (2d ed. 1988).

ROGER B. DWORKIN is Professor of Law at Indiana University School of Law-Bloomington and Nelson Poynter Scholar and Director of Medical Studies at Indiana University's Poynter Center for the Study of Ethics and American Institutions. Dworkin, who has previously served as Professor of Biomedical History at the University of Washington School of Medicine, is an expert in the relationship between law and the biomedical sciences. He is co-author of a leading casebook on Law and Medicine and numerous articles in the field.